HUMAN PERFORMANCE

Volume 15, Number 1/:

SPECIAL ISSUE: Role of General N
Industrial, Work, and Organizatic
Deniz S. Ones and Chockalingam Viswe.. ..

Subscriber Information

Human Performance is published quarterly by Lawrence Erlbaum Associates, Inc., Mahwah, NJ 07430–2262. Subscriptions for the 2002 volume are available on a calendar-year basis.

Printed journal subscription rates are $60 for individuals and $380 for institutions within the United States and Canada; $90 for individuals and $410 for institutions outside the United States and Canada. Order printed subscriptions through the Journal Subscription Department, Lawrence Erlbaum Associates, Inc., 10 Industrial Avenue, Mahwah, NJ 07430–2262.

Electronic: Full price print subscribers to Volume 15, 2002 are entitled to receive the electronic version free of charge. *Electronic only* subscriptions are also available at a reduced price of $342.00 for institiutions and $54.00 for individuals.

Claims for missing issues cannot be honored beyond 4 months after mailing date. Duplicate copies cannot be sent to replace issues due to failure to notify publisher of change of address.

This journal is abstracted or indexed in *Cambridge Scientific Abstracts: Health and Safety, Science Abstracts; Computer Abstracts; Ergonomics Abstracts; ISI: Current Contents/Social & Behavioral Sciences, Social Sciences Citation Index, Research Alert, Social SciSearch, Focus on: Industrial & Organizational Psychology;* and *PsycINFO/Psychological Abstracts*. Microform copies of this journal are available through Bell & Howell Information and Learning Sales, P.O. Box 1346, Ann Arbor, MI 48106–1346. For more information, call 1-800-521-0600 x2888.

First published by Lawrence Erlbaum Associates, Inc.

10 Industrial Avenue, Mahwah, New Jersey 07430

This edition published 2012 by Routledge
711 Third Avenue, New York, NY 10017
27 Church Road, Hove, East Sussex, BN3 2FA

HUMAN PERFORMANCE, *15*(1/2), 1–2

Introduction to the Special Issue: Role of General Mental Ability in Industrial, Work, and Organizational Psychology

Deniz S. Ones
Department of Psychology
University of Minnesota

Chockalingam Viswesvaran
Department of Psychology
Florida International University

Individual differences that have consequences for work behaviors (e.g., job performance) are of great concern for organizations, both public and private. General mental ability has been a popular, although much debated, construct in Industrial, Work, and Organizational (IWO) Psychology for almost 100 years. Individuals differ on their endowments of a critical variable—intelligence—and differences on this variable have consequences for life outcomes.

As the century drew to a close, we thought it might be useful to assess the state of our knowledge and the sources of disagreements about the role of general mental ability in IWO psychology. To this end, with the support of Murray Barrick, the 2000 Program Chair for the Society for Industrial/Organizational Psychology (SIOP), we put together a debate for SIOP's annual conference. The session's participants were Frank Schmidt, Linda Gottfredson, Milton Hakel, Jerry Kehoe, Kevin Murphy, James Outtz, and Malcolm Ree. The debate, which took place at the 2000 annual conference of SIOP, drew a standing- room-only audience, despite being held in a room that could seat over 300 listeners. The questions that were raised by the audience suggested that there was room in the literature to flesh out the ideas expressed by the debaters.

Thus, when Jim Farr, the current editor of *Human Performance,* approached us with the idea of putting together a special issue based on the "*g* debate," we were enthusiastic. However, it occurred to us that there were other important and informative perspectives on the role of cognitive ability in IWO psychology that would be valuable to include in the special issue. For these, we tapped Mary Tenopyr, Jesus Salgado, Harold Goldstein, Neil Anderson, and Robert Sternberg, and their coauthors.

The 12 articles in this special issue of *Human Performance* uniquely summarize the state of our knowledge of *g* as it relates to IWO psychology and masterfully draw out areas of question and contention. We are very pleased that each of the 12 contributing articles highlight similarities and differences among perspectives and shed light on research needs for the future. We should alert the readers that the order of the articles in the special issue is geared to enhance the synergy among them. In the last article of the special issue, we summarize the major themes that run across all the articles and offer a review of contrasts in viewpoints. We hope that the final product is informative and beneficial to researchers, graduate students, practitioners, and decision makers.

There are several individuals that we would like to thank for their help in the creation of this special issue. First and foremost, we thank all the authors who have produced extremely high quality manuscripts. Their insights have enriched our understanding of the role of *g* in IWO psychology. We were also impressed with the timeliness of all the authors, as well as their receptiveness to feedback that we provided for revisions. We also extend our thanks to Barbara Hamilton, Rachel Gamm, and Jocelyn Wilson for much appreciated clerical help. Their support has made our editorial work a little easier. Financial support for the special issue editorial office was provided by the Departments of Psychology of Florida International University and the University of Minnesota, as well as the Hellervik Chair endowment. We are also grateful to Jim Farr for allowing us to put together this special issue and for his support. We hope that his foresight about the importance of the topic will serve the literature well. We also appreciate the intellectual stimulation provided by our colleagues at the University of Minnesota and Florida International University. Finally, our spouses Saraswathy Viswesvaran and Ates Haner provided us the environment where we could devote uninterrupted time to this project. They also have our gratitude (and probably a better understanding and knowledge of *g* than most nonpsychologists).

We dedicate this issue to the memory of courageous scholars (e.g., Galton, Spearman, Thorndike, Cattell, Eysenck) whose insights have helped the science around cognitive ability to blossom during the early days of studying individual differences. We hope that how to best use measures of *g* to enhance societal progress and well-being of individuals will be better understood and utilized around the globe in the next 100 years.

HUMAN PERFORMANCE, *15*(1/2), 3–23

*g*2K

Malcolm James Ree
Center for Leadership Studies
Our Lady of the Lake University

Thomas R. Carretta
Air Force Research Laboratory
Wright-Patterson AFB, Ohio

To answer the questions posed by the organizers of the millennial debate on *g*, or general cognitive ability, we begin by briefly reviewing its history. We tackle the question of what *g* is by addressing *g* as a psychometric score and examining its psychological and physiological correlates. Then tacit knowledge and other non-*g* characteristics are discussed. Next, we review the practical utility of *g* in personnel selection and conclude by explaining its importance to both organizations and individuals.

The earliest empirical studies of general cognitive ability, *g*, were conducted by Charles Spearman (1927, 1930), although the idea has several intellectual precursors, among them Samuel Johnson (1709–1784, see Jensen, 1998, p. 19) and Sir Francis Galton (1869). Spearman (1904) suggested that all tests measure two factors, a common core called *g* and one or more specifics, $s_1, \ldots s_n$. The general component was present in all tests, whereas the specific component was test unique. Each test could have one or more different specific components. Spearman also observed that *s* could be found in common across a limited number of tests allowing for an arithmetic factor that was distinct from *g*, but found in several arithmetic tests. These were called "group factors." Spearman (1937) noted that group factors could be either broad or narrow and that *s* could not be measured without also measuring *g*.

As a result of his work with *g* and *s*, Spearman (1923) developed the principle of "indifference of the indicator." It means that when constructing intelligence tests,

Requests for reprints should be sent to Malcolm James Ree, Our Lady of the Lake University, 411 S. W. 24th Street, San Antonio, TX 78207–4689. E-mail: reemal@lake.ollusa.edu the specific content of the items is not important as long as those taking the test perceive it in the same way. Although the test content cannot be ignored, it is merely a vehicle for the measurement of g. Although Spearman was talking mostly about test content (e.g., verbal, math, spatial), the concept of indifference of the indicator extends to measurement methods, some of which were not yet in use at the time (e.g., computers, neural conductive velocity, psychomotor, oral–verbal).

Spearman (1904) developed a method of factor analysis to answer the vexing question: "Did each of the human abilities (or 'faculties' as they were then called) represent a differing mental process?" If the answer was yes, the different abilities should be uncorrelated with each other, and separate latent factors should be the sources for the different abilities. Repeatedly, the answer was no. Having observed the emergence of g in the data, an eschatological question emerged. What is g? Although the question may be answered in several ways, we have chosen three as covering broad theoretical and practical concerns. These are g as a psychometric score, as psychological correlates of g, and as physiological correlates of g.

PSYCHOMETRIC g

Spearman (1904) first demonstrated the emergence of g in a battery of school tests including Classics, French, English, Math, Pitch, and Music. During the 20th century, many competing multiple-factor theories of ability have surfaced, only to disappear when subjected to empirical verification (see, e.g., Guilford, 1956, 1959; Thurstone, 1938). Psychometrically, g can be extracted from a battery of tests with diverse content. The correlation matrix should display "positive manifold," meaning that all the scores should be positively correlated. There are three reasons why cognitive ability scores might not display positive manifold—namely, reversed scoring, range restriction, and unreliability.

Threats to Positive Manifold

Reversed scoring.   Reversed scoring is often found in timed scores such as reaction time or inspection time. In these tests, the scores are frequently the number of milliseconds necessary to make the response. A greater time interval is indicative of poorer performance. When correlated with scores where higher values are indicative of better performance, the resulting correlation will not be positive. This can be corrected by subtracting the reversed time score from a large number so that higher values are associated with better performance. This linear transformation will not affect the magnitude of the correlation, but it will associate better performance with high scores for each test.

Range restriction. Range restriction is the phenomenon observed when prior selection reduces the variance in one or more variables. Such a reduction in variance distorts the correlation between two variables, typically leading to a reduction in the correlation. For example, if the correlation between college grades and college qualification test scores were computed at a selective Ivy League university, the correlation would appear low because the range of the scores on the college qualification test has been restricted by the selectivity of the university.

Range restriction is not a new discovery. Pearson (1903) described it when he first demonstrated the product–moment correlation. In addition, he derived the statistical corrections based on the same assumptions as for the product–moment correlation. In almost all cases, range restriction reduces correlations, producing downwardly biased estimates, even a zero correlation when the true correlation is moderate or strong. As demonstrated by Thorndike (1949) and Ree, Carretta, Earles, and Albert (1994), the correlation can change sign as a consequence of range restriction. This change in sign negates the positive manifold of the matrix. However, the negation is totally artifactual. The proper corrections must be applied whether "univariate" (Thorndike, 1949) or "multivariate" (Lawley, 1943). Linn, Harnish, and Dunbar (1981) empirically demonstrated that the correction for range restriction is generally conservative and does not inflate the estimate of the true population value of the correlation.

Unreliability. The third threat to positive manifold is unreliability. It is well known[1] that the correlation of two variables is limited by the geometric mean of their reliabilities. Although unreliability cannot change the sign of the correlation, it can reduce it to zero or near zero, threatening positive manifold. Unreliable tests need not denigrate positive manifold. The solution is to refine your tests, adding more items if necessary to increase the reliability. Near the turn of the century, Spearman (1904) derived the correction for unreliability, or correction for attenuation. Application of the correction is typically done for theoretical reasons as it provides an estimate of the correlation between two scores had perfectly reliable measures been used.

Representing *g*

Frequently, *g* is represented by the highest factor in a hierarchical factor analysis of a battery of cognitive ability tests. It can also be represented as the first unrotated principal component or principal factor. Ree and Earles (1991) demonstrated that any of these three methods will be effective for estimating *g*. Ree and Earles also demonstrated that, given enough tests, the simple sum of the test scores will pro-

---

[1]Hunter and Schmidt (1990) noted, "Since the late 1890s, we have known that the error of measurement attenuates the correlation coefficient" (p. 117).

duce a measure of g. This may be attributed to Wilks's theorem (Ree, Carretta, & Earles, 1998; Wilks, 1938). The proportion of total variance accounted for by g in a test battery ranges from about 30% to 65%, depending on the composition of the constituent tests. Jensen (1980, pp. 216) provided an informative review.

Gould (1981) stated that g can be "rotated away" among lower order factors. This is erroneous, as rotation simply distributes the variance attributable to g among all the factors. It does not disappear. Interested readers are referred to a text on factor analysis.

To dispel the charge that g is just "academic intelligence" (Sternberg & Wagner, 1993), we demonstrate a complex nexus of g and nonacademic activities. The broadness of these activities, ranging from accident proneness to the ability to taste certain chemicals, exposes the falsehood that g is just academic intelligence.

PSYCHOLOGICAL CORRELATES OF g

Several psychological correlates of g have been identified. Brand (1987) provided an impressive list and summary of 48 characteristics positively correlated with g and 19 negatively correlated with g. Brand included references for all examples, listed later. Ree and Earles (1994, pp. 133–134) organized these characteristics into several categories. These categories and examples for each category follow:

- Abilities (analytic style, eminence, memory, reaction time, reading).
- Creativity/artistic (craftwork, musical ability).
- Health and fitness (dietary preference, height, infant mortality, longevity, obesity).
- Interests/ choices (breadth and depth of interest, marital partner, sports participation).
- Moral ((delinquency (–)*, lie scores (–), racial prejudice (–), values).
- Occupational (income, military rank, occupational status, socioeconomic status).
- Perceptual (ability to perceive brief stimuli, field-independence, myopia).
- Personality (achievement motivation, altruism, dogmatism (–)).
- Practical (practical knowledge, social skills).
- Other (accident proneness (–), motor skills, talking speed).
- * Indicates a negative correlation.

Noting its pervasive influence on human characteristics, Brand (1987) commented, "g is to psychology as carbon is to chemistry" (p. 257).

Cognitive and psychomotor abilities often are viewed as unrelated (Carroll, 1993; Fleishman & Quaintance, 1984). This view may be the result of dissimilarity of appearance and method of measurement for cognitive and psychomotor tests.

Several recent studies, however, have shown a modest relation between cognitive and psychomotor ability (Carretta & Ree, 1997a; Chaiken, Kyllonen, & Tirre, 2000; Rabbitt, Banerji, & Szymanski, 1989; Ree & Carretta, 1994; Tirre & Raouf, 1998), with uncorrected correlations between .20 and .69.

Although the source of the relations between cognitive and psychomotor ability is unknown, Ree and Carretta (1994) hypothesized that it might be due to the requirement to reason while taking the tests. Carretta and Ree (1997b) proposed that practical and technical knowledge also might contribute to this relation. Chaiken et al. (2000) suggested that the relation might be explained by the role of working memory capacity (a surrogate of g; see Stauffer, Ree, & Carretta, 1996) in learning complex and novel tasks.

PHYSIOLOGICAL CORRELATES OF g

A series of physiological correlates has long been postulated. Hart and Spearman (1914) and Spearman (1927) speculated that g was the consequence of "neural energy," but did not specify how that mental energy could be measured. They also did not specify the mechanism(s) that produced this energy. The speculative physiological causes of g were "energy," "plasticity," and "the blood." In a similar way, Thomson (1939) speculated that this was due to "sampling of mental bonds." No empirical studies were conducted on these speculated causes. Little was known about the human brain and g during this earlier era. Today, much more is known and there is a growing body of knowledge. We now discuss the correlates demonstrated by empirical research.

Brain Size and Structure

There is a positive correlation between g and brain size. Van Valen (1974) found a correlation of .3, whereas Broman, Nichols, Shaughnessy, and Kennedy (1987) found correlation in the range of .1 to .2 for a surrogate measure, head perimeter (a relatively poor measure of brain size). Evidence about the correlation between brain size and g was improved with the advent of more advanced measurement techniques, especially MRI. In a precedent-setting study, Willerman, Schultz, Rutledge, and Bigler (1991) estimated the brain size-g correlation at .35. Andreasen et al. (1993) reported these correlations separately for men and women as .40 and .45, respectively. They also found correlations for specific brain section volumes such as the cerebellum and the hippocampus. Other researchers have reported similar values. Schultz, Gore, Sodhi, and Anderson (1993) reported $r = .43$; Wickett, Vernon, and Lee (1994) reported $r = .39$; and Egan, Wickett, and Vernon (1995) reported $r = .48$. Willerman and Schultz (1996) noted that this cumulative evidence "provides the first solid lead for understanding g at a biological level of analysis" (p. 16).

Brain myelination has been found to be correlated with g. Frearson, Eysenck, and Barrett (1990) suggested that the myelination hypothesis was consistent with brighter people being faster in mental activities. Schultz (1991) found a correlation of .54 between the amount of brain myelination and g in young adults. As a means of explanation, Waxman (1992) suggested that myelination reduces "noise" in the neural system. Miller (1996) and Jensen (1998) have provided helpful reviews.

Cortical surface area also has been linked to g. An early postmortem study by Haug (1987) found a correlation between occupational prestige, a surrogate measure of g, and cortical area. Willerman and Schultz (1996) suggested that cortical area might be a good index based on the studies of Jouandet et al. (1989) and Tramo et al. (1995). Eysenck (1982) provided an excellent earlier review.

Brain Electrical Potential

Several studies have shown correlations between various indexes of brain electrical potentials and g. Chalke and Ertl (1965) first presented data suggesting a relation between average evoked potential (AEP) and measures of g. Their findings subsequently were supported by Ertl and Schafer (1969), who observed correlations from $-.10$ to $-.35$ for AEP and scores on the Wechsler Intelligence Scale for Children. Shucard and Horn (1972) found similar correlations ranging from $-.15$ to $-.32$ for visual AEP and measures of crystallized g and fluid g.

Speed of Neural Processing

Reed and Jensen (1992) observed a correlation of .37 between neural conductive velocity (NCV) and measured intelligence for an optic nerve leading to the brain. Faster NCV was associated with higher g. Confirming replications are needed.

Brain Glucose Metabolism Rate

Haier et al. (1988) observed a negative correlation between brain glucose metabolism and performance on the Ravens Advanced Progressive Matrices, a highly g-loaded test. Haier, Siegel, Tang, Able, and Buchsbaum (1992) found support for their theory of brain efficiency and intelligence in brain glucose metabolism research. However, Larson, Haier, LaCasse, and Hazen (1995) suggested that the efficiency hypothesis may be dependent on task type, and urged caution.

Physical Variables

There are physical variables that are related to g, but the causal mechanisms are unknown. It is even difficult to speculate about the mechanism, much less the reason, for the relation. These physical variables include the ability to curl the tongue, the ability to taste the chemical phenylthiocarbimide, asthma and other allergies, basal metabolic rate in children, blood antigens such as IgA, facial features, myopia, number of homozygous genetic loci, presence or absence of the masa intermedia in the brain, serum uric acid level, and vital (lung) capacity. For a review, see Jensen (1998) and Ree and Carretta (1998).

NONCOGNITIVE TRAITS, SPECIFIC ABILITIES, AND SPECIFIC KNOWLEDGE

The use of noncognitive traits, specific abilities, and knowledge has often been proposed as critical in personnel selection and for comprehension of the relations between human characteristics and occupational performance. Although specific abilities and knowledge are correlated with g, noncognitive traits, by definition, are not. For example, McClelland (1993) suggested that under common circumstances noncognitive traits such as "motivation" may be better predictors of job performance than cognitive abilities. Sternberg and Wagner (1993) proposed using tests of practical intelligence and tacit knowledge rather than tests of what they termed "academic intelligence." Their definition of tacit knowledge is "the practical know how one needs for success on the job" (p. 2). Sternberg and Wagner defined practical intelligence as a general form of tacit knowledge.

Schmidt and Hunter (1993), in an assessment of Sternberg and Wagner (1993), noted that their concepts of tacit knowledge and practical intelligence are redundant with the well-established construct of job knowledge and are therefore superfluous. Schmidt and Hunter further noted that job knowledge is more broadly defined than either tacit knowledge or practical intelligence and has well-researched relations with other familiar constructs such as intelligence, job experience, and job performance.

Ree and Earles (1993), in a response to Sternberg and Wagner (1993) and McClelland (1993), noted a lack of empirical evidence for the constructs of tacit knowledge, practical intelligence, and social class. Ree and Earles also noted several methodological issues affecting the interpretability of Sternberg and Wagner's and McClelland's results (e.g., range restriction, sampling error, small samples).

g AND S AS PREDICTORS OF OCCUPATIONAL CRITERIA AND IN PERSONNEL SELECTION

Although we often talk about job performance in the singular, there are several distinctive components to occupational performance. Having the knowledge, techniques, and skills needed to perform the job is one broad component. Another broad component is training or retraining for promotions or new jobs or just staying up-to-date with the changing demands of the "same" job. The application of techniques, knowledge, and skills to attain organizational goals comprises another component.

Training Performance

The first step in doing a job is to acquire the knowledge and master the skills required. We begin in elementary school with reading, writing, and arithmetic. As we progress from elementary school to secondary school, college, formal job training, and on-the-job-training, additional specialized job knowledge is acquired. g is predictive of achievement in all of these educational and training settings (Gottfredson, 1997; Jensen, 1998; Ree & Carretta, 1998).

Predictiveness of g.   The following estimates of the range of the validity of g for predicting academic success are provided by Jensen (1980, p. 319): elementary school—0.6 to 0.7; high school—0.5 to 0.6; college—0.4 to 0.5; and graduate school—0.3 to 0.4. Jensen observed that the apparent decrease in importance of g may be due to artifacts such as range restriction and selective assortment into educational track.

Thorndike (1986) presented results of a study of the predictiveness of g for high school students in six courses. Consistent with Jensen (1980), he found an average correlation of 0.53 for predicting these course grades.

In McNemar's (1964) presidential address to the American Psychological Association, he reported results showing that g was the best predictor of school performance in 4,096 studies conducted that used the Differential Aptitude Tests. Brodnick and Ree (1995) found g to be a better predictor of college performance than was socioeconomic status.

Roth and Campion (1992) provided an example of the validity of a general ability composite for predicting training success in civilian occupations. Their participants were petroleum process technicians, and the validity of the g-based composite was .50, corrected for range restriction.

Salgado (1995) used a general ability composite to predict training success in the Spanish Air Force and found a biserial correlation of 0.38 (not corrected for range restriction). Using cumulative techniques, he confirmed that there was no variability in the correlations across five classes of pilot trainees.

Jones (1988) estimated the g-saturation of 10 subtests from a multiple aptitude battery using their loadings on an unrotated first principal component. Correlating these loadings with the average validity of the subtests for predicting training performance for 37 jobs, she found a correlation of 0.76. Jones then computed the same correlation within four job families comprised of the 37 jobs and found no differences between job families. Ree and Earles (1992) later corrected the g loadings for unreliability and found a correlation of .98. Ree and Earles, in a replication in a different sample across 150 jobs, found the same correlational value.

Incrementing the predictiveness of g^2.   Thorndike (1986) studied the comparative validity of specific ability composites and measures of g for predicting training success in 35 technical schools for about 1,900 U.S. Army enlisted trainees. In prediction, specific abilities incremented g by only about 0.03. On cross-validation, the multiple correlations for specific abilities shrank below the bivariate correlation for g.

Ree and Earles (1991) showed that training performance was more a function of g than specific factors. A study of 78,041 U.S. Air Force enlisted military personnel in 82 jobs was conducted to determine if g predicted job training performance in about the same way regardless of the difficulty or the kind of the job. Hull's (1928) theory argued that g was useful only for some jobs, but that specific abilities were compensatory or more important and, thus, more valid for other jobs. Ree and Earles tested Hull's hypothesis. Linear regression models were evaluated to test if the relations of g to training performance criteria were the same for the 82 jobs. Although there was statistical evidence that the relation between g and the training criteria varied by job, these differences were so small as to be of no practical predictive consequence. The relation between g and performance was practically identical across jobs. The differences were less than one half of 1%.

In practical personnel selection settings, specific ability tests sometimes are given to qualify applicants for jobs on the assumption that specific abilities are predictive or incrementally predictive of occupational performance. Such specific abilities tests exist for U.S. Air Force computer programmers and intelligence operatives. Besetsny, Earles, and Ree (1993) and Besetsny, Ree, and Earles (1993) investigated these two specific abilities tests to determine if they measured something other than g and if their validity was incremental to g. Participants were 3,547 computer programming and 776 intelligence operative trainees, and the criterion was training performance. Two multiple regression equations were computed for each sample of trainees. The first equation contained only g, and the second equation contained g and specific abilities. The difference in R^2 between these two equations was tested to determine how much specific abilities incremented g. For the two jobs, incremental validity increases for specific abilities beyond g were a trivial 0.00 and 0.02, respectively. Although they were developed to measure specific abilities, these two tests contributed little or nothing beyond g.

Thorndike (1986) analyzed World War II data to determine the incremental value of specific ability composites versus g for the prediction of passing and failing aircraft pilot training. Based on a sample of 1,000 trainees, Thorndike found an

---

[2]Because g and s are uncorrelated, the increment to s by g reflects the same relation as the increment of g by s. The question may be asked in either direction, but the answer is constant.

increment of 0.05 (0.64 vs. 0.59) for specifics above *g*. An examination of the test content indicates that specific knowledge was tested (i.e., aviation information) rather than specific abilities (e.g., math, spatial, verbal) and that specific knowledge may have accounted for part or all of the increment.

Similarly, Olea and Ree (1994) conducted an investigation of the validity and incremental validity of *g*, specific ability, and specific knowledge, in prediction of academic and work sample criteria for U.S. Air Force pilot and navigator trainees. The *g* factor and the other measures were extracted from the Air Force Officer Qualifying Test (Carretta & Ree, 1996), a multiple aptitude battery that measures *g* and lower order verbal, math, spatial, aircrew knowledge, and perceptual speed factors. The sample was approximately 4,000 college graduate Air Force lieutenants in pilot training and 1,500 lieutenants in navigator training. Similar training performance criteria were available for the pilots and navigators. For pilots, the criteria were academic grades, hands-on flying work samples (e.g., landings, loops, and rolls), passing and failing training, and an overall performance composite made by summing the other criteria. For navigators, the criteria included academic grades, work samples of day and night celestial navigation, passing and failing training, and an overall performance composite made by summing the other criteria. As much as 4 years elapsed between ability testing and collection of the training criteria.

Similar results were found for both the pilot and navigator samples. The best predictor for all criteria was the measure of *g*. For the composite criterion, the broadest and most encompassing measure of performance, the validity of *g* corrected for range restriction was 0.40 for pilots and 0.49 for navigators. The specific, or non-*g*, measures provided an average increase in predictive accuracy of 0.08 for pilots and 0.02 for navigators. Results suggested that specific knowledge about aviation (i.e., aviation controls, instruments, and principles) rather than specific cognitive abilities was responsible for the incremental validity found for pilots. The lack of incremental validity for specific knowledge for navigators might be due to the lack of tests of specific knowledge about navigation (i.e., celestial fix, estimation of course corrections).

Meta-analyses.   Levine, Spector, Menon, Narayanan, and Cannon-Bowers (1996) estimated the average true validity of *g*-saturated cognitive tests (see their appendix 2) in a meta-analysis of 5,872 participants in 52 studies and reported a value of 0.668 for training criteria. Hunter and Hunter (1984) provided a broad-based meta-analysis of the validity of *g* for training criteria. Their analysis included several hundred jobs across numerous job families as well as reanalyses of data from previous studies. Hunter and Hunter estimated the true validity of *g* as 0.54 for job training criteria. The research demonstrates that *g* predicts training criteria well across numerous jobs and job families.

To answer the question, if all you need is *g*, Schmidt and Hunter (1998) examined the utility of several commonly used personnel selection methods in a large-scale meta-analysis spanning 85 years of validity studies. Predictors included general mental ability (GMA is another name for *g*) and 18 other personnel selection procedures (e.g., biographical data, conscientiousness tests, integrity tests, employment interviews, reference checks). The predictive validity of GMA tests was estimated as .56 for training.[3] The two combinations of predictors with the highest multivariate validity for job training were GMA plus an integrity test (*M* validity of .67) and GMA plus a conscientiousness test (*M* validity of .65). Schmidt and Hunter did not include specific cognitive abilities in their study, but they were surely represented in the selection methods allowing for the finding of utility of predictors other than *g*.

Job Performance

Predictiveness of g.   Hunter (1983b) demonstrated that the predictive validity of *g* is a function of job complexity. In an analysis of U.S. Department of Labor data, Hunter classified 515 occupations into categories based on data handling complexity and complexity of dealing with things: simple feeding/offbearing and complex set-up work. As job complexity increased, the validity of *g* also increased. The average corrected validities of g were 0.40, 0.51, and 0.58 for the low, medium, and high data complexity jobs. The corrected validities were 0.23 and 0.56, respectively, for the low complexity feeding/offbearing jobs and complex set-up work jobs. Gottfredson (1997) provided a more complete discussion.

Vineburg and Taylor (1972) presented an example of the predictiveness of *g* in a validation study involving 1,544 U.S. Army enlistees in four jobs: armor, cook, repair, and supply. The predictors were from the *g*-saturated Armed Forces Qualification Test (AFQT). Range of experience varied from 30 days to 20 years, and the job performance criteria were work samples. The correlation between ability and job performance was significant. When the effects of education and experience were removed, the partial correlations between *g*, as measured by the AFQT, and job performance for the four jobs were the following: armor, 0.36; cook, 0.35; repair, 0.32; and supply, 0.38. Vineburg and Taylor also reported the validity of *g* for supervisory ratings. The validities for the same jobs were 0.26, 0.15, 0.15, and 0.11. On observing such similar validities across dissimilar jobs, Olea and Ree (1994) commented, "From jelly rolls to aileron rolls, *g* predicts occupational criteria" (p. 848).

Roth and Campion (1992) demonstrated the validity of a general ability composite for predicting job performance for petroleum process technicians. The validity of the *g*-based composite was 0.37, after correction for range restriction.

---

[3]Schmidt and Hunter (1998) corrected their validity estimates for range restriction on the predictor and unreliability of the criterion.

Carretta, Perry, and Ree (1996) examined job performance criteria for 171 U.S. Air Force F–15 pilots. The pilots ranged in experience from 193 to 2,805 F–15 flying hr and from 1 to 22 years of job experience. The performance criterion was based on supervisory and peer ratings of job performance, specifically "situation awareness" (SA). The criterion provided a broad-based measure of knowledge of the moving aircraft and its relations to all surrounding elements. The observed correlation of ability and SA was .10. When F–15 flying experience was partialed-out, the correlation became .17, an increase of 70% in predictive efficiency.

The predictiveness of g against current performance is clear. Chan (1996) demonstrated that g also predicts future performance. In a construct validation study of assessment centers, scores from a highly g-loaded test predicted future promotions for members of the Singapore Police Force. Those who scored higher on the test were more likely to be promoted. Chan also reported correlations between scores on Raven's Progressive Matrices and "initiative/creativity" and between the Raven's Progressive Matrices and the interpersonal style variable of "problem confrontation." Wilk, Desmarais, and Sackett (1995) showed that g was a principal cause of the "gravitational hypothesis" of job mobility and promotion. They noted that "individuals with higher cognitive ability move into jobs that require more cognitive ability and that individuals with lower cognitive ability move into jobs that require less cognitive ability" (p. 84).

Crawley, Pinder, and Herriot (1990) showed that g was predictive of task-related dimensions in an assessment-center context. The lowest and highest uncorrected correlations for g were with the assertiveness dimension and the task-based problem-solving dimension, respectively.

Kalimo and Vuori (1991) examined the relation between measures of g taken in childhood and the occupational health criteria of physical and psychological health symptoms and "sense of competency." They concluded that "weak intellectual capacity" during childhood led to poor work conditions and increased health problems.

Although Chan (1996) and Kalimo and Vuori (1991) provided information about future occupational success, O'Toole (1990) and O'Toole and Stankov (1992) went further, making predictions about morbidity. For a sample of male Australian military members 20 to 44 years of age, O'Toole found that the Australian Army intelligence test was a good predictor of mortality by vehicular accident. The lower the test score, the higher the probability of death by vehicular accident. O'Toole and Stankov (1992) reported similar results when they added death by suicide. The mean intelligence score for those who died from suicide was about 0.25 standard deviations lower than comparable survivors and a little more than 0.25 standard deviations lower for death by vehicular accident. In addition, the survivors differed from the decedents on variables related to g. Survivors completed more years of education, completed a greater number of academic degrees, rose to high military rank, and were more likely to be employed in white collar occupations. O'Toole and Stankov contended the following: "The 'theoretical' parts of driver examinations in most countries acts as primitive assessments of intelligence" (p. 715). Blasco (1994) observed that similar studies on the relation of ability to traffic accidents have been done in South America and Spain.

These results provide compelling evidence for the predictiveness of g against job performance and other criteria. In the next section, we review studies addressing the incremental validity of specific abilities with respect to g.

Incrementing the predictiveness of g.[4]   McHenry, Hough, Toquam, Hanson, and Ashworth (1990) predicted the Campbell, McHenry, and Wise (1990) job performance factors for nine U.S. Army jobs. They found that g was the best predictor of the first two criterion factors, "core technical proficiency" and "general soldiering proficiency," with correlations of 0.63 and 0.65 after correction for range restriction. Additional job reward preference, perceptual–psychomotor, spatial, temperament and personality, and vocational interest predictors failed to show much increment beyond g. None added more than 0.02 in incremental validity. Temperament and personality was incremental to g or superior to g for prediction for the other job performance factors. This is consistent with Crawley et al. (1990). It should be noted, however, that g was predictive of all job performance factors.

Ree, Earles, and Teachout (1994) examined the relative predictiveness of specific abilities versus g for job performance in seven enlisted U.S. Air Force jobs. They collected job performance measures of hands-on work samples, job knowledge interviews, and a combination of the two called the "Walk Through Performance Test" for 1,036 enlisted servicemen. The measures of g and specific abilities were extracted from a multiple aptitude battery. Regressions compared the predictiveness of g and specific abilities for the three criteria. The average validity of g across the seven jobs was 0.40 for the hands-on work sample, 0.42 for the job knowledge interview, and 0.44 for the "Walk Through Performance Test." The validity of g was incremented by an average of only 0.02 when the specific ability measures were added to the regression equations. The results from McHenry et al. (1990) and Ree, Earles, & Teachout, (1994) are very similar.

Meta-analyses.   Schmitt, Gooding, Noe, and Kirsch (1984) conducted a "bare bones" meta-analysis (Hunter & Schmidt, 1990; McDaniel, Hirsh, Schmidt, Raju, & Hunter, 1986) of the predictiveness of g for job performance. A bare bones analysis corrects for sampling error, but usually does not correct for other study artifacts such as range restriction and reliability. Bare bones analyses generally are less informative than studies that have been fully corrected for artifacts. Schmitt et al. observed an average validity of 0.248 for g. We corrected this value for range re-

---

[4]See previous footnote on incrementing g.

striction and predictor and criterion unreliability using the meta-analytically derived default values in Raju, Burke, Normand, and Langlois (1991). After correction, the estimated true correlation was 0.512.

Hunter and Hunter (1984) conducted a meta-analysis of hundreds of studies examining the relation between g and job performance. They estimated a mean true correlation of 0.45 across a broad range of job families.

Building on studies of job performance (Schmidt, Hunter, & Outerbridge, 1986) and job separation (McEvoy & Cascio, 1987), Barrick, Mount, and Strauss (1994) performed a meta-analysis of the relation between g and involuntary job separation. Employees with low job performance were more likely to be separated involuntarily. Barrick et al. (1994) observed an indirect relation between g and involuntary job separation that was moderated by job performance and supervisory ratings.

Finally, as reported earlier for training criteria, Schmidt and Hunter (1998) examined the utility of g and 18 other commonly used personnel selection methods in a large-scale meta-analysis. The predictive validity of g was estimated as .51 for job performance. The combinations of predictors with the highest multivariate validity for job performance were g plus an integrity test (M validity of .65), g plus a structured interview (M validity of .63), and g plus a work sample test (M validity of .63). Specific cognitive abilities were not included in the Schmidt and Hunter meta-analysis.

Path models.   Hunter (1986) provided a major summary of studies regarding cognitive ability, job knowledge, and job performance, concluding the following: " ... general cognitive ability has high validity predicting performance ratings and training success in all jobs" (p. 359). In addition to its validity, the causal role of g in job performance has been shown. Hunter (1983a) reported path analyses based on meta-analytically derived correlations relating g, job knowledge, and job performance. Hunter found that the major causal effect of g was on the acquisition of job knowledge. Job knowledge, in turn, had a major causal influence on work sample performance and supervisory ratings. Hunter did not report any direct effect of ability on supervisory job performance ratings; all effects were moderated (James & Brett, 1984). Job knowledge and work sample performance accounted for all of the relation between ability and supervisory ratings. Despite the lack of a direct impact, the total causal impact of g was considerable.

Schmidt, Hunter, and Outerbridge (1986) extended Hunter (1983a) by including job experience. They observed that experience influenced both job knowledge and work sample measures. Job knowledge and work sample performance directly influenced supervisory ratings. Schmidt et al. did not find a direct link between g and experience. The causal impact of g was entirely indirect.

Hunter's (1983a) model was confirmed by Borman, White, Pulakos, and Oppler (1991) in a sample of job incumbents. They made the model more parsimonious, showing sequential causal paths from ability to job knowledge to task proficiency to supervisory ratings. Borman et al.(1991) found that the paths from ability to task proficiency and from job knowledge to supervisory ratings were not necessary. They attributed this to the uniformity of job experience of the participants. Borman et al.'s (1991) parsimonious model subsequently was confirmed by Borman, White, and Dorsey (1995) on two additional peer and supervisory samples.

Whereas the previous studies used subordinate job incumbents, Borman, Hanson, Oppler, Pulakos, and White (1993) tested the model for supervisory job performance. Once again, ability influenced job knowledge. They also observed a small but significant path between ability and experience. They speculated that ability led to the individual getting the opportunity to acquire supervisory job experience. Experience subsequently led to increases in job knowledge, job proficiency, and supervisory ratings.

The construct of prior job knowledge was added to occupational path models by Ree, Carretta, and Teachout (1995) and Ree, Carretta, and Doub (1996). Prior job knowledge was defined as job-relevant knowledge applicants bring to training. Ree et al. (1995) observed a strong causal influence of g on prior job knowledge. No direct path was found for g to either of two work sample performance factors representing early and late training. However, g indirectly influenced work sample performance through the acquisition of job knowledge. This study also included a set of three sequential classroom training courses where job-related material was taught. The direct relation between g and the first sequential training factor was large. It was almost zero for the second sequential training factor that builds on the knowledge of the first and low positive for the third that introduces substantially new material. Ability exerted most of its influence indirectly through the acquisition of job knowledge in the sequential training courses.

Ree et al. (1996) used meta-analytically derived data from 83 studies and 42,399 participants to construct path models to examine the roles of g and prior job knowledge in the acquisition of subsequent job knowledge. Ability had a causal influence on both prior and subsequent job knowledge.

THE IMPORTANCE OF g TO ORGANIZATIONS AND PEOPLE

Not all employees are equally productive or effective in helping to achieve organizational goals. The extent to which we can identify the factors related to job performance and use this information to increase productivity is important to organizations. Campbell, Gasser, and Oswald (1996) reviewed the findings on the value of high and low job performance. Using a conservative approach, they estimated that the top 1% of workers is 3.29 times as productive as the lowest 1% of workers.

They estimated that the value may be from 3 to 10 times the return, depending on the variability of job performance. It is clear that job performance makes a difference in organizational productivity and effectiveness.

The validity of g for predicting occupation performance has been studied for a long time. Gottfredson (1997) argued that " ... no other measured trait, except perhaps conscientiousness ... has such general utility across the sweep of jobs in the American economy" (p. 83). Hattrup and Jackson (1996), commenting on the measurement and utility of specific abilities, concluded that they "have little value for building theories about ability-performance relationships" (p. 532).

Occupational performance starts with acquisition of the knowledge and skills needed for the job and continues into on-the-job performance and beyond. We and others have shown the ubiquitous influence of g; it is neither an artifact of factor analysis nor just academic ability. It predicts criteria throughout the life cycle including educational achievement, training performance, job performance, lifetime productivity, and finally early mortality. None of this can be said for specific abilities.

ACKNOWLEDGMENT

The views expressed are those of the authors and not necessarily those of the U.S. Government, Department of Defense, or the Air Force.

REFERENCES

Andreasen, N. C., Flaum, M., Swayze, V., O'Leary, D. S., Alliger, R., Cohen, G., Ehrhardt, J., & Yuh, W. T. C. (1993). Intelligence and brain structure in normal individuals. *American Journal of Psychiatry, 150*, 130–134.

Barrick, M., Mount, M., & Strauss, J. (1994). Antecedents of involuntary turnover due to a reduction of force. *Personnel Psychology, 47*, 515–535.

Besetsny, L. K., Earles, J. A., & Ree, M. J. (1993). Little incremental validity for a special test for Air Force intelligence operatives. *Educational and Psychological Measurement, 53*, 993–997.

Besetsny, L. K., Ree, M. J., & Earles, J. A. (1993). Special tests for computer programmers? Not needed. *Educational and Psychological Measurement, 53*, 507–511.

Blasco, R. D. (1994). Psychology and road safety. *Applied Psychology: An International Review, 43*, 313–322.

Borman, W. C., Hanson, M. A., Oppler, S. H., Pulakos, E. D., & White, L. A. (1993). Role of early supervisory experience in supervisor performance. *Journal of Applied Psychology, 78*, 443–449.

Borman, W. C., White, L. A., & Dorsey, D. W. (1995). Effects of ratee task performance and interpersonal factors on supervisor and peer performance ratings. *Journal of Applied Psychology, 80*, 168–177.

Borman, W. C., White, L. A., Pulakos, E. D., & Oppler, S. H. (1991). Models of supervisory job performance ratings. *Journal of Applied Psychology, 76*, 863–872.

Brand, C. (1987). The importance of general intelligence. In S. Modgil & C. Modgil (Eds.), *Arthur Jensen: Consensus and controversy* (pp. 251–265). New York: Falmer.

Brodnick, R. J., & Ree, M. J. (1995). A structural model of academic performance, socio-economic status, and Spearman's *g*. *Educational and Psychological Measurement, 55,* 583–594.

Broman, S. H., Nichols, P. L., Shaughnessy, P., & Kennedy, W. (1987). *Retardation in young children.* Hillsdale, NJ: Lawrence Erlbaum Associates, Inc.

Campbell, J. P., Gasser, M. B., & Oswald, F. L. (1996). The substantive nature of job performance variability. In K. R. Murphy (Ed.), *Individual differences and behavior in organizations* (pp. 258–299). San Francisco: Jossey-Bass.

Campbell, J. P., McHenry, J. J., & Wise, L. L. (1990). Modeling job performance in a population of jobs. Special issue: Project A: The US Army selection and classification project. *Personnel Psychology, 43,* 313–333.

Carretta, T. R., Perry, D. C., Jr., & Ree, M. J. (1996). Prediction of situational awareness in F–15 pilots. *The International Journal of Aviation Psychology, 6,* 21–41.

Carretta, T. R., & Ree, M. J. (1996). Factor structure of the Air Force Officer Qualifying Test: Analysis and comparison. *Military Psychology, 8,* 29–42.

Carretta, T. R., & Ree, M. J. (1997a). Expanding the nexus of cognitive and psychomotor abilities. *International Journal of Selection and Assessment, 5,* 149–158.

Carretta, T. R., & Ree, M. J. (1997b). Negligible sex differences in the relation of cognitive and psychomotor abilities. *Personality and Individual Differences, 22,* 165–172.

Carroll, J. B. (1993). Human cognitive abilities: A survey of factor-analytic studies. New York: Cambridge University Press.

Chaiken, S. R., Kyllonen, P. C., & Tirre, W. C. (2000). Organization and components of psychomotor ability. *Cognitive Psychology, 40,* 198–226.

Chalke, F. C. R., & Ertl, J. (1965). Evoked potentials and intelligence. *Life Sciences, 4,* 1319–1322.

Chan, D. (1996). Criterion and construct validation of an assessment centre. *Journal of Occupational and Organizational Psychology, 69,* 167–181.

Crawley, B., Pinder, R., & Herriot, P. (1990). Assessment centre dimensions, personality and aptitudes. *Journal of Occupational Psychology, 63,* 211–216.

Egan, V., Wickett, J. C., & Vernon, P. A. (1995). Brain size and intelligence: Erratum, addendum, and correction. *Personality and Individual Differences, 19,* 113–116.

Ertl, J., & Schafer, E. W. P. (1969). Brain response correlates of psychometric intelligence. *Nature, 223,* 421–422.

Eysenck, H. J. (1982). The psychophysiology of intelligence. In C. D. Spielberger & J. N. Butcher (Eds.), *Advances in personality assessment, 1* (pp. 1–33). Hillsdale, NJ: Lawrence Erlbaum Associates, Inc.

Fleishman, E. A., & Quaintance, M. K. (1984). *Taxonomies of human performance: The description of human tasks.* Orlando, FL: Academic.

Frearson, W., Eysenck, H. J., & Barrett, P. T. (1990). The Furneaux model of human problem solving: Its relationship to reaction time and intelligence. *Personality and Individual Differences, 11,* 239–257.

Galton, F. (1869). *Hereditary genius: An inquiry into its laws and consequences.* London: Macmillan.

Gottfredson, L. S. (1997). Why *g* matters: The complexity of everyday life. *Intelligence, 24,* 79–132.

Gould, S. J. (1981). *The mismeasure of man.* New York: Norton.

Guilford, J. P. (1956). The structure of intellect. *Psychological Bulletin, 53,* 267–293.

Guilford, J. P. (1959). Three faces of intellect. *American Psychologist, 14,* 469–479.

Haier, R. J., Siegel, B. V., Nuechterlein, K. H., Hazlett, E., Wu, J. C., Pack, J., Browning, H. L., & Buchsbaum, M. S. (1988). Cortical glucose metabolic rate correlates of abstract reasoning and attention studied with positron emission tomography. *Intelligence, 12,* 199–217.

Haier, R. J., Siegel, B., Tang, C., Able, L., & Buchsbaum, M. S. (1992). Intelligence and changes in regional cerebral glucose metabolic rate following learning. *Intelligence, 16,* 415–426.

Hart, B., & Spearman, C. (1914). Mental tests of dementia. *The Journal of Abnormal Psychology, 9,* 217–264.

Hattrup, K., & Jackson, S. E. (1996). Learning about individual differences by taking situations seriously. In K. R. Murphy (Ed.), *Individual differences and behavior in organizations* (pp. 507–547). San Francisco: Jossey-Bass.

Haug, H. (1987). Brain sizes, surfaces, and neuronal sizes of the cortex cerebri: A stereological investigation of man and his variability and a comparison with some species of mammals (primates, whales, marsupials, insectivores, and one elephant). *American Journal of Anatomy, 180,* 126–142.

Hull, C.L., (1928). *Apptitude Testing.* New York: World Book Company.

Hunter, J. E. (1983a). A causal analysis of cognitive ability, job knowledge, job performance, and supervisor ratings. In F. Landy, S. Zedeck, & J. Cleveland (Eds.), *Performance measurement and theory* (pp. 257–266). Hillsdale, NJ: Lawrence Erlbaum Associates, Inc.

Hunter, J. E. (1986). Cognitive ability, cognitive aptitudes, job knowledge, and job performance. *Journal of Vocational Behavior, 29,* 340–362.

Hunter, J. E., & Hunter, R. F. (1984). Validity and utility of alternative predictors of job performance. *Psychological Bulletin, 96,* 72–98.

Hunter, J. E., & Schmidt, F. L. (1990). *Methods of meta-analysis.* Newbury Park, CA: Sage.

James, L. R., & Brett, J. M. (1984). Mediators, moderators, and tests of mediation. *Journal of Applied Psychology, 69,* 307–321.

Jensen, A. R. (1980). *Bias in mental testing.* New York: Free Press.

Jensen, A. R. (1998). *The g factor: The science of mental ability.* Westport, CT: Praeger.

Jones, G. E. (1988). *Investigation of the efficacy of general ability versus specific abilities as predictors of occupational success.* Unpublished master's thesis, Saint Mary's University of Texas, San Antonio.

Jouandet, M. L., Tramo, M. J., Herron, D. M., Hermann, A., Loftus, W. C., & Gazzaniga, M. S. (1989). Brainprints: Computer-generated two-dimensional maps of the human cerebral cortex in vivo. *Journal of Cognitive Neuroscience, 1,* 88–116.

Kalimo, R., & Vuori, J. (1991). Work factors and health: The predictive role of pre-employment experiences. *Journal of Occupational Psychology, 64,* 97–115.

Larson, G. E., Haier, R. J., LaCasse, L., & Hazen, K. (1995). Evaluation of a "mental effort" hypothesis for correlations between cortical metabolism and intelligence. *Intelligence, 21,* 267–278.

Lawley, D. N. (1943). A note on Karl Pearson's selection formulae. *Proceedings of the Royal Society of Edinburgh, Section A, 62*(Pt. 1), 28–30.

Levine, E. L., Spector, P. E., Menon, S., Narayanan, L., & Cannon-Bowers, J. (1996). Validity generalization for cognitive, psychomotor, and perceptual tests for craft jobs in the utility industry. *Human Performance, 9,* 1–22.

Linn, R. L., Harnish, D. L., & Dunbar, S. (1981). Corrections for range restriction: An empirical investigation of conditions resulting in conservative corrections. *Journal of Applied Psychology, 66,* 655–663.

McClelland, D. C. (1993). Intelligence is not the best predictor of job performance. *Current Directions in Psychological Science, 2,* 5–6.

McDaniel, M. A., Hirsh, H. R., Schmidt, F. L., Raju, N. S., & Hunter, J. E. (1986). Interpreting the results of meta-analytic research: A comment on Schmidt, Gooding, Noe, and Kirsch (1944). *Personnel Psychology, 39,* 141–148.

McEvoy, G., & Cascio, W. (1987). Do good or poor performers leave? A meta-analysis of the relationship between performance and turnover. *Academy of Management Journal, 30,* 744–762.

McHenry, J. J., Hough, L. M., Toquam, J. L., Hanson, M. A., & Ashworth, S. (1990). Project A validity results: The relationship between predictor and criterion domains. *Personnel Psychology, 43,* 335–354.

McNemar, Q. (1964). Lost our intelligence? Why? *American Psychologist, 19*, 871–882.

Miller, E. M. (1996). Intelligence and brain myelination: A hypothesis. *Personality and Individual Differences, 17*, 803–832.

Olea, M. M., & Ree, M. J. (1994). Predicting pilot and navigator criteria: Not much more than *g*. *Journal of Applied Psychology, 79*, 845–851.

O'Toole, V. I. (1990). Intelligence and behavior and motor vehicle accident mortality. *Accident Analysis and Prevention, 22*, 211–221.

O'Toole, V. I., & Stankov, L. (1992). Ultimate validity of psychological tests. *Personality and Individual Differences, 13*, 699–716.

Pearson, K. (1903). Mathematical contributions to the theory of evolution: II. On the influence of natural selection on the variability and correlation of organs. *Royal Society of Philosophical Transactions, 200 (Series A)*, 1–66.

Rabbitt, P., Banerji, N., & Szymanski, A. (1989). Space fortress as an IQ test? Predictions of learning and of practiced performance in a complex interactive video-game. *Acta Psychologica, 71*, 243–257.

Raju, N. S., Burke, M. J., Normand, J., & Langlois, G. M. (1991). A new meta-analytic approach. *Journal of Applied Psychology, 76*, 432–446.

Ree, M. J., & Carretta, T. R. (1994a). The correlation of general cognitive ability and psychomotor tracking tests. *International Journal of Selection and Assessment, 2*, 209–216.

Ree, M. J., & Carretta, T. R. (1994b). The correlation of general cognitive ability and psychomotor tracking tests. *International Journal of Selection and Assessment, 2*, 209–216.

Ree, M. J., & Carretta, T. R. (1998). General cognitive ability and occupational performance. In C. L. Cooper & I. T. Robertson (Eds.), *International review of industrial and organizational psychology* (pp. 159–184). Chichester, England: Wiley.

Ree, M. J., Carretta, T. R., & Doub, T. W. (1996). *A test of three models of the role of g and prior job knowledge in the acquisition of subsequent job knowledge*. Manuscript submitted for publication.

Ree, M. J., Carretta, T. R., & Earles, J. A. (1998). In top-down decisions, weighting variables does not matter: A consequence of Wilks' theorem. *Organizational Research Methods, 1*, 407–420.

Ree, M. J., Carretta, T. R., Earles, J. A., & Albert, W. (1994). Sign changes when correcting for range restriction: A note on Pearson's and Lawley's selection formulas. *Journal of Applied Psychology, 79*, 298–301.

Ree, M. J., Carretta, T. R., & Teachout, M. S. (1995). Role of ability and prior job knowledge in complex training performance. *Journal of Applied Psychology, 80*, 721–780.

Ree, M. J., & Earles, J. A. (1991). The stability of *g* across different methods of estimation. *Intelligence, 15*, 271–278.

Ree, M. J., & Earles, J. A. (1992). Intelligence is the best predictor of job performance. *Current Directions in Psychological Science, 1*, 86–89.

Ree, M. J., & Earles, J. A. (1993). *g* is to psychology what carbon is to chemistry: A reply to Sternberg and Wagner, McClelland, and Calfee. *Current Directions in Psychological Science, 2*, 11–12.

Ree, M. J., & Earles, J. A. (1994). The ubiquitous predictiveness of *g*. In M. G. Rumsey, C. B. Walker, & J. B. Harris (Eds.), *Personnel selection and classification* (pp. 127–135). Hillsdale, NJ: Lawrence Erlbaum Associates, Inc.

Ree, M. J., Earles, J. A., & Teachout, M. S. (1994). Predicting job performance; Not much more than *g*. *Journal of Applied Psychology, 79*, 518–524.

Reed, T. E., & Jensen, A. R. (1992). Conduction velocity in a brain nerve pathway of normal adults correlates with intelligence level. *Intelligence, 16*, 259–272.

Roth, P. L., & Campion, J. E. (1992). An analysis of the predictive power of the panel interview and pre-employment tests. *Journal of Occupational and Organizational Psychology, 65*, 51–60.

Salgado, J. F. (1995). Situational specificity and within-setting validity variability. *Journal of Occupational and Organizational Psychology, 68*, 123–132.

Schmidt, F. L., & Hunter, J. E. (1993). Tacit knowledge, practical intelligence, general mental ability, and job knowledge. *Current Directions in Psychological Science, 2,* 8–9.

Schmidt, F. L., & Hunter, J. E. (1998). The validity and utility of selection methods in personnel psychology: Practical and theoretical implications of 85 years of research findings. *Psychological Bulletin, 124,* 262–274.

Schmidt, F. L., Hunter, J. E., & Outerbridge, A. N. (1986). Impact of job experience and ability on job knowledge, work sample performance, and supervisory ratings of job performance. *Journal of Applied Psychology, 71,* 432–439.

Schmitt, N., Gooding, R. Z., Noe, R. A., & Kirsch, M. (1984). Meta analyses of validity studies published between 1964 and 1982 and the investigation of study characteristics. *Personnel Psychology, 37,* 407–422.

Schultz, R. T. (1991). *The relationship between intelligence and gray–white matter image contrast: An MRI study of healthy college students.* Unpublished doctoral dissertation, University of Texas at Austin.

Schultz, R. T., Gore, J., Sodhi, V., & Anderson, A. L. (1993). Brain MRI correlates of IQ: Evidence from twin and singleton populations. *Behavior Genetics, 23,* 565.

Shucard, D. W., & Horn, J. L. (1972). Evoked cortical potentials and measurement of human abilities. *Journal of Comparative and Physiological Psychology, 78,* 59–68.

Spearman, C. (1904). "General intelligence" objectively defined and measured. *American Journal of Psychology, 15,* 201–293.

Spearman, C. (1923). *The nature of "intelligence" and the principles of cognition.* London: Macmillan.

Spearman, C. (1927). *The abilities of man: Their nature and measurement.* New York: MacMillan.

Spearman, C. (1930). "G" and after—A school to end schools. In C. Murchison (Ed.), *Psychologies of 1930* (pp. 339–366). Worchester, MA: Clark University Press.

Spearman, C. (1937). *Psychology down the ages, volume II.* London: MacMillan.

Stauffer, J. M., Ree, M. J., & Carretta, T. R. (1996). Cognitive components tests are not much more than *g*: An extension of Kyllonen's analyses. *The Journal of General Psychology, 123,* 193–205.

Sternberg, R. J., & Wagner, R. K. (1993). The *g*-ocentric view of intelligence and job performance is wrong. *Current Directions in Psychological Science, 2,* 1–5.

Thomson, G. (1939). *The factorial analysis of human ability.* London: University of London Press.

Thorndike, R. L. (1949). *Personnel selection.* New York: Wiley.

Thorndike, R. L. (1986). The role of general ability in prediction. *Journal of Vocational Behavior, 29,* 322–339.

Thurstone, L. L. (1938). Primary mental abilities. *Psychometric Monograph, 1.*

Tirre, W. C., & Raouf, K. K. (1998). Structural models of cognitive and perceptual–motor abilities. *Personality and Individual Differences, 24,* 603–614.

Tramo, M. J., Loftus, W. C., Thomas, C. E., Green, R. L., Mott, L. A., & Gazzaniga, M. S. (1995). Surface area of human cerebral cortex and its gross morphological subdivisions: *In vivo* measurements in monozygotic twins suggest differential hemispheric effects of genetic factors. *Journal of Cognitive Neuroscience, 7,* 292–301.

Van Valen, L. (1974). Brain size and intelligence in man. *American Journal of Physical Anthropology, 40,* 417–423.

Vineburg, R., & Taylor, E. (1972). *Performance of four Army jobs by men at different aptitude (AFQT) levels: 3. The relationship of AFQT and job experience to job performance* (Human Resources Research Organization Tech. Rep. No. 72–22). Washington, DC: Department of the Army.

Waxman, S. G. (1992). Molecular organization and pathology of axons. In A. K. Asbury, G. M. McKhann, & W. L. McDonald (Eds.), *Diseases of the nervous system: Clinical neurobiology* (pp. 25–46). Philadelphia: Saunders.

Wickett, J. C., Vernon, P. A., & Lee, D. H. (1994). In vitro brain size, head perimeter, and intelligence in a sample of healthy adult females. *Personality and Individual Differences, 16,* 831–838.

Wilk, S. L., Desmarais, L. B., & Sackett, P. R. (1995). Gravitation to jobs commensurate with ability: Longitudinal and cross-sectional tests. *Journal of Applied Psychology, 80,* 79–85.

Wilks, S. S. (1938). Weighting systems for linear functions of correlated variables when there is no dependent variable. *Psychometrika, 3,* 23–40.

Willerman, L., & Schultz, R. T. (1996). *The physical basis of psychometric g and primary abilities.* Manuscript submitted for publication.

Willerman, L., Schultz, R. T., Rutledge, A. N., & Bigler, E. D. (1991). *In vivo* brain size and intelligence. *Intelligence, 15,* 223–228.

HUMAN PERFORMANCE, *15*(1/2), 25–46

Where and Why *g* Matters: Not a Mystery

Linda S. Gottfredson
School of Education
University of Delaware

g is a highly general capability for processing complex information of any type. This explains its great value in predicting job performance. Complexity is the major distinction among jobs, which explains why *g* is more important further up the occupational hierarchy. The predictive validities of *g* are moderated by the criteria and other predictors considered in selection research, but the resulting gradients of *g*'s effects are systematic. The pattern provides personnel psychologists a road map for how to design better selection batteries. Despite much literature on the meaning and impact of *g*, there nonetheless remains an aura of mystery about where and why *g* cognitive tests might be useful in selection. The aura of mystery encourages false beliefs and false hopes about how we might reduce disparate impact in employee selection. It is also used to justify new testing techniques whose major effect, witting or not, is to reduce the validity of selection in the service of racial goals.

The general mental ability factor—*g*—is the best single predictor of job performance. It is probably the best measured and most studied human trait in all of psychology. Much is known about its meaning, distribution, and origins thanks to research across a wide variety of disciplines (Jensen, 1998). Many questions about *g* remain unanswered, including its exact nature, but *g* is hardly the mystery that some people suggest. The totality—the pattern—of evidence on *g* tells us a lot about where and why it is important in the real world. Theoretical obtuseness about *g* is too often used to justify so–called technical advances in personnel selection that minimize, for sociopolitical purposes, the use of *g* in hiring.

Requests for reprints should be sent to Linda S. Gottfredson, School of Education, University of Delaware, Newark, DE 19716. E-mail: gottfred@udel.edu

THE *g* FACTOR AMONG PEOPLE

Our knowledge of the mental skills that are prototypical of *g*, of the aspects of tasks that call forth *g*, and of the factors that increase or decrease its impact on performance together sketch a picture of where and why *g* is useful in daily affairs, including paid work. They show *g*'s predictable gradients of effect. I begin here with the common thread—the *g* factor—that runs through the panoply of people's mental abilities.

Generality and Stability of the *g* Factor

One of the simplest facts about mental abilities provides one of the most important clues to the nature of *g*. People who do well on one kind of mental test tend to do well on all others. When the scores on a large, diverse battery of mental ability tests are factor analyzed, they yield a large common factor, labeled *g*. Pick any test of mental aptitude or achievement—say, verbal aptitude, spatial visualization, the SAT, a standardized test of academic achievement in 8th grade, or the Block Design or Memory for Sentences subtests of the Stanford–Binet intelligence test—and you will find that it measures mostly *g*. All efforts to build meaningful mental tests that do not measure *g* have failed.

Thus, try as we might to design them otherwise, all our mental tests measure mostly the same thing, no matter how different their manifest content is. This means that *g* must be a highly general ability or property of the mind. It is not bound to any particular kind of task content, such as words, numbers, or shapes. Very different kinds of test content can be used to measure *g* well—or badly.

This dimension of human difference in intellect—the *g* factor—does not seem bound to particular cultures, either, because virtually identical *g* factors have been extracted from test batteries administered to people of different ages, sexes, races, and national groups. In contrast, no general factor emerges from personality inventories, which shows that general factors are not a necessary outcome of factor analysis. (See Jensen, 1998, and Gottfredson, 1997, 2000a, 2002, for fuller discussion and documentation of these and following points on *g*.)

g's high generality is also demonstrated by the predictive validities of mental tests. It is the *g* component of mental tests that accounts almost totally for their predictive validity. Indeed, whole batteries of tests do little better than *g* alone in predicting school and job performance. The more *g*-loaded a test is (the better it correlates with *g*), the better it predicts performance, including school performance, job performance, and income. There are many different abilities, of course, as is confirmed by the same factor analyses that confirm the dominance of the general factor among them. Because *g* is more general in nature than the narrower group factors (such as verbal aptitude, spatial visualization, and memory), it is, not surprisingly, also broader in applicability. The clerical (i.e., non-*g*) component of clerical tests, for instance, enhances performance somewhat in clerical jobs (beyond that afforded by higher *g*), but *g* enhances performance in all domains of work.

The *g* factor shows up in nonpsychometric tests as well, providing more evidence for both its reality and generality. Exceedingly simple reaction time and inspection time tasks, which measure speed of reaction in milliseconds, also yield a strong information processing factor that coincides with psychometric *g*.

In short, the *g* continuum is a reliable, stable phenomenon in human populations. Individual differences along that continuum are also a reliable, stable phenomenon. IQ tests are good measures of individual variation in *g*, and people's IQ scores become quite stable by adolescence. Large changes in IQ from year to year are rare even in childhood, and efforts to link them to particular causes have failed. Indeed, mental tests would not have the pervasive and high predictive validities that they do, and often over long stretches of the life span, if people's rankings in IQ level were unstable.

Theorists have long debated the definition of "intelligence," but that verbal exercise is now moot. *g* has become the working definition of intelligence for most researchers, because it is a stable, replicable phenomenon that—unlike the IQ score—is independent of the "vehicles" (tests) for measuring it. Researchers are far from fully understanding the physiology and genetics of intelligence, but they can be confident that, whatever its nature, they are studying the same phenomenon when they study *g*. That was never the case with IQ scores, which fed the unproductive wrangling to "define intelligence." The task is no longer to define intelligence, but to understand *g*.

Meaning of *g* as a Construct

Understanding *g* as a construct—its substantive meaning as an ability—is essential for understanding why and where *g* enhances performance of everyday tasks. Some sense of its practical meaning can be gleaned from the overt behaviors and mental skills that are prototypical of *g*—that is, those that best distinguish people with high *g* levels from those with low *g*. Intelligence tests are intended to measure a variety of higher order thinking skills, such as reasoning, abstract thinking, and problem solving, which experts and laypeople alike consider crucial aspects of intelligence. *g* does indeed correlate highly with specific tests of such aptitudes. These higher order skills are context- and content-independent mental skills of high general applicability. The need to reason, learn, and solve problems is ubiquitous and lifelong, so we begin to get an intuitive grasp of why *g* has such pervasive value and is more than mere "book smarts."

We can get closer to the meaning of *g*, however, by looking beyond the close correlates of *g* in the domain of human abilities and instead inspect the nature of the tasks that call it forth. For this, we must analyze data on tasks, not people. Recall that the very definition of an ability is rooted in the tasks that people can perform. To abbreviate Carroll's (1993, pp. 3–9) meticulously-crafted definition, an *ability* is an attribute of individuals revealed by differences in the levels of task difficulty on a defined class of tasks that individuals perform successfully when conditions for maximal performance are favorable. Superficial inspection of *g*-loaded tests and tasks shows immediately what they are not, but are often mistakenly assumed to be—curriculum or domain dependent. Thus, the distinguishing attributes of *g*-loaded tasks must cut across all content domains.

Comparisons of mental tests and items reveal that the more *g*-loaded ones are more complex, whatever their manifest content. They require more complex processing of information. The hypothetical IQ test items in Figure 1 illustrate the point. Items in the second column are considerably more complex than those in the first column, regardless of item type and regardless of whether they might seem "academic." To illustrate, the first item in the first row requires only simple computation. In contrast, the second item in that row requires exactly the same computation, but the person must figure out which computation to make. The similarities items in the third row differ in abstractness in the similarities involved. The more difficult block design item uses more blocks and a less regular pattern, and so on.

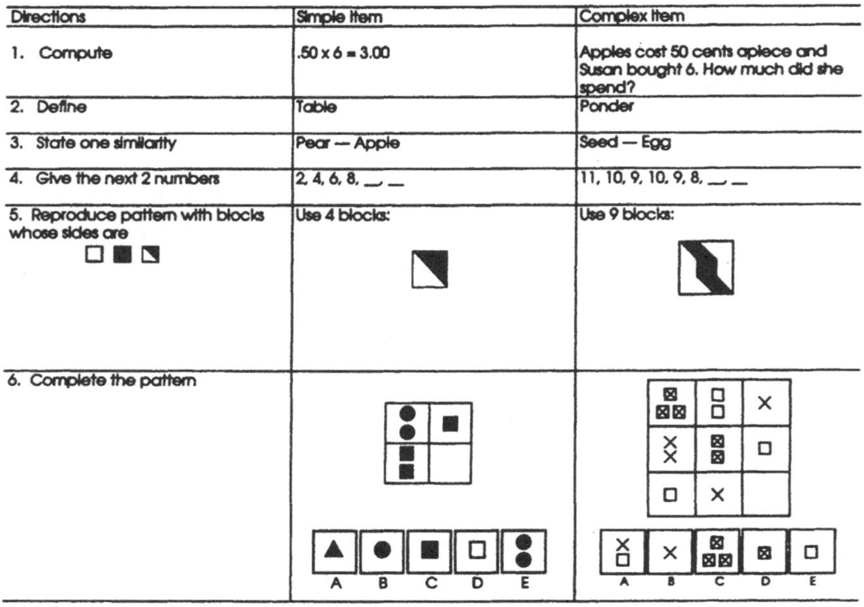

FIGURE 1   Hypothetical examples of simple versus more complex IQ test items.

Task complexity has been studied systematically in various contexts, some psychometric and some not. Researchers in the fields of information processing, decision making, and goal setting stress the importance of the number, variety, variability, ambiguity, and interrelatedness of information that must be processed to evaluate alternatives and make a decision. Wood (1986), for example, discussed three dimensions of task complexity: component complexity (e.g., number of cues to attend to and integrate, redundancy of demands), coordinative complexity (e.g., timing or sequencing of tasks, length of sequences), and changes in cause–effect chains or means–ends relations. More complex items require more mental manipulation for people to learn something or solve a problem—seeing connections, drawing distinctions, filling in gaps, recalling and applying relevant information, discerning cause and effect relations, interpreting more bits of information, and so forth.

In a detailed analysis of items on the U.S. Department of Education's National Adult Literacy Survey (NALS), Kirsch and Mosenthal (1990) discovered that the relative difficulty of the items in all three NALS scales (prose, document, quantitative) originated entirely in the same "process complexity": type of match (literalness), plausibility of distractors (relevance), and type of information (abstractness). The active ingredient in the test items was the complexity, not content, of the information processing they required. Later research (Reder, 1998) showed, not surprisingly, that the three scales represent one general factor and virtually nothing else.

One useful working definition of g for understanding everyday competence is therefore the ability to deal with complexity. This definition can be translated into two others that have also been offered to clarify g's real-world applications—the ability to learn moderately complex material quickly and efficiently and the ability to avoid cognitive errors (see the discussion in Gottfredson, 1997). Most globally, then, g is the ability to process information. It is not the amount of knowledge per se that people have accumulated. High g people tend to possess a lot of knowledge, but its accumulation is a by-product of their ability to understand better and learn faster.

They fare better with many daily tasks for the same reason. Although literacy researchers eschew the concept of intelligence, they have nonetheless confirmed g's importance in highly practical daily affairs. They have concluded, with some surprise, that differences in functional literacy (using maps, menus, order forms, and bank deposit slips; understanding news articles and insurance options; and the like) and health literacy (understanding doctors' instructions and medicine labels, taking medication correctly, and so on) reflect, at heart, differences in a general ability to process information (Gottfredson, 1997, 2002).

Clearly, there is much yet to be learned about the nature of g, especially as a biological construct. We know enough about its manifest nature already, however, to dispel the fog of mystery about why it might be so useful. It is a generic, infinitely adaptable tool for processing any sort of information, whether on the job or off, in training or after.

THE COMPLEXITY FACTOR AMONG JOBS

We also know a lot about where high *g* confers its greatest advantages. Its impact is lawful, not ephemeral or unpredictable.

Analyses of the Skills That Jobs Demand

Just as the skills that people possess have been factor analyzed, so too have the demands that jobs make. Both analyses yield analogous results, hardly a statistically necessary result. Just as there is a general ability factor among individuals, there is a general complexity factor among jobs. (See Gottfredson, 1985, on how the former may cause the latter.) The largest, most consistent distinction among jobs is the complexity of their information processing demands. In some studies, this jobs factor has been labeled "judgment and reasoning" (Arvey, 1986). In sociological research, it is usually labeled "complexity."

Table 1 reveals the meaning of the job complexity factor by listing its strongest correlates. The results in Table 1 are from a principal components analysis of 64% of the broad occupational categories (and 86% of jobs) in the 1970 census. That analysis used all job analysis data then available that could be linked to the census titles. All those job analysis attributes are listed in Table 1 so that it is clear which ones do and do not correlate with job complexity. Table 1 lists them according to whether they correlate most highly with the complexity factor rather than some other factor. (None of these items was used in actually deriving the factors. See Gottfredson, 1997, for the items used in the principal components analysis.) The data come primarily from the Position Analysis Questionnaire (PAQ), but also from the 1970 U.S. Census, ratings in *Dictionary of Occupational Titles*, and several smaller bodies of occupational data (labeled here as the Temme and Holland data). All the attributes listed in Table 1 are from the PAQ, unless otherwise noted.

Almost all of the many items pertaining to information processing correlate most highly with the complexity factor. These items represent requirements for perceiving, retrieving, manipulating, and transmitting information. Those that are generally viewed as higher level processing skills, such as compiling and combining information (.90, .88), reasoning (.86), and analyzing (.83), have the highest correlations with the complexity factor. Somewhat lower level processes, such as memory (.40) and transcribing (.51), have lower but still substantial correlations. Only the highly visual information processing activities (e.g., seeing, vigilance with machines) fail to correlate most with the complexity factor. They correlate, instead, with factors reflecting use of objects ("things") and machines, independ-

TABLE 1

Job Attributes That Correlate Most With the Job Complexity Factor

Correlate Most With "Complexity" Factor	r	Correlate Most With Another Factor	r	The Other Factor
Processing information (perceiving, retrieving, manipulating, transmitting)				
Compiling information, importance of	0.90	Seeing (DOT)	0.66	Work with complex things
Combining information, importance of	0.88	Information from events, extent of use	0.58	Vigilance with machines
Language, level of (DOT)	0.88	Vigilance—changing events, importance of	0.57	Vigilance with machines
Reasoning, level of (DOT)	0.86	Pictorial materials, extent of use	0.44	Work with complex things
Writing, importance of	0.86	Apply measurable, verifiable criteria (DOT)	0.43	Work with complex things
Intelligence (DOT)	0.84	Vigilance—infrequent events, importance of	0.41	Vigilance with machines
Written information, extent of use	0.84	Patterns, extent of use	0.41	Work with complex things
Analyzing information, importance of	0.83	Interpret others' feelings, ideas, facts (DOT)	0.22	Catering to people
Math, level of (DOT)	0.79			
Math, level of	0.70			
Quantitative information, extent of use	0.68			
Coding and decoding, importance of	0.68			
Oral information, extent of use	0.68			
Talking (DOT)	0.68			
Behavioral information, extent of use	0.59			
Apply sensory and judgmental criteria (DOT)	0.55			
Attention to detail, importance of	0.54			
Transcribing, importance of	0.51			
Short-term memory, importance of	0.40			
Recognize and identify, importance of	0.36			
Practical problem solving				
Advising, importance of	0.86	Supervising nonemployees, importance of	0.64	Catering to people
Planning and scheduling, amount of	0.83	Catering and serving, importance of	0.61	Catering to people
Decision making, level of	0.82	Entertaining, importance of	0.59	Catering to people
Negotiating, importance of	0.79	Non-job-required social contact, opportunity	0.25	Catering to people
Persuading, importance of	0.79			

(continued)

31

TABLE 1 (Continued)

Correlate Most With "Complexity" Factor	r	Correlate Most With Another Factor	r	The Other Factor
Staff functions, importance of	0.79			
Coordinate without line authority, importance of	0.74			
Public speaking, importance of	0.68			
Instructing, importance of	0.67			
Direction, control, and planning (DOT)	0.59			
Dealing with people (DOT)	0.59			
Influencing (DOT)	0.42			
Level of responsibility and respect				
Prestige (Temme)	0.82	Responsibility for materials, degree of	0.48	Vigilance with machines
General responsibility, degree of	0.76	Responsibility for safety, degree of	0.47	Vigilance with machines
Criticality of position, degree of	0.71			
Job structure				
Self-direction (Temme)	0.88	Complexity of dealings with things (DOT)	0.77	Work with complex things
Complexity of dealings with data (DOT)	0.83	Follow set procedures, importance of	0.54	Operating machines
Work under distractions, importance of	0.78	Meet set limits, tolerances, standards (DOT)	0.53	Work with complex things
Frustrating situations, importance of	0.77	Specified work pace, importance of	0.44	Operating machines
Interpersonal conflict, importance of	0.76	Cycled activities, importance of	0.42	Operating machines
Strained contacts, importance of	0.69	Perform under stress and risk (DOT)	0.27	Vigilance with machines
Complexity of dealings with people (DOT)	0.68			
Personal contact required, extent of	0.66			
Personal sacrifice, importance of	0.65			
Civic obligations, importance of	0.64			
Time pressure, importance of	0.55			
Precision, importance of	0.53			
Variety and change (DOT)	0.41			
Repetitive activities, importance of	−0.49			
Supervision, level of	−0.73			
Repetitive or continuous (DOT)	−0.74			
Structure, amount of	−0.79			

Variable	r	Variable	r	Descriptor
Focus of work and interests required				
Interest in data versus things (DOT)	0.73	"Conventional" field of work (Holland)	0.51	Coordination without sight
Interest in creative versus routine work (DOT)	0.63	"Social" field of work (Holland)	0.45	Catering to people
Interest in social welfare versus machines (DOT)	0.55	Interest in science vs. business (DOT)	0.42	Work with complex things
Interest in producing versus esteem (DOT)	-0.48	"Investigative" field of work (Holland)	0.37	Work with complex things
"Realistic" field of work (Holland)	-0.74	"Enterprising" field of work (Holland)	0.33	Selling
		"Artistic" field of work (Holland)	0.20	Work with complex things
Education and experience required				
Education, level of curriculum	0.88			
General education development level (DOT)	0.86			
Update job knowledge, importance of	0.85			
Specific vocational preparation (DOT)	0.76			
Experience, lenght of	0.62			
Training, length of	0.51			
Physical requirements				
Wet, humid (DOT)	-0.37	Outside versus inside location (DOT)	0.48	Vigilance with machines
Hazardous conditions (DOT)	-0.39	Climbing (DOT)	0.42	Controlled manual work
Fumes, odors, dust, gases (DOT)	-0.45			
Stooping (DOT)	-0.48			
Noise, vibration (DOT)	-0.53			
Physical exertion, level of	-0.56			
Reaching (DOT)	-0.66			
Other correlates				
Salary, yes or no	0.70	Commission, yes or no	0.53	Selling
Percentage government workers, men (census)	0.45	Tips, yes or no	0.50	Selling
Percentage government workers, women (census)	0.45	Licensing and certification	0.42	Catering to people
Percentage black, women (census)	-0.48	Median age, men (census)	0.31	Vigilance with machines
Percentage black, men (census)	-0.53	Mean hours, men (census)	0.31	Controlled manual
Wage, yes or no	-0.66	Median age, women (census)	-0.28	Coordination without sight
		Mean hours, women (census)	-0.34	Catering to people
		Percentage women (census)	-0.37	Controlled manual

Note.   Source of data: Gottfredson (1997). DOT = Dictionary of Occupational Titles; Temme = Temme's ratings of occupatioanl prestige and self-direction; Holland = Holland's vocational personality type codes for occupations (see Gottfredson, 1994, for description and use of these scales).

ent of the job's overall complexity. The extent of use of most forms of information (behavioral, oral, written, quantitative) is also strongly correlated with overall job complexity (.59–.84) but no other factor. The primary exception, once again, is visual (use of patterns and pictorial materials).

Many job duties can be described as general kinds of problem solving—for instance, advising, planning, negotiating, instructing, and coordinating employees without line authority. As Table 1 shows, they are also consistently and substantially correlated with job complexity (.74–.86). In contrast, the requirements for amusing, entertaining, and pleasing people mostly distinguish among jobs at the same complexity level, for they help to define the independent factor of "catering to people."

Complex dealings with data (.83) and people (.68) are more typical of highly complex than simple jobs, as might be expected. Complex dealings with things (material objects) help to define a separate and independent factor: "work with complex things" (which distinguishes the work of engineers and physicians, e.g., from that of lawyers and professors). Constant change in duties or the data to be processed ("variety and change," .41) also increase a job's complexity. As the data show, the more repetitive (−.49, −.74), tightly structured (−.79), and highly supervised (−.73) a job is, the less complex it is. Complexity does not rule out the need for tight adherence to procedure, a set work pace, cycled activities, or other particular forms of structure required in some moderately complex domains of work. As can be seen in Table 1, these attributes typify work that is high on the "operating machines" (and vehicles) factor of work.

That the overall complexity of a job might be enhanced by the greater complexity of its component parts is no surprise. However, Table 1 reveals a less well-appreciated point—namely, that job complexity also depends on the configuration of tasks, not just on the sum of their individual demands. Any configuration of tasks or circumstances that strains one's information processing abilities puts a premium on higher g. Consider dual-processing and multitasking, for instance, which tax people's ability to perform tasks simultaneously that they have no trouble doing sequentially. The data in Table 1 suggest that information processing may also be strained by the pressures imposed by deadlines (.55), frustration (.77), and interpersonal conflict (.76), and the need to work in situations where distractions (.78) compete for limited cognitive resources. Certain personality traits would aid performance in these situations, but higher g would also allow for more effective handling of these competing stresses.

The importance of performing well tends to rise with job complexity, because both the criticality of the position for the organization (.71) and the general responsibility it entails (.76) correlate strongly with job complexity. Responsibility for materials and safety are more domain specific, however, because they correlate most with the "vigilance with machines" factor.

Education and training are highly g-loaded activities, as virtually everyone recognizes. Table 1 shows, however, that more complex jobs tend not only to require higher levels of education (.88), but also lengthier specific vocational training (.76) and experience (.62). The data on experience are especially important in this context, because experience signals knowledge picked up on the job. It reflects a form of self-instruction, which becomes less effective the lower one's g level. Consistent with this interpretation, the importance of "updating job knowledge" correlates very highly (.85) with job complexity.

More complex jobs tend to require more education and pay better, which in turn garners them greater social regard. Hence, the job complexity factor closely tracks the prestige hierarchy among occupations (.82), another dimension of work that sociologists documented decades ago.

The other attributes that correlate most highly with complexity, as well as those that do not, support the conclusion that the job complexity factor rests on distinctions among jobs in their information processing demands, generally without regard to the type of information being processed. Of the six Holland fields of work, only one—Realistic—correlates best (and negatively) with the complexity factor (–.74). Such work, which emphasizes manipulating concrete things rather than people or abstract processes, comprises the vast bulk of low-level jobs in the American economy. The nature of these jobs comports with the data on vocational interests associated with the complexity factor. Complex work is associated with interests in creative rather than routine work (.63), with data (.73), and with social welfare (.55), respectively, rather than things and machines, and with social esteem rather than having tangible products (.48). This characterization of low-level, frequently Realistic work is also consistent with the data on physical requirements: All the physically unpleasant conditions of work (working in wet, hazardous, noisy, or highly polluted conditions) are most characteristic of the simplest, lowest-level jobs (–.37 to –.45). In contrast, the skill and activity demands associated with the other factors of work are consistently specific to particular functional domains (fields) of work—for example, selling with "enterprising" work and coordination without sight (such as typing) with "conventional" (mostly clerical) work. So, too, are various other circumstances of work, such as how workers are paid (salary, wages, tips, commissions), which tend to distinguish jobs that require selling from those that do not, whatever their complexity level.

As we saw, the job analysis items that correlate most highly with overall job complexity use the very language of information processing, such as compiling and combining information. Some of the most highly correlated mental demands, such as reasoning and analyzing, are known as prototypical manifestations of intelligence in action. The other dimensions of difference among jobs rarely involve such language. Instead, they generally relate to the material in different domains of work activity, how (not how much) such activity is remunerated, and the vocational interests they satisfy. They are noncognitive by contrast.

The information processing requirements that distinguish complex jobs from simple ones are therefore essentially the same as the task requirements that distinguish highly g-loaded mental tests, such as IQ tests, from less g-loaded ones, such as tests of short-term memory. In short, jobs are like (unstandardized) mental tests. They differ systematically in g-loading, depending on the complexity of their information processing demands. Because we know the relative complexity of different occupations, we can predict where job performance (when well measured) will be most sensitive to differences in workers' g levels. This allows us to predict major trends in the predictive validity of g across the full landscape of work in modern life. One prediction, which has already been borne out, is that mental tests predict job performance best in the most complex jobs.

The important point is that the predictive validities of g behave lawfully. They vary, but they vary systematically and for reasons that are beginning to be well understood. Over 2 decades of meta-analyses have shown that they are not sensitive to small variations in job duties and circumstance, after controlling for sampling error and other statistical artifacts. Complex jobs will always put a premium on higher g. Their performance will always be notably enhanced by higher g, all else equal. Higher g will also enhance performance in simple jobs, but to a much smaller degree.

This lawfulness can, in turn, be used to evaluate the credibility of claims in personnel selection research concerning the importance, or lack thereof, of mental ability in jobs of at least moderate complexity, such as police work. If a mental test fails to predict performance in a job of at least moderate complexity (which includes most jobs), we cannot jump to the conclusion that differences in mental ability are unimportant on that job. Instead, we must suspect either that the test does not measure g well or that the job performance criterion does not measure the most crucial aspects of job performance. The law-like relation between job complexity and the value of g demands such doubt. Credulous acceptance of the null result requires ignoring the vast web of well-known evidence on g, much of it emanating from industrial–organizational (I/O) psychology itself.

RELATIVE IMPORTANCE OF g FOR JOB PERFORMANCE

The I/O literature has been especially useful in documenting the value of other predictors, such as personality traits and job experience, in forecasting various dimensions of performance. It thus illuminates the ways in which g's predictive validities can be moderated by the performance criteria and other predictors considered. These relations, too, are lawful. They must be understood to appreciate where, and to what degree, higher levels of g actually have functional value on the job. I/O research has shown, for instance, how g's absolute and relative levels of predictive validity both vary according to the kind of performance criterion used. A failure to understand these gradients of effect sustains the mistaken view that g's impact on performance is capricious or highly specific across different settings and samples.

The Appendix outlines the topography of g—that is, its gradients of effect relative to other predictors. It summarizes much evidence on the prediction of job performance, which is discussed more fully elsewhere (Gottfredson, 2002). This summary is organized around two distinctions, one among performance criteria and one among predictors, that are absolutely essential for understanding the topography of g and other precursors of performance. First, job performance criteria differ in whether they measure mostly the core technical aspects of job performance rather than a job's often discretionary "contextual" (citizenship) aspects. Second, predictors can be classified as "can do" (ability), "will do" (motivation), or "have done" (experience) factors.

The Appendix repeats some of the points already made, specifically that (a) g has pervasive value but its value varies by the complexity of the task at hand, and (b) specific mental abilities have little incremental validity net of g, and then only in limited domains of activity. The summary points to other important regularities. As shown in the Appendix, personality traits generally have more incremental validity than do specific abilities, because "will do" traits are correlated little or not at all with g, the dominant "can do" trait, and thus have greater opportunity to add to prediction. These noncognitive traits do, however, tend to show the same high domain specificity that specific abilities do. The exception is the personality factor representing conscientiousness and integrity, which substantially enhances performance in all kinds of work, although generally not as much as does g.

An especially important aspect of g's topography is that the functional value of g increases, both in absolute and relative terms, as performance criteria focus more on the core technical aspects of performance rather than on worker citizenship (helping coworkers, representing the profession well, and so on). The reverse is generally true for the noncognitive "will do" predictors, such as temperaments and interests: They predict the noncore elements best. Another important regularity is that, although the predictive validities of g rise with job complexity, the opposite is true for two other major predictors of performance—length of experience and psychomotor abilities. The latter's predictive validities are sometimes high, but they tend to be highest in the simplest work.

Another regularity is that "have done" factors sometimes rival g in predicting complex performance, but they are highly job specific. Take job experience—long experience as a carpenter does not enhance performance as a bank teller. The same is true of job sample or tacit knowledge tests, which assess workers' developed competence in a particular job: Potential bank tellers cannot be screened with a sample of carpentry work. In any case, these "have done" predictors can be used to select only among experienced applicants. Measures of g (or personality) pose no such constraints. g is generalizable, but experience is not.

As for g, there are also consistent gradients of effect for job experience. The value of longer experience relative to one's peers fades with time on the job, but the advantages of higher g do not. Experience is therefore not a substitute for g. After controlling for differences in experience, g's validities are revealed to be stable and substantial over many years of experience. Large relative differences in experience among workers with low absolute levels of experience can obscure the advantages of higher g. The reason is that a little experience provides a big advantage when other workers still have little or none. The advantage is only temporary, however. As all workers gain experience, the brighter ones will glean relatively more from their experience and, as research shows, soon surpass the performance of more experienced but less able peers. Research that ignores large relative differences in experience fuels mistaken conceptions about g. Such research is often cited to support the view that everyday competence depends more on a separate "practical intelligence" than on g—for example, that we need to posit a practical intelligence to explain why inexperienced college students cannot pack boxes in a factory as efficiently as do experienced workers who have little education (e.g., see Sternberg, Wagner, Williams, & Horvath, 1995).

The foregoing gradients of g's impact, when appreciated, can be used to guide personnel selection practice. They confirm that selection batteries should select for more than g, if the goal is to maximize aggregate performance, but that g should be a progressively more important part of the mix for increasingly complex jobs (unless applicants have somehow already been winnowed by g). Many kinds of mental tests will work well for screening people yet to be trained, if the tests are highly g-loaded. Their validity derives from their ability to assess the operation of critical thinking skills, either on the spot ("fluid" g) or in past endeavors ("crystallized" g). Their validity does not depend on their manifest content or "fidelity"—that is, whether they "look like" the job. Face validity is useful for gaining acceptance of a test, but it has no relation to the test's ability to measure key cognitive skills. Cognitive tests that look like the job can measure g well (as do tests of mathematical reasoning) or poorly (as do tests of arithmetic computation).

Tests of noncognitive traits are useful supplements to g-loaded tests in a selection battery, but they cannot substitute for tests of g. The reason is that noncognitive traits cannot substitute for the information-processing skills that g provides. Noncognitive traits also cannot be considered as useful as g even when they have the same predictive validity (say, .3) against a multidimensional criterion (say, supervisor ratings), because they predict different aspects of job performance. The former predict primarily citizenship and the latter primarily core performance. You get what you select for, and the wise organization will never forego selecting for core performance.

There are circumstances where one might want to trade away some g to gain higher levels of experience. The magnitude of the appropriate trade-off, if any, would depend on the sensitivity of job performance to higher levels of g (the complexity of the work), the importance of short-term performance relative to long-term performance (probable tenure), and the feasibility and cost of training brighter recruits rather than hiring more experienced ones (more complex jobs require longer, more complex training). In short, understanding the gradients of effect outlined in the Appendix can help practitioners systematically improve—or knowingly degrade—their selection procedures.

THE FLIGHT FROM *g*

Sociopolitical goals for racial parity in hiring and the strong legal pressure to attain it, regardless of large racial disparities in *g*, invite a facade of mystery and doubt about *g*'s functional impact on performance, because the facade releases practitioners from the constraints of evidence in defending untenable selection practices. The facade promotes the false belief that the impact of *g* is small, unpredictable, or ill-understood. It thereby encourages the false hope that cognitive tests, if properly formed and used, need not routinely have much, if any, disparate impact—or even that they could be eliminated altogether. Practitioners can reduce disparate impact in ways that flout the evidence on *g*, but they, and their clients, cannot escape the relentless reality of *g*. To see why, it is useful to review the most troublesome racial gap in *g*—that between Blacks and Whites. Like *g*, its effects in selection are highly predictable.

The Predictable Impact of Racial Disparities in *g*

The roughly one standard deviation IQ difference between American Blacks and Whites (about 15 points) is well known. It is not due to bias in mental tests (Jensen, 1980; Neisser et al., 1996), but reflects disparities in the information-processing capabilities that *g* embodies (Jensen, 1998). Figure 2 shows the IQ bell curves for the two populations against the backdrop of the job complexity continuum. The point to be made with them—specifically, that patterns of disparate impact are predictable from group differences in *g*—applies to other racial–ethnic comparisons as well. The IQ bell curves for Hispanic and Native American groups in the United States are generally centered about midway between those for Blacks and Whites. The disparate impact of mental tests is therefore predictably smaller for them than for Blacks when *g* matters in selection. The bell curves for other groups (Asian Americans and Jewish Americans) cluster above those for Whites, so their members can usually be expected to be overrepresented when selection is *g* loaded. The higher the groups' IQ bell curves, the greater their overrepresentation relative to their proportion in the general population. It is the Black–White gap, however, that drives the flight from *g* in selection and thus merits closest attention.

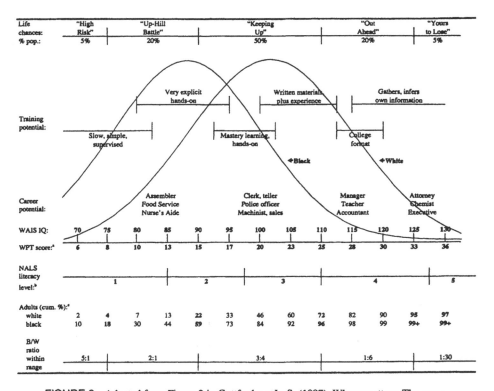

Life chances:	"High Risk"		"Up-Hill Battle"			"Keeping Up"			"Out Ahead"		"Yours to Lose"
% pop.:	5%		20%			50%			20%		5%

FIGURE 2   Adapted from Figure 3 in Gottfredson, L. S. (1997). Why *g* matters: The complexity of everyday life. *Intelligence, 24,* 79–132, with permission from Elsevier Science. [a]WPT = Wonderlic Personnel Test. [b]NALS = National Adult Literacy Survey. See Gottfredson (1997) for translation of NALS scores into IQ equivalents. [c]WAIS = Wechsler Adult Intelligence Scale. [d]See Gottfredson (1997) for calculation of percentiles.

The bell curves in Figure 2 are for representative samples of American Blacks and Whites. Racial disparities can differ somewhat from one setting to another for a host of reasons, so that the Black–White differences will sometimes be larger or smaller than those shown here. However, Figure 2 illuminates the big picture—namely, both populations in the context of the American economy. Specifically, it shows the two bell curves against the backdrop of the job complexity factor, which is arrayed along the "normal" range of the IQ continuum (from the threshold for borderline mental retardation to that for giftedness). Common occupations are arrayed along this continuum according to the IQ ranges from which they draw most of their incumbents. Those ranges therefore define the IQ ranges that make a person competitive for such work. Typical modes of training that are possible (at the higher ranges of IQ) or required (at the lower ranges) at different IQ levels are also shown.

The cumulative percentages of American Blacks and Whites at each IQ level are shown at the bottom of Figure 2. The ratios in the last row represent the proportion of all Blacks to the proportion of all Whites within five different broad ranges of IQ. Blacks are overrepresented (5:1) in the lowest range (below IQ 75, labeled here as the "high risk" zone) and extremely underrepresented (1:30) in the highest (above IQ 125, the range where "success is yours to lose"). These ratios represent racial differences in the per capita availability of applicants who will be competitive for different levels of work, and they portend a clear trend in disparate impact. Under race–neutral hiring, disparate impact will generally be high enough to fail the 80% rule (which triggers the presumption of racial discrimination under federal guidelines) in hiring for all but the simplest jobs.

When Black and White applicants are drawn from the same IQ ranges, disparate impact will therefore be the rule, not the exception, even in jobs of modest complexity. It will get progressively worse at successively higher levels of education, training, and employment, and it will be extremely high in the most desirable jobs. Cognitive tests cannot meet the 80% rule with these two populations until the threshold for consideration falls to about IQ 77 to 78 (Gottfredson, 2000b). This low estimate is consistent with other research showing that mental tests have to be virtually eliminated from test batteries to satisfy the 80% rule under typical conditions (Schmitt, Rogers, Chan, Sheppard, & Jennings, 1997). The estimate also falls below the minimum mental standard (about IQ 80) that federal law sets for inducting recruits into the military.

To take some more specific examples, about 22% of Whites and 59% of Blacks have IQs below 90, which makes considerably fewer Blacks competitive for mid-level jobs, such as firefighting, the skilled trades, and many clerical jobs. The average IQ of incumbents in such jobs is nearer IQ 100, one standard deviation above the Black average of roughly IQ 85. IQ 80 seems to be the threshold for competitiveness in even the lowest level jobs, and four times as many Blacks (30%) as Whites (7%) fall below that threshold. Looking toward the other tail of the IQ distribution, IQ 125 is about average for professionals (e.g., lawyers, physicians, engineers, professors) and high-level executives. The Black–White ratio of availability is only 1:30 at this level. Disparate impact, and therefore political and legal tension, is thus particularly acute in the most complex, most socially desirable jobs.

Actual employment ratios are not as extreme as the per capital availability ratios shown here (other factors matter in hiring), but they follow the same systematic decline up the job complexity continuum. There is considerable IQ variability among incumbents in any occupation, of course, the standard deviation among incumbents generally averaging about 8 IQ points. The average Black–White difference is twice that large, however, which guarantees that Blacks will often cluster at the lowest levels of performance when workers are hired randomly by g or with race-norming.

Minimizing Selection for g to Minimize Disparate Impact

The hope in personnel selection for a long time was that personnel psychologists could reduce disparate impact by developing technically better cognitive tests. If anything, improvements only worsened the disparate impact challenge because they resulted in more accurate measurement of g. Because good measurement has not provided the solution, it now tends to be treated as part of the problem, hence the popularity of test score banding in some quarters (it treats all scores within a specified range as equal), which reduces the reliability of measurement. Hence, also, the turning away from proven mental tests in major selection projects in favor of unproven "innovative" cognitive tests that substitute fidelity for validity and outside help for standardized conditions in taking the test. The suggestions that noncognitive tests can substitute for cognitive ones, or contextual performance for core performance, also promise to reduce the role of g in selecting workers. Such changes will do nothing, of course, to nullify the impact of lower g levels once workers are actually on the job.

One suggestion during the "Millennial Debate on g" at the Society for Industrial/Organizational Psychology convention in 2000 was that the value of good worker performance itself has been overemphasized, that we have overstated its utility. Such suggestions reflect the impact-driven claim, growing even in I/O circles, that a racially-balanced workforce is at least as important as a competent one; or that racial parity might even be a prerequisite to productivity. Going further along this line of argument, one panelist warned that Blacks simply will not put up with disparate impact, implying that balance should be our primary concern. No one at the debate argued that g was unimportant. Nonetheless, the cumulative message from its doubters, implicit but persistent, was that (without the option to race-norm) progressive practice requires cutting back on the use of g in selection.

Some of the arguments for doing so were implicit appeals to discredited theories. For instance, the claim that we ought to be more reluctant to use mental tests because Blacks suffer from stereotype threat when taking tests amounts to a claim that highly cognitive tests are biased against Blacks. We already know this claim to be false. The typical cognitive test has been exonerated of bias against low-scoring minorities. Indeed, personnel psychologists know that mental tests overpredict performance when they are used in a race-neutral manner. Another untenable claim, still offered frequently and flush with promise, is that we can create equally valid cognitive tests with considerably reduced disparate impact. Any claim to have succeeded is suspect. "Innovative" formats, item types, and scoring procedures for tests have all been offered with fanfare in recent years, but to the extent that they reduce disparate impact, we must suspect that they have degraded selection for mental skills. The same is true for any impact-driven switch in performance criteria. The vexing fact, which no tinkering with measurement can eliminate, is that Blacks and Whites differ most, on the average, on the most important predictor of job performance.

Some panelists also retreated into the unsubstantiated claim that there are multiple forms of intelligence, independent of g, that could predict job performance with less disparate impact. However, even the strongest body of evidence—that for so-called practical intelligence and its associated triarchic theory of intelligence (Sternberg et al., 2000)—provides only scant and contradictory bits of evidence for such a claim. Coming from a mere six studies (four of which remain unpublished) of five occupations, those data provide no support whatsoever (see Gottfredson, in press; also Brody, in press) for Sternberg et al.'s (2000, p. xi) assertion that "practical intelligence is a construct that is distinct from general intelligence and ... is at least as good a predictor of future success as is the academic form of intelligence [g]".

Reducing disparate impact is a worthy goal to which probably all selection professionals subscribe. What is troubling are the new means being promulgated: minimizing or eliminating the best overall predictor of job performance. They amount to a call for reducing test validity and thereby violating personnel psychology's primary testing standard. Reducing the role of g in selection may be legally and politically expedient in the short term, but it delays more effective responses to the huge racial gaps in job-relevant skills, abilities, and knowledges.

REFERENCES

Arvey, R. D. (1986). General ability in employment: A discussion. *Journal of Vocational Behavior, 29*, 415–420.

Brody, N. (in press). Construct validation of the Sternberg Triarchic Abilities Test. (STAT): Comment and reanalysis. *Intelligence, 30.*

Carroll, J. B. (1993). *Human cognitive abilities: A survey of factor-analytic studies.* New York: Cambridge University Press.

Gottfredson, L. S. (1985). Education as a valid but fallible signal of worker quality: Reorienting an old debate about the functional basis of the occupational hierarchy. In A. C. Kerckhoff (Ed.), *Research in sociology of education and socialization, Vol. 5* (pp. 119–165). Greenwich, CT: JAI.

Gottfredson, L.S. (1994). *The role of intelligence and education in the division of labor.* Report No. 355. Baltimore, MD: Johns Hopkins University, Center for Social Organization of Schools.

Gottfredson, L. S. (1997). Why g matters: The complexity of everyday life. *Intelligence, 24*, 79–132.

Gottfredson, L. S. (2000a). Intelligence. In E. F. Borgatta & R. J. V. Montgomery (Eds.), *Encyclopedia of sociology, revised edition* (pp. 1359–1386). New York: Macmillan.

Gottfredson, L. S. (2000b). Skills gaps, not mental tests, make racial proportionality impossible. *Psychology, Public Policy, and Law, 6*, 129–143.

Gottfredson, L. S. (2002). g: Highly general and highly practical. In R.J. Sternberg & E. L. Grigorenko (Eds.), *The general intelligence factor: How general is it?* (pp. 331-380) Mahwah, NJ: Lawrence Erlbaum Associates, Inc.

Gottfredson, L. S, Sternberg J. & Grigorenko E. L. (Eds.), *The general intelligence factor: How general is it?* Mahwah, NJ: Lawrence Erlbaum Associates, Inc.

Gottfredson, L. S. (in press). Dissecting practical intelligence theory: Its claims and evidence. *Intelligence, 30.*

Jenson, A.R. (1980). *Bias in mental testing.* New York; Free Press.

Jensen, A. R. (1998). *The g factor: The science of mental ability.* Westport, CT: Praeger.

Kirsh I. S., & Mosenthal P. B. (1990). Exploring document literacy: Variables underlying the performance of young adults. *Reading Research Quarterly, 25,* 5-30.

Neisser, U., Boodoo, G., Bouchard, T. J., Jr., Boykin, A. W., Brody, N., Ceci, S. J., Halpern, D. F., Loehlin, J. C., Perloff, R., Sternberg, R. J., & Urbina, S. (1996). Intelligence: Knowns and unknowns. *American Psychologist, 51,* 77–101.

Reder, S. (1998). Dimensionality and construct validity of the NALS assessment. In M. C. Smith (Ed.), *Literacy for the twenty–first century* (pp. 37–57). Westport, CT: Praeger.

Schmitt, N., Rogers, W., Chan, D., Sheppard, L., & Jennings, D. (1997). Adverse impact and predictive efficiency of various predictor combinations. *Journal of Applied Psychology, 82,* 719–730.

Sternberg, R. J., Forsythe, G. B., Hedlund, J., Horvath, J. A., Wagner, R. K., Williams, W. M., Snook, S. A., & Grigorenko, E. L. (2000). *Practical intelligence in everyday life.* New York: Cambridge University Press.

Sternberg, R. J., Wagner, R. K., Williams, W. M., & Horvath, J. A. (1995). Testing common sense. *American Psychologist, 50,* 912–926.

Wood, R. E. (1986). Task complexity: Definition of the construct. *Organizational Behavior and Human Decision Processes, 37,* 60–82.

APPENDIX 1
Major Findings on *g*'s Impact on Job Performance a Utility of *g*

1. Higher levels of *g* lead to higher levels of performance in all jobs and along all dimensions of performance. The average correlation of mental tests with overall rated job performance is around .5 (corrected for statistical artifacts).

2. There is no ability threshold above which more *g* does not enhance performance. The effects of *g* are linear: successive increments in *g* lead to successive increments in job performance.

3. (a) The value of higher levels of *g* does not fade with longer experience on the job. Criterion validities remain high even among highly experienced workers. (b) That they sometimes even appear to rise with experience may be due to the confounding effect of the least experienced groups tending to be more variable in relative level of experience, which obscures the advantages of higher *g*.

4. *g* predicts job performance better in more complex jobs. Its (corrected) criterion validities range from about .2 in the simplest jobs to .8 in the most complex.

5. *g* predicts the core technical dimensions of performance better than it does the non-core "citizenship" dimension of performance.

---

[a]See Gottfredson (2002) for fuller discussion and citations.

6. Perhaps as a consequence, *g* predicts objectively measured performance (either job knowledge or job sample performance) better than it does subjectively measured performance (such as supervisor ratings).

Utility of *g* Relative to Other "Can Do" Components of Performance

7. Specific mental abilities (such as spatial, mechanical, or verbal ability) add very little, beyond *g,* to the prediction of job performance. *g* generally accounts for at least 85-95% of a full mental test battery's (cross-validated) ability to predict performance in training or on the job.

8. Specific mental abilities (such as clerical ability) sometimes add usefully to prediction, net of *g,* but only in certain classes of jobs. They do not have general utility.

9. General psychomotor ability is often useful, but primarily in less complex work. Its predictive validities fall with complexity while those for *g* rise.

Utility of *g* Relative to the "Will Do" Component of Job Performance

10. *g* predicts core performance much better than do "non-cognitive" (less *g*-loaded) traits, such as vocational interests and different personality traits. The latter add virtually nothing to the prediction of core performance, net of *g.*

11. *g* predicts most dimensions of non-core performance (such as personal discipline and soldier bearing) much less well than do "non-cognitive" traits of personality and temperament. When a performance dimension reflects both core and non-core performance (effort and leadership), *g* predicts to about the same modest degree as do non-cognitive (less *g*-loaded) traits.

12. Different non-cognitive traits appear to usefully supplement *g* in different jobs, just as specific abilities sometimes add to the prediction of performance in certain classes of jobs. Only one such non-cognitive trait appears to be as generalizable as *g*: the personality trait of conscientiousness/integrity. Its effect sizes for core performance are substantially smaller than *g*'s, however.

Utility of *g* Relative to the Job Knowledge

13. *g* affects job performance primarily *indirectly* through its effect on job-specific knowledge.

14. *g*'s direct effects on job performance increase when jobs are less routinized, training is less complete, and workers retain more discretion.

15. Job-specific knowledge generally predicts job performance as well as does *g* among experienced workers. However, job knowledge is not generalizable (net

of its g component), even among experienced workers. The value of job knowledge is highly job specific; g's value is unrestricted.

Utility of g Relative to the "Have Done" (Experience) Component of Job Performance

16. Like job knowledge, the effect sizes of job-specific experience are sometimes high but they are not generalizable.

17. In fact, experience predicts performance less well as all workers become more experienced. In contrast, higher levels of g remain an asset regardless of length of experience.

18. Experience predicts job performance less well as job complexity rises, which is opposite the trend for g. Like general psychomotor ability, experience matters least where g matters most to individuals and their organizations.

HUMAN PERFORMANCE, *15*(1/2), 47–74

Asking the Right Questions About *g*

Charlie L. Reeve
Department of Psychological Sciences
Perdue University

Milton D. Hakel
Department of Psychology
Bowling Green State University

It is our position that a complete understanding of human intellectual development is of ultimate interest to researchers and of great import to society. In this article, we ask questions that reflect common themes seen in the debate regarding the nature and importance of general cognitive ability (i.e., the *g* factor), sources of individual and group differences, and the viability of arguments against *g* theory. We also examine questions reflecting aspects of these debates that are commonly ignored or misconstrued. Our goal is to help researchers and debaters continue or begin to ask clear, critical, and dispassionate questions about *g* that will stimulate productive research and promote informed public policy.

Consideration of human intelligence likely arose in step with the rise of human civilization. Indeed, formal philosophical treatment of individual differences in intelligence can be traced back to at least Plato, and evidence indicates that testing for individual differences, borne out of the recognition of differences in intelligent behavior, arose as early as 2357 B.C.E. in what is now China (Nitko, 1983). Although scientific treatment of intelligence did not appear until the late 19th century (Jensen, 1998), theory development and a wealth of empirical data accumulated since that time supports two conclusions: (a) intelligence is of great functional importance in virtually every aspect of life (Brand, 1996b; Brody, 1996; Gordon, 1997; Gottfredson, 1997b; Herrnstein & Murray, 1994; Jensen, 1998), and (b) a general cognitive ability factor, *g,* underlies all specific cognitive abilities (Brand,

Requests for reprints should be sent to Charlie L. Reeve, Department of Psychological Sciences, 1364 Psychological Science Building, Purdue University, West Lafayette, IN 47907–1364. E-mail: creeve@bgnet.bgsu.edu or mhakel@bgnet.bgsu.edu

1996a; Carroll, 1993, 1997; Jensen, 1998; Spearman, 1904). Nonetheless, an enormous amount remains to be understood about the nature of intelligence; its development across the life span; the specific genetic and environmental factors that either hinder or spur its development; and how abilities, personality, and preferences (i.e., values, interests) combine and interact with facets of the environment to determine both intraindividual and interindividual differences in the acquisition of domain-specific knowledge, leading to effective performance.

In this article, we ask questions that reflect common themes seen in the debate regarding the nature and importance of the g factor, sources of individual and group differences, and the viability of arguments against g theory. We also examine questions reflecting aspects of these debates that are commonly ignored or misconstrued. Our goal is to help researchers and debaters continue or begin to ask questions about g that will stimulate productive research. We hope this leads to informed public policy, particularly regarding employee selection and other employment practices. Not all of the questions we address have answers at this time; others do. We do not, however, pretend to have any unique insight to the issues. We have based our answers on a reading of the evidence.

IS THERE A g FACTOR?

Often the debate over intelligence questions the existence of g. Is there a single general mental factor underlying individual differences in specific mental abilities? In short, the answer is yes. Arguably, no other psychometric question has been scrutinized and empirically tested more than this one. The evidence is clear: There is a g factor that underlies human mental functioning (Brand, 1996a; Carroll, 1993; Gottfredson, 1997a; Jensen, 1980a, 1998; Spearman, 1904; Thurstone, 1947). The g factor has been shown to be remarkably invariant across (a) different test batteries (Ree & Earles, 1991b; Thorndike, 1987); (b) the method of factor extraction (Jensen, 1998; Jensen & Weng, 1994); and (c) racial, cultural, ethnic, and nationality groups (Carroll, 1993; Irvine & Berry, 1988; Jensen, 1985; Jensen, 1998; Jensen & Reynolds, 1982). Occasionally, a theory antithetical to g-theory is proposed, but so far, these efforts have failed to produce data that confirm an alternative theory (e.g., Gardner, 1983; see Campbell, 1996; Carroll, 1997; and Jensen, 1998, for criticisms), contradict the construct validity of the g factor, or undermine the practical importance of individual differences in g (Jensen, 1998).

Despite the evidence, as is proper in science, attempts to discredit g continue. Gould (1996), for example, argued that g is purely an arbitrary mathematical artifact, and by conducting research on g, psychologists are guilty of "reification." This argument is fallacious, however, as pointed out by Carroll (1997), Jensen (1980a, 1982), and Jensen and Weng (1994). All constructs are abstractions, purposely invoked to describe coherent classes of phenomena that co-occur in nature.

For instance, gravity is a mathematical construct that describes one of the four classes of forces associated with matter. Similarly, g is a psychometric and psychological construct that describes a class of phenomena associated with results of human mental functioning. Both of these constructs are abstract ideas; both are latent. However, because the phenomena ascribed to these constructs can be observed, the constructs are subject to conceptual refinement, measurement, and verification. Constructs are, in essence, minitheories, and testing them is equivalent to theory testing (Binning & Barrett, 1989; Carroll, 1993; Cronbach & Meehl, 1955). Constructs need not be "hard objects" to be real in a scientific sense (Meehl, 1991).

Failing to discredit the evidence of g, others have added the redundant adjective "psychometric" in an attempt to imply that "psychometric g" is merely a statistical phenomenon and thus has no practical importance (e.g., Sternberg, Wagner, Williams, & Horvath, 1995). However, because all factors are "psychometric," one wonders about the implications of this line of reasoning for Sternberg's conceptualization of "practical intelligence." The evidence is clear and overwhelming: "Psychometric g" is something very much worth measuring.

IS g IMPORTANT?

You might ask, "Important for what?," but that does not much matter. A wealth of data has confirmed that there is virtually no circumstance, no life outcome, no criterion for which even minimal cognitive functioning is required in which g is not at least moderately predictive of individual differences (Brand, 1996a; Gordon, 1997; Gottfredson, 1997b; Herrnstein & Murray, 1994; Jensen, 1998). We can think of no reason why this question should continue to be debated: g is important.

IS g IMPORTANT ONLY BECAUSE WE MEASURE IT?

This question conveys an idea that has been forwarded by a few, even in the scientific literature (e.g., Sternberg & Kaufman, 1998). The argument is that correlations between g and criteria only exist because people have been preselected on the basis of g. This is a false argument. The influence of individual differences in g will manifest whether or not we acknowledge and measure them. The correlations observed between measures of intelligence and various criteria reflect natural covariation. The covariation does not suddenly exist because we measure g and a criterion. (Interestingly, no one has ever argued that the criteria are important only because we measure them.) Again, consider gravity—no one was around to measure gravity (or even conceptualize the construct) for billions of years, but do we seriously question whether gravity exerted any influence on the universe until Newton discovered it? In addition, this argument is flawed from a statistical viewpoint. To the extent that a sample is preselected on any given trait, the correlation between that trait and any criterion will diminish due to restriction of range in variance.

The importance of *g* comes not from our assessment of it per se, but rather from its relations with a vast array of important criteria. It is the breadth and depth of the *g* nexus and the robustness of that nexus across cultures, countries, time, and environments that make *g* important. It is true that we now take advantage of our understanding of intelligence and our ability to assess it. Indeed, no other social intervention has been as successful at breaking down class-based privilege and moving underprivileged, intelligent youth into higher education than the standardized assessment of intelligence (Benbow & Stanley, 1996; J. Gardner, 1984; Jensen, 1980a). *g* is not important because we measure it; we measure it because it is important.

IF *g* IS SO IMPORTANT, WHY NOT TEST EVERY 6-YEAR-OLD AND GIVE PHD DEGREES TO THE BRIGHTEST?

Sometimes it is easy to misinterpret or overinterpret research findings. When a title includes a phrase such as "Not much more than *g*" (Ree & Earles, 1991a), it is tempting to gloss over methodological details and to jump to the conclusion that only *g* is important. Observed practice in education suggests, however, that high *g* is not sufficient. Obtaining a PhD is based on demonstrated knowledge and skill. Although above-average *g* is probably necessary for mastering the performance demands of a PhD program, a number of other factors are necessary as well. For instance, an individual must have enough interest in the domain to select the area and to help sustain motivation once enmeshed in the drudgeries of graduate school. Similarly, in many cases individuals will need a specific combination of personality factors that give rise to the resilience, stubbornness, and humility necessary to put up with the demands of the program and the idiosyncrasies of one's advisor. Not every high *g* person deserves, is capable of, or wants a PhD.

SO WHY DO WE USE *g*-LOADED TESTS FOR SELECTION INTO PHD PROGRAMS?

The training, resources, and time that universities can provide to doctoral candidates are limited. Although the desire to receive a PhD is important, it is not sufficient. To perform well in the research environment, a minimum level of ability is required. Allowing anyone who wants a PhD to enter a program would be extremely costly, both economically and psychologically. Individuals who are intellectually unequipped for graduate school are quite likely to suffer failure. This wastes resources for both parties and also is a punishing experience for failing individuals. (We also acknowledge that earning a PhD may in part be a punishing experience for those who do so.)

IS *g* THE ONLY IMPORTANT DIFFERENCE AMONG PEOPLE?

No, of course not. Although one cannot ignore the huge influence of individual differences in *g*, acknowledging that *g* is important does not imply that other factors are unimportant codeterminants of valued outcomes. Similarly, saying that other factors are highly important does not suggest that *g* is not highly important. Obviously *g* does not predict everything perfectly.

IS *g* THE MOST IMPORTANT DIFFERENCE AMONG PEOPLE?

The phrase "most important" is somewhat misleading and probably creates much unnecessary debate. If we define "most important" specifically in terms of accounting for the most variance in "job performance" (for jobs typically studied by industrial–organizational [I–O] psychologists) or "academic performance," then *g* is almost always the "most important" factor. In the aggregate, individual differences in *g* predict a wider array of criteria and do so better than any other single variable. If I–O psychologists could know only one thing about individuals, we would be best served by choosing to know *g*.

But what a different world it would be! Think about it—a one-dimensional psychology, with only one predictor. Fortunately, we are not limited to a single variable, and we do not have to limit our criteria to the common variance among measures of job or academic performance. We are adept at assessing a wide range of individual differences, and also we know that an assessment of individual differences on a wide array of factors will always predict a single criterion, or an array of criteria, better than any single variable, whether that single variable is *g* or any other construct. Why then is there much contentious debate over the nature of the single best predictor?

This is not to say that we see no value in investigating single predictor–criterion relations to understand the full range and nature of a variable's impact. However, there are presumably many determinants of any criterion, and accurately measuring individual differences in a larger constellation of traits will always be more informative (Lubinski, 2000; Murphy, 1996). Debating which one is "most important" appears to be of little value. The better question is to ask, "For a given domain, what combination of traits and environmental conditions afford the best probability of acquiring expertise and demonstrating effective performance?"

IS A SINGLE FACTOR MODEL THE BEST REPRESENTATION OF THE PREDICTOR SPACE?

The construct space of mental abilities is best described, not by a single factor model, but rather by a factor hierarchy with numerous specific abilities occupying the lower levels, a small number of group factors at an intermediate level, and a single general factor at the top (Carroll, 1993). The appropriate level of measurement within the hierarchy will depend on the purpose of prediction and the nature of the criterion or criteria that one seeks to predict. Although each of the specific abilities is g-loaded, they each yield reliable, unique variance that may differentially relate to various classes of criteria. The assessment of specific abilities may be especially useful in personnel classification (Murphy, 1996), academic and career counseling (Dawis, 1992; Lubinski, 2000), and predicting specific achievement factors (Gustafsson & Balke, 1993).

Furthermore, even a hierarchical model is inadequate if we consider the larger predictor space relevant to work psychology. As exemplified by Dawis and Lofquist's (1984) Theory of Work Adjustment, abilities, personality, and preferences (i.e., values, interests) will all interact with the environmental features of a job to determine a breadth of individual outcomes (e.g., satisfaction, competence). The goals of differential psychology are ultimately based on a multivariate assessment of individuals (Dawis, 1992; Lubinski, 2000, Wachs, 1993).

IS A SINGLE FACTOR MODEL THE BEST REPRESENTATION OF THE CRITERION SPACE?

Although "performance" is often thought of and discussed as a unitary construct, there is little doubt that the criterion space is also multidimensional. Defining job performance as the class of behaviors exhibited by employees that are relevant to the goals of the job or the organization (Campbell, McHenry, & Wise, 1990; Murphy & Shiarella, 1997), researchers have shown that a multidimensional model is most appropriate (Campbell, McCloy, Oppler, & Sager, 1993; Campbell et al., 1990). Indeed, although finer gradations are appropriate, a broad distinction is commonly made between the technical performance of core tasks and more "contextualized" behaviors that are not specific for task accomplishment but are necessary for the normal functioning of a team or organization (Borman & Motowidlo, 1993; Motowidlo & Van Scotter, 1994). Although g tends to predict technical and core performance better than other factors in virtually every job studied (Hunter & Hunter, 1984; Schmidt & Hunter, 1998), noncognitive factors tend to outperform g as predictors of the other aspects of performance (Borman, Hanson, & Hedge, 1997; Campbell et al., 1990).

The relevant point here is that the g debate tends to place almost sole focus on the predictor side of the equation, whereas criteria have been virtually ignored. Differentiating, validating, and understanding criterion constructs is as important as doing so for predictor constructs. Poor specification of criterion constructs can obfuscate meaningful relations between criteria and predictors (Gustafsson & Snow, 1997). Some of the contentiousness of the g debate is likely a direct result of poor specification of criteria.

HOW IS g IMPORTANT? (THIS IS *NOT* ASKING, "HOW IMPORTANT IS *G*?")

We know that individual differences in g have extremely important consequences. However, our understanding of how g comes to yield such broad and strong impact is negligible. Many important questions remain unanswered, and the evidence is sparse. What are the biological and physiological correlates of g that account for individual differences in cognitive performance? How do those correlates come to be associated with individual and group differences in academic, work, and social outcomes? How broad and deep is the g nexus? Why is the predictive validity of g so robust in the face of other individual and situational differences? There is no question that g is important. We need to be asking how g achieves this importance.

IS g THE PRIMARY DETERMINANT OF INTERINDIVIDUAL DIFFERENCES IN DOMAIN-SPECIFIC PERFORMANCE?

Within a specific domain (i.e., a defined area of organized knowledge or activities, a field of study, or job type), individual differences in g typically account for a lot of variance in performance (e.g., Ree & Earles, 1991a, 1991b). Thus, if we define "primary determinant" as the strongest predictor of domain-specific performance differences, then g is typically the "primary determinant." To stop here, however, is a mistake. Domain-specific deliberate-practice has also been shown to be the primary direct determinant of expert and exceptional performance (Ericsson, Krampe, & Tesch-Römer, 1993). In many domains, attainment of expert or exceptional performance capability requires thousands of hours of focused, intensive deliberate-practice; in some cases, the threshold level of practice for attaining expert performance exceeds 10,000 hr (Ericsson & Lehmann, 1996). Does this mean g is not an important determinant of domain-specific performance? Not at all.

These seemingly contradictory positions can be reconciled easily. Whereas *g* is primarily a *distal* antecedent of performance, practice is a key *proximal* determinant of effective performance. Practice makes real the investment of *g* in a domain. Differences in *g* give rise to important differences in the rate and depth of knowledge and skill acquisition, which in turn are direct antecedents of performance differences (Campbell et al., 1993). At the same time, differences in *g* are likely to create differences in the extent to which experiences afford positive reinforcement (Lubinski & Benbow, 2000). In a complex domain, initial efforts to learn by high *g* individuals are more likely to be successful and thus evaluated as positive, interesting, and pleasurable experiences. This will bolster motivation to continue to seek out and persist in opportunities for further skill acquisition within that domain; that is, they are more likely to engage in and sustain deliberate practice. Thus, differences in knowledge, skill, interest, and motivation associated with differences in *g* ultimately give rise to differences in the propensity to engage in deliberate practice, which in turn give rise to differences in performance (see Winner, 2000, for similar arguments). Practice will lead to better performance for virtually everyone; however, higher *g* people are more likely to initiate, sustain, and benefit from practice, especially in complex domains. In this sense, *g* is an important determinant of performance differences, but it is arguably not a "primary" direct determinant.

The aforementioned discussion should not be construed as arguing that other individual difference factors do not play an important role in the acquisition of domain-specific expertise. Differential psychological research has shown reliable influence of individual differences in interests (Rathunde & Csikszentmihalyi, 1993; Reeve & Hakel, 2000; Schiefele, Krapp, & Winteler, 1992), work values (Dawis & Lofquist, 1984), personality (Barrick & Mount, 1991; Eysenck, 1995), and specific cognitive abilities (Gustafsson & Balke, 1993; Prediger, 1989) on domain-specific learning, achievement, and work performance. The same rationale applies. The extent to which experiences within a domain are reinforcing or punishing is determined by the fit between these factors and the specific demands and supplies of the environment. To the extent that efforts to invest *g* in a domain are experienced as rewarding (rather than punishing), the more likely the person is to engage in deliberate practice.

It should be noted that *g*, or any other individual difference factor, may be more or less important for any given domain. Indeed, Simonton (1999) developed an emergenic and epigenic model of domain-specific talent development that posits the existence of threshold levels for individual difference factors that vary across domains. The model specifies a multiplicative relation among the determinants of performance such that if any one of the antecedent traits is subthreshold, the person will fail to develop talent in that domain. Viewed in this framework, individuals with high *g* are likely to develop talent in any domain they select because their *g* level is likely to surpass the threshold for virtually all domains. That is, increasingly higher levels of *g* result in increasingly higher probabilities of successful talent development in any chosen domain. An obvious implication of this model is that, in domains for which the g threshold is low, other factors have more opportunity to compensate for low g than they would in domains for which the g threshold is high. If the g threshold is relatively high compared to other antecedent factors, g will be a primary determinant of the development of performance capacities. However, in cases where the g-threshold value is high, the variance in g may be so restricted that its impact will not be evident in correlations. Of course, these same points apply to any relevant factor. Any trait for which it is not possible to compensate for low values (i.e., the trait has a high threshold value) may be considered a primary determinant in the development of domain-specific performance capacities.

IS g THE PRIMARY DETERMINANT OF INTRAINDIVIDUAL PERFORMANCE DIFFERENCES ACROSS DOMAINS?

For a moment, think about g as a determiner of one's profile of skills, without norm-based reference to others' profiles. For a given individual, does g differentially determine the development of performance capacities across domains? This brings us back to the representation of the predictor space, and if one focuses only on g, the answer is necessarily "no" because g has no within-person variance. Only when the group or specific levels of mental abilities are studied does the question become meaningful. Multiple developmental theories provide a theoretical basis from which to evaluate this question (Bouchard, Lykken, Tellegen, & McGue, 1996; Lubinski & Benbow, 2000; Scarr, 1996; Scarr & McCartney, 1983). These theories suggest that, because of a variety of genotype-environment interactions, individual differences in cognitive and noncognitive predispositions tend to create the environments in which people find themselves. For instance, people having low quantitative reasoning abilities and high artistic interests are unlikely to find themselves presented with opportunities to pursue careers in quantum physics because of the educational choices and accomplishments afforded by their abilities and interests. Whereas their abilities and interests are unlikely to lead to reinforcing experiences in quantitative scientific domains, those factors are likely to afford the types of reinforcing experiences necessary to sustain the motivation to develop performance capabilities in other areas.

From this perspective, one can see why g may not always be the relevant cognitive variable of interest. Intraindividual differences in the profile of specific cognitive abilities, interests, and personality may substantially influence one's choice to allocate effort and cognitive resources in a given domain. Thus, although g is likely to be a primary determining factor of interindividual differences in performance within a domain, the domain to which people choose to apply the capacity afforded by g is largely determined by other factors (Ackerman, 1996; Cattell, 1943). Reeve and Hakel (2000), for example, showed that intraindividual differences in interests are meaningfully associated with intraindividual differences in acquired domain-specific knowledge.

However, this is not to say that interindividual differences in *g* are completely irrelevant in the study of intraindividual profiles. The gravitational hypothesis (McCormick, DeNisi, & Staw, 1979) holds that individuals will sort themselves into jobs that are congruent with their levels of ability. Individuals with low *g* are likely to be frustrated by high complexity jobs, and high *g* individuals are likely to find low complexity jobs boring (i.e., both situations are punishing experiences). Similarly, low *g* individuals in high complexity jobs are likely to be unsatisfactory to the organization. Research shows that high *g* people do in fact gravitate toward increasingly complex jobs, whereas low *g* people gravitate toward increasingly less complex jobs (Wilk, Desmarais, & Sackett, 1995; Wilk & Sackett, 1996). This suggests that interindividual differences in *g* may influence the development of intraindividual differences if the domains under study are not of relatively equal complexity levels.

IS *g* NECESSARY FOR EFFECTIVE OR EXCEPTIONAL DOMAIN-SPECIFIC PERFORMANCE?

The answer clearly is yes for virtually every domain studied by psychologists to date. Although the relative importance of *g* may vary across domains, there is always some minimal level of *g* required, and as the environment becomes increasingly complex, the minimum requirement increases. That is, if we view the cognitive complexity of the environment as analogous to the difficulty of a test item (i.e.,   ), the probability of a successful response (i.e., demonstrating effective performance) decreases for any specific theta value. For virtually any level of environmental complexity, the probability of a successful response will eventually approach zero at some point on the theta continuum. Second, as shown in Simonton's (1999) model of talent development, compensating for a factor at a subthreshold level is not possible. Given that *g* is a significant predictor of performance in even the lowest complexity domains (Hunter & Hunter, 1984; Jensen, 1998), it can be said that *g* is necessary for performance in any domain, but the minimal level of *g* required will vary across domains. That is, the degree to which low levels of *g* can be compensated by other factors will decrease as the complexity of the environment increases.

IS *g* SUFFICIENT FOR EFFECTIVE OR EXCEPTIONAL DOMAIN-SPECIFIC PERFORMANCE?

Clearly, the answer is no. Even a moderate understanding of the development of performance capabilities requires the addition of multiple factors. For instance, interindividual and intraindividual differences in non-g factors appear to be the key determinants of the way people choose to invest the personal resources afforded by g and are largely responsible for much of the motivation needed to develop expertise within a domain. It would seem that recognition of high g as a necessary but not sufficient condition for exceptional performance has existed among researchers for over 100 years. Indeed, Galton (1869) noted that, in addition to high intelligence, achieving eminence required factors giving rise to zeal and persistence.

IS g THE PRIMARY DETERMINANT OF INDIVIDUAL DIFFERENCES IN MERIT?

Assuming that merit is based on a person's demonstrated capacities and accomplishments, we can understand that g is an important influence. Higher g people are more likely to be able to develop capacities to demonstrate meritorious accomplishments; individual differences in g are going to account for a large part of the variance in any criterion used to assess merit. However, it should also be obvious that accomplishments are the result of a multitude of interacting factors that are genetic and environmental, cognitive and noncognitive, and distal and proximal. g is not a sole determinant, and having high g does not guarantee that one will exhibit meritorious behavior. The ambiguous nature of the word *primary* in this context probably introduces much unnecessary debate. g provides a meaningful contribution to individual differences in merit.

WHICH IS MORE IMPORTANT, NATURE OR NURTURE?

Discussions of individual and group differences all too often embrace a false dichotomy. It makes no sense to debate "genetic versus environmental" factors. Both are necessary. Human traits, both physical and psychological, develop through a longitudinal interaction between genetic and environmental factors. A trait will not develop if the necessary genetic code is not present. Likewise, a trait will not develop if the environment does not afford its development; environments must lie within a "normal" range for most human traits to develop. The right questions to be asking are (a) how does nature nurture one's environment?, and (b) how does the environment nurture one's nature? (Scarr, 1993).

Three basic mechanisms underlie the symbiotic relations among genetic factors and environmental factors (Scarr & McCartney, 1983). First, *passive* genetic–environment (g–e) interaction occurs because parents provide both the genetic code and the environment for a child. For example, a child with parents who have high verbal abilities and like to read is likely to receive (a) a genotype for above average verbal abilities and interest in reading and (b) a home environment filled with books and role models who read and express joy in reading. Second, *evocative* genetic–environment interaction occurs because individual differences in intellectual abilities, personality, and interests will evoke different responses from the environment, and thus differences in experienced environments. For example, students who are more attentive, cooperative, and bright are likely to receive more positive attention from instructors than will students who are lazy, argumentative, and dull. Although a group of students is exposed to the same objective environment, differences in the experienced environment are evoked by trait differences. Third, *active* genetic–environment interaction, also called "niche-picking" or "niche-building," occurs because people attend to information and seek out experiences that afford pleasantness, such as success, excitement, or flow states (Csikszentmihalyi, 1988). They are likely to withdraw from or avoid experiences that result in frustration, confusion, boredom, or consistent failure (Lubinski & Benbow, 2000). Multiple individuals with access to the same objective environment will differentially select, attend to, and seek the myriad of opportunities and information provided in that environment. Again, the experienced environments are varied.

The relative impact of these three mechanisms is not static. As people mature and experience increasing freedom to make choices that determine their own environments, passive g–e interactions are less influential, and active g–e interactions are more influential (Bouchard et al., 1996; Scarr & McCartney, 1983). Thus, the shift in importance from passive to active g–e interactions affords increasing opportunities for the expression of talents, personality, and interests. That is, to the degree that full and unimpeded access to a wide range of environments is available, the relative impact of genotypic differences will increase with age (Bouchard, 1997; Plomin, 1990; Plomin & Petrill, 1997).

Behavioral genetic research examines the relative importance of genetic and environmental influences on individual differences from a symbiotic and longitudinal perspective (Plomin, Petrill, & Cutting, 1996; reviewing this methodology is beyond the scope of this article. Readers are directed to texts on the subject such as Plomin, 1990). Unfortunately, the common desire to see intellectual development from a "nature versus nurture" perspective results in misinterpretations of this research. For instance, research has established that, within most adult populations, genetic factors are the primary sources of phenotypic variance in intelligence (Betsworth et al., 1994; Bouchard, 1997; Chorney et al., 1998; Jensen, 1998; Plomin, 1990). That is, given the environmental variation present within adult populations, the heritability (h^2) of g is between .60 and .80 (Bouchard, 1997; Jensen, 1998). A common misconception is to interpret a h^2 as the part of an individual's IQ score, for instance, due to genetic factors. This is incorrect. A heritability estimate is a population statistic concerning variance; it does not apply to an individual or a single test score. Similarly, the h^2 statistic is relative to the environmental variation in the population it reflects. That is, to the degree that h^2 is large, relevant environmental variation (i.e., any variation in environmental factors that have an influence on phenotypic individual differences) is minimal for that population. If substantial variation exists in the environmental factors that influence the expression of genetic factors, the h^2 statistic would be smaller. Of importance, although h^2 estimates are informative of the relative contribution of both genetic and environmental variation, it can only be interpreted in its reference context. h^2 estimates can change over time and across populations and can be changed by social interventions that increase or decrease open access to a wide range of environments.

Another misconstrued assumption is that because the relative importance of genetic and environmental differences is known, the causes are also known. This is not necessarily true. The specific genetic factors responsible for individual differences in g and intellectual functioning are still largely unknown. Likewise, few hypotheses regarding environmental influences on individual differences in g have been confirmed. Knowing that there are genetic and environmental factors that influence individual differences is one thing; actually knowing those factors and how they interact over time is quite another.

Another important distinction must be made here. There are known environmental interventions that do evidence increases in mean intelligence levels. For example, some evidence suggests that the complexity of the rearing environment has meaningful impact on important physiological attributes of the nervous system associated with the speed of information processing (Reed, 1993). Similarly, Lynn (1998) described various pieces of evidence supporting the association between improved nutrition and increases in mean IQ scores. However, this is in no way contradictory to the finding of substantial heritabilities. Heritability describes why individuals differ within groups; it does not describe the potential of individuals, changes in average intelligence, or group differences. Behavioral genetics tells us "what is," not "what will be" or "what should be." (Petrill & Wilkerson, 2000).

The debate regarding intelligence has often suffered from such misunderstandings. However, the more fundamental point is that the "nature versus nurture" perspective is naive and prevents proper interpretation of research regarding the nature of individual and group differences. The right question is not "nature or nurture," but rather "how do we nurture nature for everyone?" Optimal development of talent requires substantial effort to ensure that everyone is provided with appropriate opportunities to promote innate potential (Benbow & Stanley, 1996; Scarr, 1996).

WHAT IS OUR CURRENT UNDERSTANDING OF RACIAL DIFFERENCES IN MEASURED INTELLIGENCE?

We address the question of racial differences out of a sense of necessity, and assuredly not because we are eager to experience the politically and emotionally heated attacks launched against others who discuss race. We believe that dealing with and understanding this issue is vitally important. There is much we do not know about the sources of racial differences in assessed intelligence. However, there is much we do know. It is through scientific research that answers and understanding can be achieved. Furthermore, I–O psychologists need to be informed regarding research on the nature of race differences. It would seem difficult to use intelligence tests ethically or advise others about policy regarding adverse impact without being knowledgeable about the nature of group and individual differences.

In the interest of promoting critical consideration of adverse impact issues within work psychology, we review major lines of evidence regarding hypotheses about observed race differences and hope to clarify common misunderstandings and misconceptions, covering the full extent of racial differences, not just the Black–White (B–W) difference. Although the B–W difference captures most of the media attention in the United States, it is important to consider all differences. The reason will become clear later. However, as an example, consider that many of the "test bias hypotheses" predict that White Americans should be the highest scoring group. The evidence is clear; they are most certainly not the highest scoring group. Focusing only on the B–W difference is, at best, misleading—it can be a serious error. Unfortunately, the vast majority of research on racial differences in test scores has studied only the B–W difference anyway, and as such, much of this section focuses on the B–W difference. (Incidentally, please note that the length of this section reflects more about the societal importance of the question than its scientific importance to I–O psychologists.)

Before reviewing the evidence, four points need to be addressed. First, "race" is not a biological variable. Rather, race is a construct based on biological and morphological differences that are the result of differing polymorphic gene frequencies among human populations. (There are approximately 100,000 genes that have one or more alleles and thus contribute to genetic variation within the human species.) These frequency differences arose from natural genetic variation interacting with environmental selection and the relative isolation of various human subpopulations throughout the last 70,000 to 80,000 years (Futuyma, 1986). That is, the spread of *homo s. sapiens* across the planet and subsequent long-term isolation of the various subgroups' genetic pools resulted in the development of identifiable differences in polymorphic gene frequencies associated with various traits, some of which are readily visible and highly heritable (e.g., skin pigmentation, hair color, specific skeletal features, number and shape of teeth; Baker, 1974), as well as others that are not so visible (e.g., susceptibility to certain diseases, color blindness, metabolic reactions to medicines and toxins; Lin, Poland, & Nakasaki, 1993). Furthermore, the "genetic distance" between historically isolated subgroups can be mapped by quantitative assessment of specific allelic frequencies (Nei & Roychoudhury, 1982). Thus, although there is no biological or genetic litmus test for racial identity, race can be a useful scientific concept. Racial classifications should be considered to be "fuzzy sets" of statistically distinguishable groups, in which individual membership is not identifiable by any single criterion. The concept of race, defined in this way, is used in many sciences such as psychology, sociology, anthropology, biology, medicine, forensic pathology, and so forth.

Second, contrary to claims by Gould (1996), theorizing about race differences was evident prior to the development of intelligence tests (Brand, 1996a). Intelligence tests are a vehicle that provide direct empirical evidence. Indeed, the measured racial and ethnic group differences among people of western European ancestry (i.e., Caucasian or "White"), Jewish people, peoples of East Asian ancestry, and peoples of African ancestry (i.e., "Black") are largely as Galton estimated them in 1869, prior to the advent of reliable intelligence tests: Compared to European White norms, Jewish people reliably average around 1.0 to 0.75 SDs higher, East Asians average 0.66 to 0.33 higher, and Blacks average around 0.75 to 1.0 lower (Jensen, 1998; Osborne & McGurk, 1982). These relative values have been confirmed on a worldwide basis (Lynn, 1997). The psychometric assessment of intelligence has not created racial differences, but rather has allowed reliable measurement of those differences.

Third, knowing that average test score differences exist, and knowing the causes of those differences, are two very different things. There is clear evidence of reliable differences in mean scores based on racial classifications, but there is no shortage of hypotheses regarding the causes of observed differences.

Finally, race differences have provided the flash point for debates about g because they seem to contravene popular notions of equality. The Declaration of Independence proclaims the following: "We hold these truths to be self evident, that all men are created equal, that they are endowed by their creator with certain unalienable rights, that among these are life, liberty, and the pursuit of happiness." "Created equal" means equality before the law, a concept that has found expression in the 5th and 14th amendments of the U.S. Constitution and been given operational force in both legislation and judicial opinion. A great deal of the heat in the debate about g in general and cognitive selection tests in particular comes from trying to reconcile equal employment opportunity with a B–W difference that is about one standard deviation on g-saturated tests. g-saturated selection test scores seem to some to define precisely which applicants are "similarly situated" and therefore entitled to the "equal protection of the laws." Even if they are a bit narrow in terms of coverage of the predictor domain, such tests are "objective" and therefore color blind. However, to others they epitomize institutionalized racism and oppression, due to marked adverse impact. Moreover, because g is not a sufficient determinant of performance, and performance may be multidimensional, selection tests become the focus for complaints about outcome inequality and unfairness. Balancing procedural and distributive justice is difficult. Wigdor and Garner (1982) noted the following:

> The diminished prospects of the average American give the debate about testing an especially sharp edge. Because they are visible instruments of the process of allocat-

ing economic opportunity, tests are seen as creating winners and losers. What is not as readily appreciated, perhaps, is the inevitability of making choices: whether by tests or some other mechanism, selection must take place. (p. 205)

Although a comprehensive review of race differences in *g* is well beyond the scope of this article, we outline evidence about a number of popular hypotheses concerning such differences. So that the complexity of the situation can be witnessed, and certain false claims can be identified, we also discuss the relation between evidence concerning within-group heritability and between-group heritability, and we discuss an eminently important, yet often ignored phenomenon concerning group differences for which any causal hypothesis must account—namely the Spearman–Jensen Effect. We strongly encourage reading original sources as well as more comprehensive reviews.

Test Bias

There is no reliable evidence that professionally developed intelligence tests, or the factor scores derived from such tests, are subject to cultural or measurement test bias. Jensen's (1980a) tome on the issue still stands as the definitive account, and research since then has only confirmed his conclusions. There is some evidence of predictive bias in favor of Blacks, due to using a common regression equation. Intelligence tests typically show the same reliability and validity for all groups assessed.

An often ignored yet eminently important fault in the cultural test bias argument is that White Americans are not the top-scoring group. One version of the test bias argument claims that tests measure nothing more than knowledge of the dominant (i.e., "White") culture and therefore all non-White, non-Americans are unfairly disadvantaged. Nonetheless, East Asians and Jews consistently outscore White Americans. This finding holds whether these groups are Americans themselves or live in other countries, and whether they speak English or another language (Silegman, 1994, chapter 10).

Economic and Social Class

The hypotheses of poverty or low social class as causes of racial differences in *g* have yielded very little supportive data (Eysenck, 1971; Jensen, 1998; Lynn, 1997). Although the correlation between economic success and intelligence has been cited as evidence for this hypothesis, the causal arrow may point in either direction. This correlation is of little value by itself. Furthermore, economic and social class hypotheses are contradicted by historical evidence. For instance, Jews arrived in America in poverty after fleeing persecution in Russia and Poland in the early part of the century. Despite language and economic barriers, as a group Jews

ASKING THE RIGHT QUESTIONS   63

scored well on the early mental tests and soon prospered (Jensen, 1980a; Seligman, 1994). Similarly, a number of studies reported Chinese children consistently scored above American and British norms of the same age, despite living in general poverty (see Silegman, 1994, for summary). Furthermore, when Black and White children are matched on schooling and parental socioeconomic status, a 12-point difference remains (Eysenck, 1971; Jensen, 1980b). Although living in lower social class or poverty has other deleterious social consequences, the evidence suggests it is not a likely cause of racial differences in intelligence.

Cultural Alienation

This hypothesis states that growing up with a different cultural heritage, speaking a nonstandard form of English, and experiencing hostility from the dominant culture creates intelligence differences. For instance, it has been shown that the B–W difference shrinks (and the averages of both groups increase) as one moves from the American southeast to the Pacific Northwest (Lynn, 1997). Although it is often assumed that this reflects regional differences in racial attitudes and overt racial discrimination, this same pattern is apparent in the IQs of preschool children (Jensen, 1998). Furthermore, racism or cultural alienation hypotheses do not tend to hold when applied to other groups. As noted previously, Asian Americans consistently out-score their White counterparts in America despite historical racism. For instance, after experiencing a century of racial prejudice that banned access to community resources and trade unions, the Japanese of the west coast suffered extreme racism during World War II, were stripped of their possessions, lost their businesses, and placed in "relocation camps" in the desert. Despite this, Japanese Americans reliably outscore White Americans on intelligence tests and are over-represented in "highly g-loaded" professions, such as science and engineering (Jensen, 1998; Vernon, 1982).

Two other considerations are damaging to this hypothesis. First, the construct of "culture" is typically left undefined and reliable measurement of the degree of "cultural alienation" is absent. Alienation is usually assumed to exist. It is possible that this hypothesis has some validity, but the poor operationalization and specification of the constructs or the specific causal processes has rendered it useless.

Second, longitudinal studies of transracial adoptions (Scarr & Weinberg, 1976; Scarr, Weinberg, & Waldman, 1993; Weinberg, Scarr, & Waldman, 1992) show that, despite being reared in "the culture of the tests and schools" by adoptive parents with above average IQs, the pattern of racial differences among the adopted children was consistent with the typical worldwide pattern when assessed at age 7 and at age 17. The longitudinal results showed the following: (a) Black children reared by White adoptive parents with above average IQs have essentially the same, or only slightly higher, average IQ at age 17 as their relative norm population; (b) the B–W IQ difference between adoptees and adoptive siblings (i.e., biological offspring of adoptive parents) was about equal to the B–W difference in the general population; (c) the B–W IQ difference did not shrink across time although the children were raised in the same family environments; and (d) adoptee IQ at age 17 was best predicted by biological mother's race and education (Scarr et al., 1993; Weinberg et al., 1992). Although there has been some contention over the exact meaning of these results (cf. Levin, 1994; Lynn, 1994; Waldman, Weinberg, & Scarr, 1994), it is clear that whether children are reared in "the culture of the tests and schools" does not have an appreciable influence on mean IQ differences. Overall, there is little evidence supporting this hypothesis.

Stereotype Threat

Steele (1997; Steele & Aronson, 1995) proposed a hypothesis suggesting that performance on ability tests by individual members of a racial group may be undermined by stereotypes associated with that racial group. According to Steele (1997), fear or anxiety about negative stereotypes interferes with performance on standardized tests of the stigmatized domain. Of the published studies testing this hypothesis, most report finding that a decrement in mean performance of a stereotype-threatened group can be created, compared to control groups (e.g., Aronson et al., 1999; Stangor, Carr, & Kiang, 1998; Steele & Aronson, 1995; Stone, Lynch, Sjomeling, & Darley, 1999). Of importance, recent studies have extended these findings to other racial group stereotypes, gender groups, and social class differences (e.g., Croizet, & Claire, 1998; Shih, Pittinsky, & Ambady, 1999; Spencer, Steele, & Quinn, 1999). These extensions have shown that the effects of stereotype threat manipulations are generally consistent with the direction of the stereotype. Shih et al. (1999), for example, showed that an Asian group "threatened" with a positive stereotype (i.e., confronted with the stereotype that Asians perform well in mathematics) performed better than an Asian control group (i.e., a group of Asians not confronted with the stereotype) on mathematics tests. This, importantly, shows that the effect conforms to the direction of social stereotypes.

Although the phenomenon shown in these studies is highly intriguing and deserving of further research, many questions remain regarding the validity of this hypothesis. First, it should be noted that the effects demonstrated in these studies are typically very small. For instance, Croizet and Claire (1998) demonstrated that, over a 30-min testing session, the threatened group correctly answered an average of only two items fewer than the three control groups, attempted an average of only one item less, and had an average accuracy decrement of .08. Steele and Aronson (1995) found that the threatened group, compared to control groups, attempted an average of two items less in one study but found no difference in a follow-up, and found no meaningful differences in accuracy in either study. Aronson et al. (1999) reported a significant finding for stereotype threat manipulation on a sample of White men for a math test; however, two additional manipulations predicted to nullify the threat resulted in the same pattern of group performances (discussed later). Although other studies have found somewhat larger effects, the typical differences reported, although potentially meaningful under specific conditions, do not appear able to account for any appreciable portion of typically observed race differences.

Second, evidence concerning the proposed causal mechanisms is either lacking or has been disconfirmatory. Studies examining causal mechanisms, such as increased anxiety or self-handicapping, have either showed no difference between stereotyped groups and control groups or the difference has actually been contrary to the hypothesized direction of the effect (e.g., Aronson et al., 1999; Croizet & Claire, 1998; Steele & Aronson, 1995; Stone et al., 1999). Other issues concerning external and internal validity as well as contradictory evidence has been commented on by Whaley (1998; see Steele, 1998, for reply).

Early Education Interventions

A number of early intervention programs have been attempted in America, such as Head Start, the Abecedarian Project, and the Milwaukee Project. Although none of these programs were specifically aimed at increasing intelligence per se, many assumed that they would help to reduce the B–W difference in academic performance and presumably intelligence test scores. However, despite evidence of short-term IQ gains for youngsters enrolled in these programs compared to age-mates not enrolled, these gains typically do not last beyond a few years after the intervention has ended and rarely exceed a 5-point increase (Jensen, 1998; Spitz, 1986). After 30 years, mainstream scholars now accept that, although programs such as Head Start do have significant and lasting effects on social and academic adjustment (e.g., decreases in delinquency rates), they do not appear to have any lasting effect on measured intelligence or achievement differences (Scarr, 1993). It should be noted that this does not reflect a failure of these programs. As Edward Zigler, one of Head Start's founders, stated, "Everybody thinks we're in the business of raising IQs. Finally, after 35 years, Congress said the goal of Head Start is school readiness." (as quoted in Weaver, 2000). Indeed, these programs appear to be very successful in many aspects when evaluated in terms of what they were designed to do (Jensen, 1998).

Cumulative Environmental Deficits

The cumulative deficit hypothesis posits that environmental deprivation progressively decreases the mean IQ of individuals reared in those environments (Jensen, 1974). Although early studies failed to find any supportive evidence, Jensen (1974, 1977) provided an exceptionally rigorous confirmation of the hypothesis that ruled out alternative explanations. By showing that the effect was present in a poor, rural Georgian school district but not present in a large, more prosperous urban sample, and that the effect increased with age (Jensen, 1974, 1977), the results confirmed that specific, exceedingly poor, rural environments can result in developmental deficits. Furthermore, Jensen's studies confirm the effect could only be explained by specific, but as yet unknown, environmental factors associated with the exceptionally poor environments. Jensen's studies provide very strong evidence for this hypothesis. However, it also simultaneously suggests that this effect cannot account for an appreciable part of the overall B–W IQ difference in nationally representative samples, but may be highly important in localized samples.

Prenatal and Infant Care

A relatively robust research base has confirmed the importance of nutrition in human and animal development, although direct study of the association between nutrition and the development of cognitive skills is not as common as one might think (Sigman & Whaley, 1998). Nonetheless, there is sufficient evidence to conclude that nutritional deficiencies during prenatal and early child development can have substantial and lasting influences on motor and cognitive development (e.g., Broman, Nichols, & Kennedy, 1975). Other studies have shown that specific factors in infant care such as whether babies received mother's milk or formula was strongly associated with IQ of preterm and low-birth-weight babies (e.g., Lucas, Morley, Cole, Lister, & Leeson-Payne, 1992). Similarly, the use of drugs or alcohol during pregnancy has been shown to have considerable influence on adult IQ, even after controlling for some background variables (e.g., Reinisch, Sanders, Mortensen, & Rubin, 1995). It is clear that prenatal and early childhood nutrition plays an important role in intellectual development.

What is less clear is the role of these factors in explaining racial differences. For instance, Montie and Fagan (1988) matched Black and White 3-year-old children by the mother's level of education, pregnancy complications (e.g., due to drug addiction), weight at birth, gestational length, and the early health of the child. Doing so resulted in only a 2-point reduction of the usual group mean difference. Others, however, have suggested that these factors are key nongenetic causes of the B–W difference (e.g., Eysenck, 1991). For instance, Black mothers are at a higher risk for low-birth-weight babies, and Black mothers breast-fed less frequently on average than White mothers (Ryan et al., 1991). Similarly, it has been shown that when children with specific mineral deficiencies received supplements, they exhibited significant gains on tests of abstract reasoning and problem solving (i.e., fluid g; Eysenck & Schoenthaler, 1997). Interestingly, these specific deficiencies were found in middle-class children with "normal diets."

Constraints on Causal Hypotheses: Degree of g-Saturation

The nature of the test does impact the size of the observed racial differences. The most notable phenomenon is known as the Spearman–Jensen effect—the size of the racial difference on any test is directly proportional to the g-saturation of the test (Jensen, 1985, 1987, 1998). The more a test is g-saturated (e.g., inductive or deductive reasoning tests), the larger the associated racial difference; the less it is g-saturated (e.g., rote memory, simple reaction time), the smaller the associated racial difference. This association is reliably strong, averaging about $r = .60$ across 149 different tests (Jensen, 1998, chapter 11). Furthermore, this association has been shown to hold even when the tests' g-saturations are estimated in a Japanese sample and the B–W differences are estimated in American samples (Jensen, 1998), as well as in a sample of 3-year-old children (Peoples, Fagan, & Drotar, 1995). Although only a handful of studies has tested the Spearman–Jensen effect by using other racial classifications, results from those studies support the extension of this effect to these racial differences as well. The data regarding the Spearman–Jensen effect strongly suggest that racial intelligence differences are driven primarily (although not completely) by biological factors (either genetic or environmental in origin) relating to g, and not surface level features of the tests.

Similarly, research has confirmed that the degree of g-saturation is proportional to the correlation between test scores and a host of factors such as head size, brain volume, average evoked potential habituation and complexity, glucose metabolic rate as measured by PET scan, and average reaction time to elementary cognitive tasks, as well as the heritability of the test (see Jensen, 1998, for summary of research).

These findings are critically important to the evaluation of causal hypotheses. Any causal hypothesis must be able to explain how the putative causal factor creates racial differences on phenotypic measurements in direct proportion to the degree that the test is g-loaded, for all age ranges. Similarly, any hypothesized factor that claims to account for differences in g must be able to explain these other relations as well. Although rarely recognized in the research literature, these phenomena render untenable many causal hypotheses based on attitudinal, cultural, or experiential factors.

The Relevance of Within-Group Evidence

Because it is known beyond a reasonable doubt that, among American adults, 60% to 80% of within-group differences in intelligence are due to genetic factors for all racial groups assessed (Bouchard & McGue, 1981; Jensen, 1980b; Jensen, 1998; Nagoshi & Johnson, 1987), some have mistakenly assumed that between-group differences must also be largely genetic. However, evidence of within-group heritability has no direct relevance to inferences about the source of between-group differences. Of course, what is usually missed is that the same thing applies to environmental evidence; any evidence for the influence of environmental factors on within-group differences cannot provide any direct evidence concerning between-group differences.

Nonetheless, it is incorrect to say that there is no relation between within-group heritability (WGH) and between-group heritability (BGH). The formal relation between BGH and WGH is the following:

$$BGH = WGH \frac{r_g(1 - r_p)}{r_p(1 - r_g)}$$

where r_g is the genetic intraclass correlation within groups, and r_p is the phenotypic intraclass correlation within groups (Defries, 1972; Jensen, 1973, 1998; Loehlin, Lindzey, & Spuhler, 1975). Of course, this formula is not empirically applicable because we know neither r_g nor BGH. Nonetheless, it shows that for any hypothesized value of r_g (other than $r_g = 0$), the relation between BGH and WGH is monotonically increasing. This relation makes no formal assumptions regarding the genetic and environmental sources of variance in BGH and WGH, and it does not assume that those sources are the same between BGH and WGH. Jensen (1998) provided a thorough discussion of the important implications of this relation on environmental and genetic arguments (pp. 447–462).

Summary

Although the evidence to date is far from complete, certain conclusions about the causes of observed racial differences are warranted. First, it is clear that group differences are not due *solely* to genetic, biological, or environmental factors. This is hardly surprising, however. Given the symbiotic relations among them, it would seem surprising if these factors were not all contributors to the manifestation of group differences. Second, the environmental and genetic factors that appear to be the most viable sources of group differences are those that influence biological and physiological factors associated with g. That is, microenvironmental factors (e.g., prenatal, perinatal, and neonatal conditions and nutritional factors) and genetic factors that have effects on the biological development of the nervous system appear to have the strongest empirical support as causes of racial differences. Third, it is clear that there are specific circumstances where other factors have real and detectable effects on local populations (e.g., cumulative deficit effect) or in specific circumstances (e.g., stereotype threat). Although these additional factors should be of concern to the public and practitioners, they do not provide plausible explanations for all of the long-standing, worldwide racial differences in g.

Perhaps more so than any other aspect of intelligence, the debate over racial differences absolutely requires clear, critical, and dispassionate consideration. Although we did not attempt to provide a comprehensive summary of research on race differences, we hope our discussion was sufficient to encourage readers to consider that they are complex, multiply determined, and should not be ignored. There are no easy, simple answers. Our degree of understanding and ability to deal effectively with racial differences hinges on the courage of our questions and the depth of our answers.

CONCLUSION

If readers remember only one point from our discussion, we hope it is the following: Differences in *g* and other interindividual and intraindividual differences interact with environmental conditions to give rise to a cascade of events that determine interindividual and intraindividual differences in performance within and across domains. However, we hope all the points we have made spur both scientists and the public to ask critically important and insightful questions about the development of adult intellectual capabilities. It should be apparent that there is much we know about intelligence. It should be equally apparent that there is much still to be learned.

It is our position that a complete understanding of human intellectual development is of ultimate interest to researchers and of great import to society. Although the intensity and longevity of the debate surrounding intelligence might be evidence that others share our view, it seems that this energy is driven more by dogmatic opinions and political criticism than by a genuine zeal for greater understanding of human development. In his 1999 Galton Lecture to the Zoological Society of London, Arthur Jensen discussed the link in the public's mind between eugenics and the horrific acts committed in its name during World War II, noting that the link has "contributed to making research on intelligence ... stigmatized to a degree not seen for scientific research on other natural phenomena, save perhaps for evolution as perceived by biblical fundamentalists" (as quoted in Holden, 1999).

Indeed, scientific research on intelligence has often met with fierce public opposition. Even within the scientific community, the debate is often sidetracked by misunderstandings and misconceptions. The same questions are asked repeatedly, false claims and criticisms are based on misconstrued or misunderstood evidence, and important questions remain ignored. This wastes the resources, time, and energy of partisans, scientists, and the public. If we are ever to understand the nature of intelligence and its influence on individual differences in performance, we need to be asking the right questions.

ACKNOWLEDGMENT

Parts of this article are based on Milton Hakel's presentation at a symposium at the 15th Annual Conference for the Society of Industrial Organizational Psychology, in New Orleans.

REFERENCES

Ackerman, P. L. (1996). A theory of adult intellectual development: Process, personality, interests, and knowledge. *Intelligence, 22,* 227–257.

Aronson, J. A., Lustina, M. J., Good, C., Keough, K., Steele, C. M., & Brown, J. (1999). When White men can't do math: Necessary and sufficient factors in stereotype threat. *Journal of Experimental Social Psychology, 35,* 29–46.

Baker, J. R. (1974). *Race.* New York: Oxford University Press.

Barrick, M. R., & Mount, M. K. (1991). The big-five personality dimensions and job performance. *Personnel Psychology, 44,* 1–26.

Benbow, C. P., & Stanley, J. C. (1996). Inequity in equity: How "equity" can lead to inequity for high-potential students. *Psychology, Public Policy, and Law, 2,* 149–291.

Betsworth, D. G., Bouchard, T. J., Cooper, C. R., Grotevant, H. D., Hansen, J. C., Scarr, S., & Weinberg, R. A. (1994). Genetic and environmental influences on vocational interests assessed using adoptive and biological families and twins reared apart and together. *Journal of Vocational Behavior, 44,* 263–278.

Binning, J., & Barrett, G. (1989). Validity of personnel decisions: A conceptual analysis of the inferential and evidential bases. *Journal of Applied Psychology, 74,* 478–494.

Borman, W. C., Hanson, M. A., & Hedge, J. W. (1997). Personnel selection. *Annual Review of Psychology, 48,* 299–337.

Borman, W. C., & Motowidlo, S. J. (1993). Expanding the criterion domain to include elements of contextual performance. In N. Schmitt & W. C. Borman (Eds.), *Personnel selection in organizations* (pp. 71–98). San Francisco: Jossey-Bass.

Bouchard, T. J. (1997). IQ similarity in twins reared apart: Findings and responses to critics. In R. Sternberg & E. Grigorenko (Eds.), *Intelligence, heredity and environment* (pp. 126–160). New York: Cambridge University Press.

Bouchard, T. J., Lykken, D. T., Tellegen, A., & McGue, M. (1996). Genes, drives, environment, and experience: EPD theory revisited. In C. P. Benbow & D. Lubinski (Eds.), *Intellectual talent: Psychometric and social issues* (pp. 5–43). Baltimore: John Hopkins University Press.

Bouchard, T. J., & McGue, M. (1981). Familial studies of intelligence: A review. *Science, 212,* 1055–1059.

Brand, C. (1996a). *The g factor: General intelligence and its implications.* New York: Wiley.

Brand, C. (1996b). The importance of intelligence in western societies. *Journal of Biosocial Science, 28,* 387–404.

Brody, N. (1996). Intelligence and public policy. *Psychology, Public Policy, and Law, 2,* 473–485.

Broman, S. H., Nichols, P. L., & Kennedy, W. A. (1975). *Preschool IQ: Prenatal and early development correlates.* Hillsdale, NJ: Lawrence Erlbaum Associates, Inc.

Campbell, J. P. (1996). Group differences, and personnel decisions: Validity, fairness, and affirmative action. *Journal of Vocational Behavior, 49,* 122–158.

Campbell, J. P., McCloy, R. A., Oppler, S. H., & Sager, C. E. (1993). A theory of performance. In N. Schmitt & W. C. Borman (Eds.), *Personnel selection in organizations* (pp. 35–70). San Francisco: Jossey-Bass.

Campbell, J. P., McHenry, J. J., & Wise, L. L. (1990). Modeling job performance in a population of jobs. *Personnel Psychology, 43,* 313–333.

Carroll, J. B. (1993). *Human cognitive abilities: A survey of factor-analytic studies.* New York: Cambridge University Press.

Carroll, J. B. (1997). Psychometrics, intelligence, and public perception. *Intelligence, 24,* 25–52.

Cattell, R. B. (1943). The measurement of adult intelligence. *Psychological Bulletin, 40,* 153–193.

Chorney, M. J., Chorney, K., Seese, N., Owen, M. J., Daniels, J., McGuffin, P., et al. (1998). A quantitative trait locus associated with cognitive ability in children. *Psychological Science, 9,* 159–166.

Croizet, J-C., & Claire, T. (1998). Extending the concept of stereotype and threat to social class: The intellectual underperformance of students from low socioeconomic backgrounds. *Personality and Social Psychology Bulletin, 24*, 588–594.

Cronbach, L. J., & Meehl, P. E. (1955). Construct validity in psychological tests. *Psychological Bulletin, 52*, 281–302.

Csikszentmihalyi, M. (1988). Motivation and creativity: Towards a synthesis of structural and energistic approaches to cognition. *New Ideas in Psychology, 6*, 159–176.

Dawis, R. V. (1992). The individual differences tradition in counseling psychology. *Journal of Counseling Psychology, 39*, 7–19.

Dawis, R. V., & Lofquist, L. H. (1984). *A psychological theory of work adjustment.* Minneapolis: University of Minnesota Press.

Defries, J. C. (1972). Quantitative aspects of genetics and environment in the determination of behavior. In L. Ehrman, G. S. Omenn, & E. Caspari (Eds.), *Genetics, environment, and behavior* (pp. 5–16). New York: Academic.

Ericsson, K. A., Krampe, R. T., & Tesch-Römer, C. (1993). The role of deliberate practice in the acquisition of expert performance. *Psychological Review, 100*, 309–324.

Ericsson, K. A., & Lehmann, A. C. (1996). Expert and exceptional performance: Evidence of maximal adaptation to task constraints. *Annual Review of Psychology, 47*, 273–305.

Eysenck, H. (1971). *Race, intelligence and education.* London: Maurice Temple Smith.

Eysenck, H. (1991). Race and intelligence: An alternative hypothesis. *Mankind Quarterly, 32*, 123–125.

Eysenck, H. (1995). *Genius: The natural history of creativity.* Cambridge, England: Cambridge University Press.

Eysenck, H., & Schoenthaler, S. J. (1997). Raising IQ level by vitamin and mineral supplementation. In R. J. Sternberg & E. Grigorenko (Eds.), *Intelligence, heredity, and environment* (pp. 363–392). New York: Cambridge University Press.

Futuyma, D. J. (1986). *Evolutionary biology.* Sunderland, MA: Sinauer Associates.

Galton, F. (1869). *Hereditary genius: An enquiry into its laws and consequences.* London: Collins.

Gardner, H. (1983). *Frames of mind.* New York: Basic Books.

Gardner, J. W. (1984). *Excellence: Can we be equal & excellent too?* New York: Norton.

Gordon, R. A. (1997). Everyday life as an intelligence test: Effects of intelligence and intelligence context. *Intelligence, 24*, 203–320.

Gottfredson, L. S. (1997a). Editorial: Mainstream science on intelligence: An editorial with 52 signatories, history, and bibliography. *Intelligence, 24*, 13–23.

Gottfredson, L. S. (1997b). Why g matters: The complexity of everyday life. *Intelligence, 24*, 79–132.

Gould, S. J. (1996). *The mismeasure of man.* New York: Norton.

Gustafsson, J-E., & Balke, G. (1993). General and specific abilities as predictors of school achievement. *Multivariate Behavioral Research, 28*, 407–434.

Gustafsson, J-E., & Snow, R. E. (1997). Ability profiles. In R. F. Dillion (Ed.), *Handbook on testing* (pp. 107–135). Westport, CT: Greenwood.

Herrnstein, R. J., & Murray, C. (1994). *The bell curve: Intelligence and class structure in American life.* New York: Free Press.

Holden, C. (1999, November 12). The IQ taboo. *Science, 286*, 1285.

Hunter, J. E., & Hunter, R. F. (1984). Validity and utility of alternative predictors of job performance. *Psychological Bulletin, 96*, 72–98.

Irvine, S. H., & Berry, J. W. (Eds.). (1988). *Human abilities in cultural context.* Cambridge, England: Cambridge University Press.

Jensen, A. R. (1973). *Educability and group differences.* London: Methuen.

Jensen, A. R. (1974). Cumulative deficit: A testable hypothesis? *Developmental Psychology, 10*, 996–1019.

Jensen, A. R. (1977). Cumulative deficit in IQ of blacks in the rural south. *Developmental Psychology, 13*, 184–191.

Jensen, A. R. (1980a). *Bias in mental testing.* New York: Free Press.

Jensen, A. R. (1980b). Uses of sibling data in educational and psychological research. *American Educational Research Journal, 17*, 153–170.

Jensen, A. R. (1982). The debunking of scientific fossils and straw persons [Review of the book *The mismeasure of man*]. *Contemporary Education Review, 1*, 121–135.

Jensen, A. R. (1985). The nature of the black–white difference on various psychometric tests: Spearman's hypothesis. *Behavioral and Brain Sciences, 8*, 193–219.

Jensen, A. R. (1987). Further evidence for Spearman's hypothesis concerning the black–white differences on psychometric tests. *Behavioral and Brain Sciences, 10*, 512–519.

Jensen, A. R. (1998). *The g factor.* Westport, CT: Praeger.

Jensen, A. R., & Reynolds, C. R. (1982). Race, social class and ability patterns on the WISC–R. *Personality and Individual Differences, 3*, 423–438.

Jensen, A. R., & Weng, L-J. (1994). What is a good g? *Intelligence, 18*, 231–258.

Levin, M. (1994). Comment on the Minnesota Transracial Adoption Study. *Intelligence, 19*, 13–20.

Lin, K-M., Poland, R. E., & Nakasaki, G. (1993). *Psychopharmacology and psychobiology of ethnicity.* Washington, DC: American Psychiatric Press.

Loehlin, J. C., Lindzey, G., & Spuhler, J. N. (1975). *Race differences in intelligence.* New York: Freeman.

Lubinski, D. (2000). Scientific and social significance of assessing individual differences: "Sinking shafts at a few critical points". *Annual Review of Psychology, 51*, 405–444.

Lubinski, D., & Benbow, C. P. (2000). States of excellence. *American Psychologist, 55*, 137–150.

Lucas, A., Morley, R., Cole, T. J., Lister, G., & Leeson-Payne, C. (1992). Breast milk and subsequent intelligence quotient in children born preterm. *Lancet, 339*, 261–264.

Lynn, R. (1994). Some reinterpretations of the Minnesota Transracial Adoption Study. *Intelligence, 19*, 21–27.

Lynn, R. (1997). Geographical variation in intelligence. In N. Helmuth (Ed.), *The scientific study of human nature: Tribute to Hans J. Eysenck at eighty.* Oxford, England: Pergamon.

Lynn, R. (1998). In support of the nutrition theory. In U. Neisser (Ed.), *The rising curve: Long-term gains in IQ and related measures* (pp. 207–218). Washington, DC: American Psychological Association.

McCormick, E., DeNisi, A., & Staw, J. (1979). Use of the position analysis questionnaire for establishing the job component validity of tests. *Journal of Applied Psychology, 64*, 51–56.

Meehl, P. E. (1991). Four queries about factor reality. *History and Philosophy of Psychology Bulletin, 3*, 16–18.

Montie, J. E., & Fagan, J. F., (1988). Racial differences in IQ: Item analysis of the Stanford–Binet at 3 years. *Intelligence, 12*, 315–332.

Motowidlo, S. J., & Van Scotter, J. R. (1994). Evidence that task performance should be distinguished from contextual performance. *Journal of Applied Psychology, 79*, 475–480.

Murphy, K. R. (1996). Individual differences and behavior in organizations: Much more than g. In K. R. Murphy (Ed.), *Individual differences and behavior in organizations* (pp. 3–30). San Francisco: Jossey-Bass.

Murphy, K. R., & Shiarella, A. H. (1997). Implications of the multidimensional nature of job performance for the validity of selection tests: Multivariate frameworks for studying test validity. *Personnel Psychology, 50*, 823–854.

Nagoshi, C. T., & Johnson, R. C. (1987). Between- versus within-family factor analyses of cognitive abilities. *Intelligence, 11*, 305–316.

Nei, M., & Roychoudhury, A. K. (1982). Genetic relationship and evolution of human races. *Evolutionary Biology, 14*, 1–59.

Nitko, A. J. (1983). *Educational tests and measurement: An introduction.* New York: Harcourt Brace.

Osborne, R. T., & McGurk, F. (1982). *The testing of Negro intelligence*. Athens, GA: Foundation for Human Understanding.

Peoples, C. E., Fagan, J. F., & Drotar, D. (1995). The influence of race on 3-year-old children's performance on the Stanford–Binet: Fourth edition. *Intelligence, 21*, 69–82.

Petrill, S. A., & Wikerson, B. (2000). Intelligence and achievement: A behavioral genetic perspective. *Educational Psychology Review, 12*, 185–199.

Plomin, R. (1990). *Nature and nurture*. Belmont, CA: Brooks/Cole.

Plomin, R., & Petrill, S. A. (1997). Genetics and intelligence: What's new? *Intelligence, 24*, 53–77.

Plomin, R., Petrill, S. A., & Cutting, A. L. (1996). What genetic research on intelligence tells us about the environment. *Journal of Biosocial Science, 28*, 587–606.

Prediger, D. J. (1989). Ability differences across occupations: More than *g*. *Journal of Vocational Behavior, 34*, 1–27.

Rathunde, K. R., & Csikszentmihalyi, M. (1993). Undivided interest and the growth of talent: A longitudinal study of adolescents. *Journal of Youth & Adolescence, 22*(4), 385–405.

Ree, M. J., & Earles, J. A. (1991a). Predicting training success: Not much more than *g*. *Personnel Psychology, 44*, 321–332.

Ree, M. J., & Earles, J. A. (1991b). The stability of convergent estimates of *g*. *Intelligence, 15*, 271–278.

Reed, T. E. (1993). Effect of enriched (complex) environment on nerve conduction velocity: New data and a review of implications for the speed of information processing. *Intelligence, 17*, 533–540.

Reeve, C. L., & Hakel, M. D. (2000). Toward understanding adult intellectual development: Investigating within-individual convergence of interest and knowledge profiles. *Journal of Applied Psychology, 85*, 897–908.

Reinisch, J. M., Sanders, S. A., Mortensen, E. L., & Rubin, D. B. (1995). In utero exposure to phenobarbital and intelligence deficits in adult men. *Journal of the American Medical Association, 274*, 1518–1525.

Ryan, A. S., Pratt, W. F., Wysong, J. L., Lewandowski, G., McNally, J. W., & Krieger, F. W. (1991). A comparison of breast-feeding data from the National Surveys of Family Growth and the Ross Laboratories mothers' surveys. *American Journal of Public Health, 81*, 1049–1052.

Scarr, S. (1993). Biological and cultural diversity: The legacy of Darwin for development. *Child Development, 64*, 1333–1353.

Scarr, S. (1996). How people make their own environments: Implications for parents and policy makers. *Psychology, Public Policy, and Law, 2*, 204–228.

Scarr, S., & McCartney, K. (1983). How people make their own environments: A theory of genotype ® environment effects. *Child Development, 54*, 424–435.

Scarr, S., & Weinberg, R. A. (1976). IQ test performance of black children adopted by white families. *American Psychologist, 31*, 726–739.

Scarr, S., Weinberg, R. A., & Waldman, I. D. (1993). IQ correlations in transracial adoptive families. *Intelligence, 17*, 541–555.

Schiefele, U., Krapp, A., & Winteler, A. (1992). Interest as a predictor of academic achievement: A meta-analysis of research. In K. A. Renninger, S. Hidi, & A. Krapp (Eds.), *The role of interest in learning and development*. Hillsdale, NJ: Lawrence Erlbaum Associates, Inc.

Schmidt, F. L., & Hunter, J. E. (1998). The validity and utility of selection methods in personnel psychology: Practical and theoretical implications of 85 years of research findings. *Psychological Bulletin, 124*, 262–274.

Shih, M., Pittinsky, T. L., & Ambady, N. (1999). Stereotype susceptibility: Identity salience and shifts in quantitative performance. *Psychological Science, 10*, 80–83.

Sigman, M., & Whaley, S. E. (1998). The role of nutrition in the development of intelligence. In U. Neisser (Ed.), *The rising curve: Long-term gains in IQ and related measures* (pp. 155–182). Washington, DC: American Psychological Association.

Silegman, D. (1994). *A question of intelligence: The IQ debate in America*. New York: Citadel Press.

Simonton, D. K. (1999). Talent and its development: An emergenic and epigenetic model. *Psychological Review, 106*, 435–457.

Spearman, C. (1904). General intelligence, objectively determined and measured. *American Journal of Psychology, 15*, 201–293.

Spencer, S. J., Steele, C. M., & Quinn, D. M. (1999). Stereotype threat and women's math performance. *Journal of Experimental Social Psychology, 35*, 4–28.

Spitz, H. (1986). *The raising of intelligence: A selected history of attempts to raise retarded intelligence.* Hillsdale, NJ: Lawrence Erlbaum Associates, Inc.

Stangor, C., Carr, C., & Kiang, L. (1998). Activating stereotypes undermines task performance expectations. *Journal of Personality and Social Psychology, 75*, 1191–1197.

Steele, C. M. (1997). A threat in the air: How stereotypes shape intellectual identity and performance. *American Psychologist, 52*, 613–629.

Steele, C. M. (1998). Stereotyping and its threat are real. *American Psychologist, 53*, 680–681.

Steele, C. M., & Aronson, J. (1995). Stereotype threat and the intellectual test performance of African Americans. *Journal of Personality and Social Psychology, 69*, 797–811.

Sternberg, R. J., & Kaufman, J. C. (1998). Human abilities. *Annual Review of Psychology, 49*, 479–502.

Sternberg, R. J., Wagner, R. K., Williams, W. M., & Horvath, J. A. (1995). Testing common sense. *American Psychologist, 50*, 912–927.

Stone, J., Lynch, C., Sjomeling, M., & Darley, J. M. (1999). Stereotype threat effects on Black and White athletic performance. *Journal of Personality and Social Psychology, 77*, 1213–1227.

Thorndike, R. L. (1987). Stability of factor loadings. *Personality and Individual Differences, 8*, 585–586.

Thurstone, L. L. (1947). *Multiple factor analysis: A development and expansion of. The Vectors of the Mind.* Chicago: University of Chicago Press.

Vernon, P. E. (1982). *The abilities and achievements of Orientals in North America.* New York: Academic.

Wachs, T. D. (1993). Determinants of intellectual development: Single-determinant research in a multidetermined universe. *Intelligence, 17*, 1–9.

Waldman, I. D., Weinberg, R. A., & Scarr, S. (1994). Racial-group differences in IQ in the Minnesota Transracial Adoption Study: A reply to Levin and Lynn. *Intelligence, 19*, 29–44.

Weaver, B. (2000, July/August). Social competence, not IQ. *APS Observer, 13*(6), 16, 31.

Weinberg, R. A., Scarr, S., & Waldman, I. D. (1992). The Minnesota Transracial Adoption Study: A follow-up of IQ test performance in adolescence. *Intelligence, 16*, 117–135.

Whaley, A. L. (1998). Issues of validity in empirical tests of stereotype threat theory. *American Psychologist, 53*, 679–680.

Wigdor, A. K., & Garner, W. R. (Eds.). (1982). *Ability testing: Uses, consequences, and controversies.* Washington, DC: National Academy Press.

Wilk, S. L., Desmarais, L. B., & Sackett, P. R. (1995). Gravitation to jobs commensurate with ability: Longitudinal and cross-sectional tests. *Journal of Applied Psychology, 80*, 79–85.

Wilk, S. L., & Sackett, P. R. (1996). Longitudinal analysis of ability-job complexity fit and job change. *Personnel Psychology, 49*, 937–967.

Winner, E. (2000). The origins and ends of giftedness. *American Psychologist, 55*, 159–169.

HUMAN PERFORMANCE, *15*(1/2), 75–96

Cognitive and GMA Testing in the European Community: Issues and Evidence

Jesús F. Salgado
Department of Social Psychology
University of Santiago de Compostela, Spain

Neil Anderson
Department of Psychology
Goldsmiths College, University of London, UK

This article reviews the evidence on General Mental Ability (GMA) and cognitive ability tests in connection with employment in the European Community (EC). Five themes are reviewed: prevalence, applicant reactions, testing standards, criterion validity, and recent advances. The first section shows that GMA and cognitive ability tests are used more often in Europe than in America. The second section, regarding applicant reactions, shows that the studies carried out in the EC have shown that there are no differences between Europe and America. The third section shows that there is an initiative to harmonize the standards used across the European countries. In the fourth section, we report on a validity generalization study carried out using the primary studies conducted in Great Britain and Spain. The results showed that GMA and cognitive tests are valid predictors of job performance and training success in both countries and they generalize validity across occupations. Furthermore, the size of the observed validity estimates is similar to those found in the American meta-analyses. Finally, two recent advances are mentioned: the British "Project B" and the use of virtual reality technology for predicting job performance.

Requests for reprints should be sent to Jesús F. Salgado, Departamento de Psicología Social, Universidad de Santiago de Compostela, 15706 Santiago de Compostela, Spain. E-mail: psjesal@usc.es Requests for reprints could also be sent to Neil Anderson, Department of Psychology, Goldsmiths College, University of London, New Cross London SE14 6NW, Great Britain. E-mail: pss01na@gold.ac.uk

General Mental Ability (GMA) tests, sometimes called cognitive ability tests, have a long history in personnel selection and assessment in several European Community (EC) countries. Different tests of cognitive abilities (i.e., verbal, numerical, spatial, perceptual) or GMA have been used for hiring purposes for a century. In the early 20th century, cognitive and GMA tests were used in the majority of European countries for selecting and assessing people. For example, in 1901, the Italian psychologist Ugo Pizzoli used professional examinations with apprentices (Baumgartem, 1949), and in Paris in 1907, Jean M. Lahy used tests for selecting drivers (Viteles, 1932). During the first World War (WWI), also called the Great or European War, ability tests were used by the Belgian, German, and Italian armies. In Italy, for example, Agostino Gemelli (1916; see Viteles, 1932) used ability tests for selecting pilots. After WWI, ability tests were frequently used in all European countries, especially in the most developed at that time: France, Germany, Great Britain, Italy, and Spain, but also in a lot of other European countries such as Belgium, Holland, Poland, Czechoslovakia, the USSR, and Austria. In addition to this, eight conferences were held in Europe between 1920 and 1934 to communicate the experiences and results of the European laboratories devoted to "psychotechnik." This word, created in 1903 by the German psychologist W. Stern and used by H. Münsterberg (1913), was the name used at those times for the field known today as Industrial and Organizational (I/O) Psychology in the United States and Work and Organizational (W/O) Psychology in Europe.

Despite these strong beginnings, European research with regard to the validity of GMA and cognitive tests has progressively declined since the 1930s due to political and economic reasons. This has regrettably produced an absence of studies summarizing the use and validity of these personnel selection procedures (e.g., GMA tests, personality tests, and interviews) in Europe. Simultaneously, thousands of studies have been conducted in the United States, showing that GMA and cognitive ability tests predict job performance and training criteria (see Ghiselli 1966, 1973), the results of which have been meta-analytically integrated in a number of studies (e.g., Hunter & Hunter, 1984; Levine, Spector, Menon, Narayanon, & Cannon-Bowers, 1996; Pearlman, Schmidt, & Hunter, 1980; Schmitt, Gooding, Noe, & Kirsch, 1984; Schmidt & Hunter, 1977). However, although perhaps surprising to colleagues in the United States, no study in the EC has meta-analyzed the criterion validity of GMA and cognitive ability tests in different European countries.

This lack of meta-analytical studies in Europe has had two negative consequences. First, the Situational Specificity Hypothesis (SSH) was largely accepted and remained unchallenged for many years. Consequently, many European researchers thought that the tests should be locally validated. According to the SSH, the measurement instruments used for personnel selection must be individually validated for each job, organization, and human group. In other words, it is assumed that it is possible that valid tests for a job could not be valid for another job, although the two jobs are very similar in tasks and functions. Ghiselli (1966, 1973) found great variability in validity coefficients, and these results were considered to support this hypothesis. Schmidt and Hunter (1984) affirmed that the SSH makes two predictions: (a) that there will be a high degree of variability in the validity coefficients obtained in different settings (i.e., organizations, jobs, tests, and applicant pools), and (b) if the setting does not change, the observed validity will not change. Schmidt and Hunter (1977) stated an alternative hypothesis called the Validity Generalization Hypothesis (VGH). According to VGH, the variability and the size of the observed validity coefficients are affected by several artifactual errors, including criterion and predictor unreliability, range restriction in the criterion and predictor, criterion and predictor dichotomization, sample size, and several others (see Hunter & Schmidt, 1990, for a complete list of error sources). However, it is possible to find validity generalization when these sources of error are removed. With respect to this, psychometric meta-analysis (Hunter & Schmidt, 1990; Schmidt & Hunter, 1977) is the method used to aggregate numerous studies, while removing some of the artifactual errors introduced into the data by these error sources.

As mentioned previously, a number of meta-analyses of validity coefficients of GMA and cognitive tests have been conducted in the United States since the 1970s, to check whether validity might be generalizable (e.g., Hartigan & Wigdor, 1989; Hunter & Hunter, 1984; Levine et al., 1996; McDaniel, Schmidt, & Hunter, 1988; Pearlman et al., 1980; Schmitt et al., 1984; Schmidt & Hunter, 1977; Schmidt, Hunter, Pearlman, & Shane, 1979). Most of these studies have found that the variability in the observed validities has been due to artifacts, mainly sampling error, which explains a range of variance between 50% to 100%. Thus, it might be hypothesized that criterion validity can be generalized across settings for a large group of occupational families. Using civilian occupations, the three largest meta-analyses were carried out by Hunter and Hunter (1984; see also Hunter, 1986), by the panel of the U.S. National Research Council (Hartigan & Wigdor, 1989), and by Levine et al. (1996). Hunter and Hunter found an average corrected validity of .45 for job performance and .54 for training success. They used a criterion reliability estimate of .60 for overall job performance, .80 for training, and .60 for range restriction corrections. The panel of the U.S. National Research Council (Hartigan & Wigdor, 1989) subsequently replicated Hunter and Hunter's work. This new study contained three main differences with Hunter and Hunter's meta-analysis, as the number of validity studies was enlarged by 264 additional coefficients ($n = 38,521$), the estimate of job performance ratings was assumed to be .80, and range restriction was not corrected for. Under these conditions, the panel found an estimate of the average operational validity of .22 ($K = 755, n = 77,141$) for predicting job performance. However, if Hunter and Hunter's figures for criterion reliability and range restriction were to be applied to the mean observed validity found by the panel, then the average operational validity would be .38 for job performance ratings, a figure closer to Hunter and Hunter's results. In addition to these, Levine et al. conducted a very relevant meta-analysis for crafts jobs in the utility industry. They used a value of .585 for range restriction and .756 for criterion reliability of job performance ratings. Levine et al. found an operational validity of .43 for job performance and .67 for training success. However, applying Hunter and Hunter's estimates for criteria reliability and range restriction once again to Levine et al.'s observed validity, the results would be .47 for job performance ratings and .62 for training success, indicating a great similarity between Hunter and Hunter's and Levine et al.'s results. Hunter (1986) also meta-analyzed an impressive database of military studies in which training success was used as the criterion. He found an average validity of .62 ($k = 828$, $n = 472, 539$). This validity was corrected for range restriction, but was not corrected for unreliability in the criterion. As a whole, the results of these meta-analyses confirmed that GMA tests are the best predictors for entry-level jobs and that they have generalized validity across occupations in the U.S. economy. In this sense, the SSH was strongly disconfirmed by the U.S. validity studies. At present, however, given the paucity of comparable meta-analyses of GMA tests across Europe, it is not possible to say the same for European validity studies.

The second negative consequence of the lack of European meta-analyses was that the results of the American meta-analyses of GMA and cognitive tests (and other selection procedures) were taken as granted without considering possible cross-cultural differences in the characteristics of companies and in the practices of human resources management, both of which could affect the validity coefficient. For example, the majority of European companies are medium and small companies (less than 500 employees). Another reason is that, within the EC, individualistic (e.g., Germany, Holland, United Kingdom) and collectivist cultures (e.g., France, Italy, and Spain; Hofstede, 1980) coexist. Consequently, such a mix of cultural typographies could produce a differential impact on the validity of GMA and cognitive tests due to the fact that different systems of values, approaches to power, supervision styles, and interpersonal communication may be operating simultaneously. These different cultural systems could produce a country-specific effect on validity and result in a lack of validity generalization across the EC. Therefore, to assume that the American results are unreservedly generalizable to the multifarious cultural context of the EC would be an erroneous practice. Herriot and Anderson (1997) suggested the following:

> The findings from [the American] meta-analyses have been unreservedly cited by personnel psychologists in other countries and appear to have been unquestioningly accepted as being generalizable to different national contexts. Social, cultural, legislative and recruitment and appraisal differences have been overlooked, and certainly in many European countries the results of meta-analyses conducted in the United States have been cited without caveat. These findings may indeed be transferable to

other countries, but then again they may not be, given the pervasive cultural differences. (p. 28)

For example, as we describe later in this article, survey data appear to show that there are somewhat different practices of assessment in North America and the EC.

Taking into account these two negative consequences resulting from the lack of meta-analytic studies in Europe, this article has two main objectives. First, we review the current evidence concerning the use and prevalence of GMA tests and cognitive ability tests for selecting people in the EC. In doing so, the review will provide a picture of current practices within personnel selection in the EC, with an emphasis on the use of GMA and cognitive tests, to compare these practices with those of the United States. Furthermore, data will be presented regarding the perception of fairness and justice of GMA and cognitive ability tests for hiring personnel. The second objective will be to present the first results of a large-scale study looking at the validity generalization of GMA and cognitive tests for predicting work criteria. These form part of a larger research project we are conducting, looking at the validity studies conducted in all EC countries, the aim of which is to establish whether criterion validity is country-specific or whether validity is generalizable across the EC countries. In addition to this, we also look to see whether the validity magnitudes for predicting overall job performance and training success are similar to those found in the United States. However, at present, it is only possible to report the results of the first countries analyzed, which are those of Spain and the United Kingdom. We also comment on recent moves toward ensuring common standards of test administration across Europe. Finally, we discuss recent developments in Europe concerning emerging media for assessing cognitive abilities (e.g., video tests, virtual reality tests).

PERSONNEL SELECTION PRACTICES IN THE EC: THE ROLE OF GMA AND COGNITIVE TESTS

Use of Ability Tests in Europe

There have been a number of surveys of organizational use of selection methods in European countries, most of which have included cognitive ability tests in the list of methods surveyed (e.g., Bartram, Lindley, Marshall, & Forster, 1995; Hodgkinson & Payne, 1998; Keenan, 1995; Robertson & Makin, 1986; Ryan, McFarland, Baron, & Page, 1999; Schuler, Frier, & Kaufman, 1993; Shackleton & Newell, 1991, 1994; Smith & Abrahamsen, 1992, amongst others). Some of these surveys have focused on single country selection practices (e.g., Keenan, 1995), whereas others have included multiple countries (Ryan et al., 1999, being the most extensive, covering 20 countries worldwide). Several surveys have investigated selection method use for all types of applicant and levels of organizational entry (e.g., Ryan et al., 1999), whereas others have addressed specific levels of organizational entry—for instance, graduate selection (e.g., Keenan, 1995; Shackleton & Newell, 1991, 1994) or managerial selection (e.g., Eleftheriou & Robertson, 1999). Finally, several surveys present data by size of organization or scale of the recruitment activity in the organization (e.g., Robertson & Makin, 1986; Shackleton & Newell, 1991), providing useful information on method popularity depending on the size of the organization.

Table 1 summaries the results of the major survey findings. We located a number of published surveys covering 16 European countries, although there are almost certainly other unpublished surveys that have been conducted but are not generally available. Cross-country differences in ability test use are apparent from this table, with generally more frequent use of ability tests in Belgium, Britain, The Netherlands, Portugal, and Spain than in France, Germany, Greece, Ireland, or Italy. These differences are not great, however, in comparison with the range of frequency differences into test usage for different levels of applicant groups. Ability tests seem to be used considerably more for graduate and managerial level appointments than for general selection procedures. This seems to be particularly the case in Britain. Hodgkinson and Payne (1998), for instance, reported that 78.4% of those surveyed used ability tests for graduate selection (i.e., selection specifically directed at recruiting individuals who have completed an undergraduate degree), whereas Keenan (1995) found an even higher percentage use of 91%. This compares with the findings of Ryan et al. (1999), where, on a 5-point scale of usage, the mean was 3.41 (21%–50% of occasions) for general use of ability tests in Britain. In addition, there is unsurprising evidence that larger organizations use ability tests more frequently than smaller ones (Bartram, Lindley, et al., 1995; Robertson & Makin, 1986; Shackleton & Newell, 1991).

One of the inherent difficulties, however, in interpreting data from these surveys is that different surveys have used different response scales to record frequency of method usage. In addition, we should be mindful of Fletcher's (1994) critique of the reliability of such survey findings. Nevertheless, it is instructive to be able to at least identify overarching trends in the use of ability tests across Europe and, moreover, to be able to compare these findings with surveys of practice in the United States. Fortunately, the most extensive surveys conducted by Ryan et al. (1999) provided directly comparable data. Table 2 sets out frequency responses in test use rank-ordered by country. (We have included only European countries and the United States here.)

It produces some surprising and anomalous findings. The United States ranks only 10th in ability test usage, behind several European countries, including, less surprisingly, the Netherlands, Spain, and Britain, but, more surprisingly, behind countries such as Portugal, Ireland, and Greece. Whether the exact rankings produced from this data are strictly accurate is a moot point (e.g., it is highly unlikely

TABLE 1
Use of Cognitive Ability Tests in Different European Countries

| Country and Survey | Sample | | Percentage | Average |
	Type	n	Use[a]	
Belgium				
Ryan, McFarland, Baron, & Page (1999)	General	68	21–50	[3.85][b]
Shackleton & Newell (1994)				
French speaking	Management	24	54.5	
Flemish speaking	Management	48	58.1	
Bruchon & Lievens (1989)				
French speaking	General	89	71	
De Witte, Van Laese, & Vewecke (1992)				
Flemish speaking	General	53	74	
Denmark				
Price–Waterhouse–Cranfield (1994)	General	330	17	
Finland				
Price–Waterhouse–Cranfield (1994)	General	225	42	
France				
Ryan et al. (1999)	General	35	1–20	[2.29][b]
Hodgkinson & Payne (1998)	Graduates	26	80.7	
Shackleton & Newell (1991)	Graduates	52	22.5	
Smith & Abrahamsen (1992)	General		33	
Clark (1993)[c]	Executive search	23	34.8	
Price–Waterhouse–Cranfield (1994)	General	651	28	
Schuler, Frier, & Kauffmann (1993)	General	44		
Great Britain				
Ryan et al. (1999)	General	108	21–50	[3.08][b]
Hodgkinson & Payne (1998)	Graduates	120	78.4	
Keenan (1995)	Graduates	236	91	
Bartram, Lindley, et al. (1995)	Small businesses	307	15.3	
Shackleton & Newell (1991)	Graduates	73	41.1	
Smith & Abrahamsen (1992)	General		11	
Robertson & Makin (1986)	Graduates	105	35.3	
Clark (1993)[c]	Executive search	420	40	
Price–Waterhouse–Cranfield (1994)	General	1243	45	
Schuler et al. (1993)	General		44	
Germany				
Ryan et al. (1999)	General	35	1–20	[1.90][b]
Shackleton & Newell (1994)	Managements	67	9.7	
Smith & Abrahamsen (1992)	General		21	
Clark (1993)[c]	Executive search	15	40	
Price–Waterhouse–Cranfield (1994)	General	884	8	
Schuler et al. (1993)	General		8	
Greece				
Ryan et al. (1999)	General	27	1–20	[2.54][b]
Eleftheriou & Robertson (1999)	Management	48	35	

(continued)

TABLE 1 *(Continued)*

Country and Survey	Sample Type	n	Percentage Use[a]	Average
Ireland				
Ryan et al. (1999)	General	49	1–20	[2.79][b]
Price–Waterhouse–Cranfield	General	140	41	
Italy				
Ryan et al. (1999)	General	29	Never	[1.33][b]
Shackleton & Newell	Management	27	16	
Clark (1993)[c]	Executive search	17	37.5	
The Netherlands				
Ryan et al. (1999)	General	66	21–50	[3.76][b]
Hodgkinson & Payne (1998)	Graduates	46	67.4	
Smith & Abrahamsen (1992)	General		21	
Price–Waterhouse–Cranfield (1994)	General	128	19	
Norway				
Smith & Abrahamsen (1992)	General		25	
Price–Waterhouse–Cranfield (1994)	General	280	19	
Portugal				
Ryan et al. (1999)	General	31	21–50	[3.27][b]
Price–Waterhouse–Cranfield	General	93	17	
Spain				
Ryan et al. (1999)	General	24	21–50	[3.75][b]
Schuler et al. (1993)	General		47	
Price–Waterhouse–Cranfield	General	260	72	
Sweden				
Ryan et al. (1999)	General	91	1–20	[3.75][b]
Price–Waterhouse–Cranfield	General	322	14	
Switzerland				
Schuler et al. (1993)	General		25	
Turkey				
Price–Waterhouse–Cranfield (1994)	General	112	33	
Sinangil, Ones & Jockin (1999)	General	200	22	

[a]Percentage use refers to responding organizations reporting using cognitive ability measures "almost always," "always," on "more than half" of applicants, or "sometimes" used. [b]Ryan et al. (1999) used a 5-point response scale: 1 = never, 2 = rarely (1–20), 3 = occasionally (21–50), 4 = often (51–80), 5 = almost always or always (81–100). [c]Clark (1993) combines all types of testing, including ability and personality.

that ability tests are utilized more in Portugal than Britain, or in Greece than the United States), but the mean rating 0f 2.09 for United States organizations is considerably less than several European countries. This equates on Ryan et al.'s (1999) scale to between 1% and 20% of selection processes within U.S. organizations using ability tests. One possible explanation is that fears over claims of adverse impact may be suppressing ability tests' use in the U.S. compared to Europe, where in

TABLE 2
Rank Order Frequencies of Ability Test Use: Europe and the United States

Rank	Country	M^a	SD
1	Belgium	3.85	1.30
2	The Netherlands	3.76	1.41
3	Spain	3.75	1.44
4	Portugal	3.27	1.75
5	Britain	3.08	1.52
6	Sweden	2.86	1.37
7	Ireland	2.79	1.42
8	Greece	2.54	1.56
9	France	2.29	1.72
10	United States	2.09	1.26
11	Germany	1.90	1.52
12	Italy	1.33	0.82

Note. Data from Ryan, McFarland, Baron, and Page (1999), Table 5, pp. 375–377.
[a]Ryan et al. (1999) used a 5-point response scale: 1 = never, 2 = rarely (1–20%), 3 = occasionally (21–50%), 4 = often (51–80%), 5 = almost always or always (81–100%).

many countries the equal opportunities legislation is far less stringent and only sporadically enforced. Ironically, almost without exception, the findings from meta-analytic investigations into cognitive test validity have been based on American validity studies and have certainly been a major contribution to our understanding of selection method of efficacy. Yet, it appears that the organizational use of ability tests in the United States is less than in many European countries where meta-analytic evidence is absent. This anomaly is a curious finding, but one that we believe clearly illustrates the impact of legislative and social–cultural factors on the take-up of validity study findings by selection practitioners, and one to which we return later in this article.

Applicant Reactions to GMA Tests

Various studies have recently been carried out into applicant reactions to personnel selection procedures in the EC countries (see Steiner & Gilliland, in press, and Anderson, Born, & Cunningham-Snell, in press, for recent reviews). These studies have partially replicated an early study by Steiner and Gilliland (1996), in which these authors examined the perceived fairness of eight selection procedures: interviews, personality tests, ability tests, work sample tests, integrity tests, Curriculo Vitaes or resumés, graphology, job knowledge tests, and informal contacts. Steiner and Gilliland found that interviews, resumés, and work-sample tests consistently receive favorable ratings in France and the United States. Ability tests, personal references, and personality tests are rated in the middle of the scales. Honesty tests and biodata are also moderately well-rated, and graphology is poorly rated. In a practical replication and extension of Steiner and Gilliland's study, Salgado and Moscoso (2000) used Steiner and Gilliland's survey in Spain and Portugal. The findings with regard to GMA and cognitive tests do not show significant differences among the European countries or between the European countries and the United States. Steiner and Gilliland (in press) reported similar results in Germany. Thus, this failure to find cross-cultural differences in perceived fairness of cognitive tests indicates that perceived fairness does not seem to contribute a specific influence on the criterion validity of cognitive tests for predicting job performance and training criteria.

Testing Standards in Europe

The standards for test use, user qualification, and test construction vary considerably between European counties. Generally speaking, in individualistic cultures such as north–west European counties (e.g., Britain, The Netherlands, and Germany), psychometric testing standards have been longer-established, as tests have been used in selection for several decades, whereas in more collectivist Southern European countries (e.g., Italy, Greece) and in Eastern European countries (e.g., Poland, Hungary, Czech Republic), testing is less regulated by the relevant professional psychological bodies. Certainly in Britain, for instance, the British Psychological Society (BPS) now has in force a detailed and comprehensive framework of test user competency requirements (Bartram, 1995, 1996). Test users are certified in Britain only after they have satisfactorily passed test training programs (where the programs themselves are verified independently as meeting BPS standards) at two levels of certification: "Level A" and "Level B". Level A covers seven competency areas relating to cognitive ability test construction and use, whereas Level B relates to personality instruments, interest inventories, and other instruments. Much of the credit for developing and implementing these competency-based standards is attributable to the work of Bartram (e.g., Bartram, 1995, 1996) and the panel of BPS verifiers. Today, the position adopted by most responsible test suppliers is that relevant Level A or Level B certificates need to be held by purchasers before they can be supplied with cognitive ability or personality instruments. Another strand to this framework is the BPS-published reviews of tests in print, similar in purpose to the Buros compendium in the United States. Reviews of both Level A tests (Bartram, Lindley, & Foster, 1992) and Level B tests (Bartram, Anderson, Kellet, Lindley, & Robertson, 1995) have been published, allowing test users to access independent reviews of popular occupational tests.

At the European level of analysis, the European Federation of Professional Psychologists' Associations (EFPPA) has been particularly active in researching and promoting cross-national harmonization of testing standards (see, e.g., Bartram, 1998; Bartram & Coyne, 1998). EFPPA established its task force on Tests and

Testing in 1995, although this covered clinical, forensic, and educational testing as well as work-related psychometric testing (see Bartram, 1998, for an accessible account). Given the cultural and legislative diversity present across different European countries, however, it may prove to be problematic to move toward a completely harmonized set of European standards (Bartram & Coyne, 1998). Indeed, these deeply historic cultural differences, not to mention the multitude of languages present in different countries, make the European context for work-related testing substantially more complex and challenging than in the United States. These moves are to be welcomed, nevertheless, and the EFPPA initiative toward providing a pan-European framework for testing standards are clearly a positive development.

Possibly, as a result of this lack of harmonization of legislative structures across Europe, there has been far less research into subgroup differences and adverse impact on all types of tests, including GMA tests, in Europe compared with the United States (see, e.g., Ones & Anderson, 2000). Because the threat of legal action is perceived by employers and selection psychologists to be far less likely in many European countries compared to the United States, research into subgroup differences has been sorely lacking in several European countries (te Nijenhuis, 1997). Yet this lack of evidence does not dispel concerns that the same or similar degrees of subgroup differences on applicant raw scores on GMA tests may be found in European countries. Rather, existing data tends to be held by the test publishers themselves who are naturally sensitive over allowing access to such findings or publishing subgroup differences in tests' manuals or any other medium. In several European countries, there are of course substantial minority group communities either native to the country or who have immigrated as migrant workers over more recent years (e.g., Black and Asian communities in Great Britain, many of whom are now third and fourth generation British citizens; Turkish "guest workers" in Germany and the Netherlands; Moroccan and Algerian migrant workers in Spain; French, Brazilian, and Angolan immigrants in Portugal; and migrant workers from Surinam who now reside in the Netherlands). Although it is beyond the scope of this study to examine such subgroup differences, this whole area of research in selection in Europe has been largely neglected, and it is an issue that appears to us as an important and potentially fruitful area for future research studies to address. Nevertheless, two relevant studies by te Nijenhuis (1997; Nijenhuis & van der Flier, 1997) must be cited here with regard to adverse impact. In the first study, te Nijenhuis and van der Flier (1997) investigated the comparability of General Aptitude Test Battery (GATB) scores for immigrants and majority group members in the Netherlands. Specifically, they studied the impact of group differences with respect to the construct validity of the GATB. Their samples consisted of several groups of immigrants (Surinam = 535, Dutch Antilles = 126, North Africa = 167, Turkey = 275, others = 219) and a large sample of the majority group ($n = 816$). Te Nijenhuis and van der Flier found very small differences with respect to the construct validity of each individual test and the battery as a whole (except for the vocabulary test). In another study, te Nijenhuis compared the predictive validity of the GATB for training success of a minority and a majority group. The findings demonstrated that the mean scores on the GATB were less favorable for the minority group. With the exception of the vocabulary test, the effect sizes for the other seven tests included in the GATB ranged from −.25 to −.86, with an average effect size of .53. For the vocabulary test, the effect size was −1.63, and for the battery as a whole, the effect size was −.99. However, the immigrants scored on average a quarter of a standard deviation lower on the training criteria than the majority group. Te Nijenhuis (1997) found that the line of regression of immigrants was under the line of regression of the majority group. This finding means that when a common regression line is used, immigrants are overpredicted and majority group members are underpredicted.

Criterion Validity of GMA and Cognitive Tests

In the first section of this article, we suggested that cross-cultural differences could have an impact on the validity of personnel selection procedures. However, to date, this possibility has not been checked with regard to the EC. The multinational and multicultural community, which is the EC, is a very challenging field in which to test both the SSH and the VGH, the reason being that, in the EC, there coexist countries with different languages, cultures, and legislative systems, and a complete union has still not been achieved, although there is a common currency (i.e., Euro) and common legislative and executive systems. For example, there are over 20 different languages among the current members of the EC, and in some countries more than one culture or language also coexist, as is the case in Belgium, Great Britain, and Spain. Therefore, if the SSH is correct, there should be substantially greater variability in the size of the validity coefficients found in the EC countries than in the United States, this variability being due to the societal and cultural variations present within the EC context.

We are currently leading a European team of researchers with the purpose of studying the validity generalization of GMA and cognitive tests across the EC countries. At present, however, we have only analyzed data collected from the validity studies conducted in Great Britain and Spain. Although they represent only a small part of the studies conducted in the EC, at the same time they are two very relevant countries, as they have two very different languages (English vs. Spanish) and cultures (Individualistic vs. Collectivistic). However, as our study progresses, it is possible that some effect sizes may change slightly due to the increase in the number of studies.

We have conducted a search of published and unpublished studies that could be relevant to our purposes. Our literature search began with the scientific journals of psychology published in Great Britain and Spain. After that, we sought unpublished reports and technical reports in which validity coefficients were reported.

This task was accomplished by contacting relevant researchers in the United Kingdom and Spain. In addition, we checked the technical manuals of cognitive ability tests published in both the United Kingdom and Spain. Once all the studies had been obtained, we applied the formulas of psychometric meta-analysis as developed by Hunter and Schmidt (1990). We conducted separated meta-analyses for job performance and training success for occupational groups. To do that, we used distributions for criterion reliability as well as for range restriction. For job performance, we used the interrater reliability reported by Viswesvaran, Ones, and Schmidt (1996), with an average estimate of .52 $(SD = .10)$. For training success, we used the .80 $(SD = .10)$ estimate of reliability reported by Hunter and Hunter (1984). We developed specific empirical distributions for range restriction using the data reported in the studies. For the United Kingdom studies, .609 $(SD = .24)$ was the weighted-sample average of range restriction. For the Spanish studies, the average was .795 $(SD = .21)$. Therefore, considering both countries as a whole, the average range restriction weighted by the number of studies in each country was .66. For predictor reliability, we used .85 $(SD = .05)$ as our estimate. This was the average test–retest reliability reported in the studies that we found.

Table 3 presents the results of the meta-analyses for the GMA-criterion combinations for each country separately and jointly. From left to right, the first four columns report the number of studies (K), the total sample size (N), the weighted-sample average observed validity (r), and the weighted-sample observed standard deviation (SDr). The next four columns report the operational validity (rho); the standard deviation of the operational validity (Sdrho); the percentage of variance accounted for by criterion and predictor unreliability, range restriction, and sam-

TABLE 3
Meta-Analysis Results of Cognitive Ability–Criterion Combinations

Criterion	K	N	r	SDr	Rho	SDrho	%VE	CV	LRHO	LSD	LCV
JPR–SPA	9	1239	.36	.11	.61	.00	111	.61	.55	.18	.31
JPR–UK	45	7283	.18	.14	.41	.23	46	.11	.37	.25	.05
JPR UK+SPA	54	8522	.21	.15	.42	.23	45	.13	.38	.25	.07
TRA–SPA	25	2405	.35	.17	.47	.17	47	.25	.42	.23	.14
TRA–UK	61	20305	.34	.12	.56	.08	87	.46	.51	.18	.28
TRA–UK+SPA	86	22710	.34	.13	.53	.09	80	.48	.48	.18	.25

Note. K = number of independent samples; N = total sample size; r = weighed-sample average observed validity; Sdr = weighted-sample observed standard deviation; RHO = operational validity (observed validity corrected for criterion unreliability and range restriction); Sdrho = rho standard deviation; %VE = percentage of observed variance accounted for by artifactual errors; CV = 90% credibility value; JPR–UK = job performance ratings–United Kingdom studies; JPR–SPA = job performance ratings–Spain studies; TRA–UK = training success–United Kingdom studies; TRA–SPA = training success–Spain studies; LRHO = lowest rho value; LSD = standard deviation for the lowest rho value; LCV = 90% credibility value for the lowest rho value.

pling error (*%VE*); and the 90% credibility value (*90%CV*). Because in some of the cells the number of studies is small, we cannot be sure that our review contains all relevant studies. With regard to this point, Ashworth, Osburn, Callender, and Boyle (1992) developed a method for assessing the vulnerability of validity generalization results to unrepresented or missing studies. Ashworth et al. (1992) suggested calculating the effects on validity when 10% of studies are missing and their validity is zero. Therefore, we calculated additional estimates to represent what the validity would be if we were unable to locate 10% of the studies carried out and if these studies showed zero validity. The last three columns report these new estimates: lowest rho value, standard deviation, and the 90% credibility value. The operational validity was estimated as the observed validity corrected for criterion unreliability and range restriction. Finally, each study within the meta-analysis represents an independent sample.

For the criterion of job performance, we found 45 studies in the United Kingdom and 9 studies in Spain, contributing to a total sample of 8,522 individuals. In the United Kingdom, the operational validity was .41, a value similar to the one found in the American meta-analyses (e.g., Hunter & Hunter, 1984; Levine et al., 1996). Artifactual errors explained 46% of the variability in the observed validities, and the 90% credibility value was .11. This value means that there is validity generalization in the United Kingdom studies. In the case of the Spanish studies, the operational validity was .61, a value higher than the one found in the United Kingdom and American meta-analyses. The observed variability was completely explained by artifactual errors, but there was also second-order sampling error. The 90%CV was also .61; therefore, the Spanish studies showed that there is also validity generalization in this group of studies. Taking together the United Kingdom and Spanish studies, the operational validity resulted in an estimate of .42, the explained variance was 45%, and the 90% credibility value was .13. Consequently, these figures are very close to the values reported by Hunter and Hunter (1984).

For the training success criterion, we found 61 studies in the United Kingdom and 25 studies in Spain, representing a total sample of 22,710 individuals. The observed validities were practically the same in both countries, and the operational validity changed a bit due to the different range restriction estimates used for the United Kingdom and Spain. However, the results were very similar in both countries. In the United Kingdom, the operational validity was .56, and in the Spanish studies, the operational validity was .47. These results are similar to those found in the United States by Hunter and Hunter (1984; Hunter, 1986), Levine et al. (1996), and the panel of the U.S. National Research Council (when corrected for criterion unreliability and range restriction; Hartigan & Wigdor, 1989). Artifactual errors accounted for 87% of the variance in the United Kingdom studies and 47% in the Spanish studies. Finally, the credibility values were .46 and .25 for the United Kingdom and Spain, respectively. Consequently, we found that validity is generalizable across jobs and samples in both countries. The analysis of the coefficients of both countries taken as a whole showed an operational validity of .53 ($SD = .09$) and a 90% credibility value of .48. Comparatively, Hunter (1986) reported a value of .57 for the occupation family of medium complexity. This group of occupations represents about 65% of the total number of occupations in the U.S. economy.

Table 4 presents the results of the meta-analyses of cognitive ability–criterion–occupation combinations. To be able to compare the results between the United Kingdom and Spanish validity studies, we only report the results for occupations with data in both countries. In general, the meta-analyses were carried out with a small number of studies, for both the job performance and training success criteria. For the criterion of job performance, the occupational group "clerical" is the only occupation represented in both countries. In both cases, the number of studies is small. The operational validities were .50 and .21 for the Spanish and British studies, respectively. The 90% credibility values showed that there is validity generalization in both countries, as the estimates are .34 and .21 for Spain and the United Kingdom, respectively. The artifactual errors explained 68% of the variance in the Spanish studies. However, in the United Kingdom studies, there is an extremely large second-order sampling error, as the percentage of variance accounted for by artifactual errors is extremely large. For the training success criterion, we found three occupations with validity studies in Spain and the United Kingdom. These occupations were clerical, drivers, and trade jobs. For clerical jobs, the operational validities were .77 and .55 in Spain and the United Kingdom,

TABLE 4
Meta-Analysis Results of Cognitive
Ability–Criterion–Occupation Combinations

Jobs	K	N	r	SDr	Rho	SDrho	%VE	CV	LRHO	LSD	LCV
Job performance ratings											
Clerical–SPA	4	487	.29	.13	.50	.15	68	.34	.45	.20	.19
Clerical–UK	6	860	.09	.02	.21	.00	1524	.21	.19	.06	.11
Training success											
Clerical–SPA	4	394	.55	.09	.77	.04	89	.72	.64	.20	.37
Clerical–UK	8	1989	.33	.13	.55	.11	75	.41	.50	.19	.26
Driver–SPA	7	737	.25	.10	.35	.00	206	.35	.32	.10	.19
Driver–UK	3	1674	.28	.06	.47	.00	129	.47	.43	.14	.25
Trade–SPA	4	282	.25	.13	.34	.06	90	.27	.31	.11	.16
Trade–UK	12	3086	.33	.14	.55	.14	65	.38	.50	.21	.24

Note. K = number of independent samples; N = total sample size; r = weighed-sample average observed validity; Sdr = weighted-sample observed standard deviation; RHO = operational validity (observed validity corrected for criterion unreliability and range restriction); Sdrho = rho standard deviation; %VE = percentage of observed variance accounted for by artifactual errors; CV = 90% credibility value; SPA = Spain; UK = United Kingdom; LRHO = lowest rho value; LSD = standard deviation for the lowest rho value; LCV = 90% credibility value for the lowest rho value.

respectively, and the 90% credibility values were very large, also—.72 and .41 for Spain and the United Kingdom, respectively. Therefore, these findings indicate that there is validity generalization in clerical occupations for the training success criterion. Furthermore, the figures found here for job performance and training criteria are similar to those reported by Pearlman et al. (1980), as they found an operational validity of .52 and .71 for job performance and training success, respectively, when all types of clerical jobs are combined. For driver jobs, the operational validities were .35 and .47 for Spain and the United Kingdom, respectively, and the 90% credibility values were the same, as all the observed variance was explained by artifactual errors, although there is second-order sampling error in both countries. Once again, the findings indicate that there is validity generalization in Spain and the United Kingdom. Trade jobs were the third type of occupations analyzed. In this case, the operational validity was .34 for the Spanish studies and .55 for the British studies. In both cases, the 90% credibility value showed evidence of validity generalization, as the estimates were .27 and .38 for Spain and the United Kingdom, respectively. The operational validity estimates found are comparable with those found by Schmidt, Hunter, and Caplan (1981) for maintenance trade jobs in the petroleum industry. Schmidt et al. (1981) reported a validity of .56, although it should be noted that the jobs included in our database are different.

Despite Spain and the United Kingdom being two countries with clearly different cultures, equal opportunities legislation, and languages, as a whole, there are apparently large similarities in the validity generalization results found for both countries. The results presented here suggest that cultural differences do not produce large differences in the magnitude and variability of validity coefficients, when the effects of artifactual errors are removed. The evidence also suggests that our findings are quite similar to those found in the largest meta-analyses of cognitive ability test studies conducted in the United States. In this sense, a relevant finding is the cross-cultural and cross-country consistency in the validity magnitude of cognitive abilities for predicting job performance and training success. Further research is called for to extend these questions to other countries and job roles within the EC, although this is one of the main aims of our ongoing collaborative project.

Recent European Developments for Assessing Cognitive Abilities

Recent advances and developments with regard to GMA and cognitive tests must be mentioned, as they may show the current state of affairs in Europe concerning cognitive testing and personnel selection. First, various European armies (e.g., British and French armies) are currently conducting research to validate existing measures and to produce new batteries for personnel selection and classification. For example, in the United Kingdom, a series of reviews into soldier selection was undertaken as part of "Project B" in the last few years, although, due to the strictly confidential nature of this project, the output reports to date have been internal technical reports (e.g., Anderson & Asprey, 1997; Anderson & Fletcher, 1998; Fletcher, Anderson, & Perkins, 1999).

A second interesting advance is related to cognitive tests based on virtual reality technology (VRT). VRT is a computer-simulated multisensory environment in which the perceiver feels as if he or she is actually present in an environment generated by a computer. VRT has been suggested as an alternative technology to conventional and video-based tests. VRT could be used as either a predictor or a criterion. Considered as a criterion, VRT scores may serve in validational studies as a sort of work sample measure and are seen by some researchers as the most appropriate criterion measures for validity studies (e.g., Hunter, 1986). The big problem of VRT is that it is prohibitively expensive. However, a European consortium of test publishers from Germany, Italy, Spain, and Switzerland have developed a VRT-based test for selecting people for dangerous occupations. This VRT test primarily assesses distributed attention. Pamos (1999) reported a concurrent validity study in which measures of distributed attention, as assessed by the VRT test, were correlated with some aspects of work behavior. For example, Pamos (1999) reported a correlation of .53 between the distributed attention score and the rating of stress tolerance. The distributed attention score also correlated .53 with the number of incidents headed. Pamos (1999) also reported a significant correlation between the number of alarms solved and stress tolerance $r = .41$) and between efficiency scores and team working ratings $r = .45$).

DISCUSSION

The aim of this article was to present a general view and evidence on the use, testing standards, legislative provisions, fairness, validity generalization, and recent developments of GMA and cognitive ability tests in Europe. We presented the European perspective based on the most current available data in the EC. Specifically, we tried to provide an answer to the following questions: (a) How widely are ability tests used in Europe?, (b) How fairly are ability tests perceived in the EC?, (c) What progress toward the harmonization of test administration standards has been achieved?, (d) What is the comparative legislative framework for ability testing between EC countries and the United States?, (e) Is there validity generalization for GMA and cognitive tests in the countries of the EC, and are the magnitudes and variability of GMA validity coefficients for predicting job performance and training success in the EC similar to those found in the U.S. meta-analyses?, and (f) What are the most recent developments for assessing GMA and cognitive abilities?

Summarizing the numerous surveys across EC countries into GMA and cognitive ability test use, we reported differences in popularity between countries and levels of jobs. These findings, to some extent, reflect the cultural differences within the EC noted earlier, with individualistic cultures (e.g., Britain, The Netherlands, Belgium, Germany) reporting more use of tests than collectivistic cultures (e.g., Italy, Greece). Tests are also more frequently used for more senior job roles, especially in Britain for managerial and graduate selection. Perhaps most interesting, however, are the findings that test use in many EC countries appears to be substantively higher than in the United States. This conclusion accords with that of Schuler et al. (1993), who summarized data suggesting that, on average in EC countries, 37% of companies use cognitive tests for personnel selection. This value is over two times greater than the estimate found in North America (see Gowin & Slivinski, 1994).

The single published survey covering both the United States and several EC countries (Ryan et al., 1999) placed only Germany and Italy behind the United States in terms of cognitive test use by employer organizations (see Table 2). Despite the lack of meta-analytic findings in support of GMA tests in Europe, it appears that they are generally more widely utilized than in the United States. This, as we previously noted, may well be a reflection of the less extensive equal opportunities legislation in EC countries, with employers being less concerned over potential legal case challenges of adverse impact. The results of this meta-analysis for GMA tests in Spain and Britain give somewhat post-hoc scientific support for the popularity of GMA tests among European employers. These findings are arguably of scientific and practical importance to selection practices in EC countries, as they not only lend support to the VGH, but also vindicate post hoc the faith placed in the use of GMA tests by European organizations.

The first results of our cross-nation meta-analysis of the criterion validity of GMA and cognitive ability tests indicate that they are predictors of job performance and training (success and outcomes) for various occupations in two European countries (Spain and the United Kingdom) with large cultural differences. For both countries, we found similar magnitudes in the size and variability of the operational validity, and in all cases analyzed, we found evidence of validity generalization. In addition, we found that the magnitude of the operational validity for these two European countries is similar to the one found in the largest meta-analyses of the criterion validity of GMA and cognitive abilities carried out in the United States (e.g., Hunter, 1986; Hunter & Hunter, 1984; Levine et al., 1996; Pearlman et al., 1980; Schmidt et al., 1981). Consequently, we see small room for speculating about the situational specificity of these validity coefficients.

These findings are particularly relevant, as they suggest that validity generalization is not only possible within a country, it is also possible to have cross-national validity generalization for GMA and cognitive ability tests. With respect to this, it should be taken into account that the economic structure of the countries within the EC is quite different to that of the United States. In the EC, the most typical organization is a company with a smaller number of employees. In such a situation, it is very problematic and expensive to conduct validity studies. However, based on the findings shown here, we can suggest to European practitioners that they use cognitive ability tests and the average validity estimates found here. In other words, as Schmidt (1993) did, we see meta-analysis and validity generalization studies as a good alternative for those situations with very small sample size, which are very frequent in the EC.

Another important implication of the validity generalization findings in the EC, together with similar findings in the United States, is that they provide support for a general theory of performance at work, independent of national boundaries. In this sense, it seems to us that cultural differences may be less relevant for the criterion validity of cognitive tests than had previously been supposed. Our research showed that the criterion validity is quite similar for two very different cultures, one individualistic (United Kingdom) and another collectivist (Spain; Hofstede, 1980). However, we are clearly not arguing that cultural differences are irrelevant for personnel selection.

Currently, we are faced with some limitations in answering other important questions related to GMA and cognitive ability tests. Due to the fact that we are in the first steps of our cross-national project, we have insufficient validity data to appropriately answer questions such as the following: (a) Do these findings generalize to other EC countries beyond Britain and Spain?, (b) What is the relative importance of *g* versus specific abilities for predicting job performance, training, and other work-relevant criteria (e.g., accident, turnover)?, and (c) What are the perspectives on adverse impact issues in Europe? However, our initial findings suggest that specific abilities do not improve the validity of GMA tests, or, in the best case, the incremental validity of the specific abilities beyond *g* is very small (Bertua, 2000). With regard to adverse impact, this is currently a less cumbersome problem for the majority of the EC countries compared with the United States. This is due to the fact that many EC countries are relatively homogenous and have smaller proportions of ethnic minority applicants than in the United States. However, in the near future, it is possible that adverse impact issues may become more important as a result of European laws providing citizens of the EC with the freedom to work in any country of the EC. Nevertheless, this will be a qualitatively different type of adverse impact as presently construed in the United States. In the EC, the problem will be between EC citizens that are national and non-national of a specific country, not between majority and minority groups within a country. To conclude, however, it is apt for us to highlight the most important finding thus far of our collaborative project, meta-analyzing European cognitive ability test validity findings. Comparing our results for the average corrected validity of tests in Spain and Britain, we found they are directly comparable to earlier U.S. meta-analytic results.

ACKNOWLEDGMENT

The preparation of this article was supported by the Xunta de Galicia (Spain) Grant XUGA PGIDT00PX121104PR to Jesús F. Salgado.

REFERENCES

Anderson, N. R., & Asprey, E. (1997). *Project B: Investigating interrelationships between selection predictors and criterion measures on the British Army Recruit Database* (internal report commissioned by DERA from Department of Psychology, Goldsmiths College, University of London).

Anderson, N. R., Born, M., & Cunningham-Snell, N. (2001). Recruitment and selection: Applicant perspectives and outcomes. In N. Anderson, D.S. Ones, M. K. Sinangil, & C. Viswesvaran (Eds.), *Handbook of Industrial, Work and Organizational Psychology, 1*, 200–218. London: Sage.

Anderson, N. R., & Fletcher, C. (1998). *A study to review the British Army soldier selection process* (internal report commissioned by ATRA from Department of Psychology, Goldsmiths College, University of London).

Ashworth, S. D., Osburn, H. G., Callender, J. C., & Boyle, K. A. (1992). The effects of unrepresented studies on the robustness of validity generalization results. *Personnel Psychology, 45*, 341–361.

Bartram, D. (1995). The development of standards for the use of psychological tests in occupational settings: The competence approach. *The Psychologist, 8*, 219–223.

Bartram, D. (1996). Test qualifications and test use in the United Kingdom: The competence approach. *European Journal of Psychological Assessment, 12*, 62–71.

Bartram, D. (1998). The need for international guidelines for test use: A review of European and international initiatives. *European Psychologist, 3*, 155–163.

Bartram, D., Anderson, N., Kellett, D., Lindley, P.A., & Robertson, I. (1995). *Review of personality assessment instruments (Level B) for use in occupational settings*. Leicester, England: BPS Books.

Bartram, D., & Coyne, I. (1998). The ITC/EFPPA survey of testing and test use within Europe. *Proceeding of the British Psychological Society's Occupational Psychology Conference*, 12–18.

Bartram, D., Lindley, P. A., & Foster, J. (1992). *Review of psychometric tests for assessment in vocational training*. Leicester, England: BPS Books.

Bartram, D., Lindley, P. A., Marshall, I., & Foster, J. (1995). The recruitment and selection of young people by small business. *Journal of Occupational and Organizational Psychology, 68*, 339–358.

Baumgartem, F. (1949). Rapport sur l'activite de l'Association Internationale de Psychotechnique depuis 1934, presenté par la Secretaire Generale du Congress [Report on the activity of the International Association of Psychotechnics since 1934, presented by the General Secretary of the Congress]. IX Congress de l'Association International de Psychotechnique. Berne.

Bertua, C. (2000). *Validity generalization of general mental ability (GMA) tests as predictors of job performance ratings and training success in the UK*. Unpublished master's thesis, Goldsmiths College, University of London.

Bruchon-Schweiter, M., & Lievens, D. (1989). Le recrutement en Europe [Recruitment in Europe]. *Psychologie et Psychometrie, 12*, 2.

Clark, T. (1993). Selection methods used by executive search consultancies in four European countries: A survey and critique. *International Journal of Selection and Assessment, 1*, 41–49.

Dany, F., & Torchy, V. (1994). Recruitment and selection in Europe: Policies, practices and methods. In C. Brewster & A. Hegewisch (Eds.), *Policy and practice in European human resource management: The Price–Waterhouse–Cranfield Survey*. London: Routledge & Kegan Paul.

De Witte, K., van Laese, B., & Vervecke, P. (1992, June). *Assessment techniques: Toward a new perspective*. Paper presented at the workshop on psychological aspect of employment, Sofía, Bulgaria.

Eleftheriou, A., & Robertson, I. T. (1999). A survey of management practices in Greece. *International Journal of Selection and Assessment, 7*, 203–208.

Fletcher, C. (1994). Questionnaire surveys of organizational assessment practices: A critique of their methodology and validity, and a query about their future relevance. *International Journal of Selection and Assessment. 2.* 172–175.

Fletcher, C., Anderson, N. R., & Perkins, A. (1999). *A research strategy for soldier selection* (internal report commissioned by the Ministry of Defence from Department of Psychology, Goldsmiths College, University of London).

Ghiselli, E. E. (1966). *The measurement of occupational aptitude.* Berkeley: University of California Press.

Ghiselli, E. E. (1973). The validity of aptitude tests in personnel selection. *Personnel Psychology, 26,* 461–477.

Gowin, M. K., & Slivinski, L. W. (1994). A review of North American selection procedures: Canada and United States of America. *International Journal of Selection and Assessment, 2,* 103–114.

Hartigan, J. A., & Wigdor, A. K. (1989). *Fairness in employment testing.* Washington, DC: National Academy Press.

Herriot, P., & Anderson, N. (1997). Selecting for change: How will personnel selection psychology survive? In N. Anderson & P. Herriot (Eds.), *International handbook of selection and assessment* (pp. 1–34). London: Wiley.

Hodgkinson, G. P., & Payne, R. L. (1998). Short research note: Graduate selection in three countries. *Journal of Occupational and Organizational Psychology 71,* 359–365.

Hofstede, G. (1980). *Culture's consequences: International differences in work-related values.* Beverly Hills, CA: Sage.

Hunter, J. E. (1986). Cognitive ability, cognitive aptitudes, job knowledge, and job performance. *Journal of Vocational Behavior, 29,* 340–362.

Hunter, J. E., & Hunter, R. F. (1984). Validity and utility of alternative predictors of job performance. *Psychological Bulletin, 96,* 72–98.

Hunter, J. E., & Schmidt, F. L. (1990). *Methods of meta-analysis. Correcting error and bias in research findings.* Newbury Park, CA: Sage.

Keenan, T. (1995). Graduate recruitment in Britain: A survey of selection methods used by organizations. *Journal of Organizational Behavior, 16,* 303–317.

Levine, E. L., Spector, P. E., Menon, P. E., Narayanon, L., & Cannon-Bowers, J. (1996). Validity generalization for cognitive, psychomotor, and perceptual tests for craft jobs in the utility industry. *Human Performance, 9,* 1–22.

McDaniel, M. A., Schmidt, F. L., & Hunter, J. E. (1988). Job experience correlates of job performance. *Journal of Applied Psychology, 73,* 327–330.

Münsterberg, H. (1913). *Psychology and industrial efficiency.* Boston: Houghton Mifflin.

Ones, D. S., & Anderson, N. (2000). *Gender and ethnic group differences on personality scales.* Manuscript submitted for publication.

Pamos, A. (1999). Virtual reality at a power plant. Technical chapter. In VAT Consortium (TEA, SA–Spain, OS–Italy, Hogrefe Verlag–Germany, & GM–Switzerland). *Virtual reality assisted psycho-attitude testing handbook.* Esprit project Number 22119. Bruxells, Belgium: The European Commission.

Pearlman, K., Schmidt, F. L., & Hunter, J. E. (1980). Validity generalization results for tests used to predict job proficiency and training success in clerical occupations. *Journal of Applied Psychology, 65,* 373–406.

Robertson, I., & Makin, P. (1986). Management selection in Britain: A survey and critique. *Journal of Occupational Psychology, 59,* 45–57.

Ryan, A. M., MacFarland, L., Baron, H., & Page, R. (1999). An international look at selection practices: Nation and culture as explanations for variability in practice. *Personnel Psychology, 52,* 359–391.

Salgado, J. F., & Moscoso, S. (2000, September). *Reacciones a las técnicas de selección de personal en España y Portugal [Reaction to personnel selection techniques in Spain and Portugal].* Paper presented at the VII Congreso Nacional de Psicología Social, Oviedo, Spain.

Schmidt, F. L., & Hunter, J. E. (1977). Development of a general solution to the problem of validity generalization. *Journal of Applied Psychology, 62,* 529–540.

Schmidt, F. L., & Hunter, J. E. (1984). A within setting test of the situational specificity hypothesis in personnel selection. *Personnel Psychology, 37*, 317–326.

Schmidt, F. L., Hunter, J. E., & Caplan, J. R. (1981). Validity generalization results for two groups in the petroleum industry. *Journal of Applied Psychology, 66*, 261–273.

Schmidt, F. L., Hunter, J. E., Pearlman, K., & Shane, G. S. (1979). Further tests of the Schmidt–Hunter bayesian validity generalization procedure. *Personnel Psychology, 32*, 257–281.

Schmitt, N., Gooding, R. Z., Noe, R. A., & Kirsch, M. (1984). Metaanalyses of validity studies published between 1964 and 1982 and the investigation of study characteristics. *Personnel Psychology, 37*, 407–422.

Schuler, H., Frier, D., & Kauffmann, M. (1993). *Personalauswahl in europäischen vergleich [Eleccion de personal en el ámbito europeo]* [On-line]. Available: http://www.jobpilot.es

Shackleton, V., & Newell, S. (1991). Management selection: A comparative survey of methods used by top British and French companies. *Journal of Occupational Psychology, 64*, 23–36.

Shackleton, V., & Newell, S. (1994). European management selection methods: A comparison of five countries. *International Journal of Selection and Assessment, 2*, 91–102.

Sinangil, H. K., Ones, D. S., & Jockin, V. (1999). *Survey of personnel selection tools and techniques in Turkey*. Paper presented at the Ninth European Congress on Work and Organizational Psychology, Helsinki, Finland.

Smith, M., & Abrahamsen, M. (1992). Patterns of selection in six countries. *The Psychologist, 5*, 205–207.

Steiner, D. D., & Gilliland, S. W. (1996). Fairness reactions to personnel selection techniques in France and United States. *Journal of Applied Psychology, 81*, 134–141.

Steiner, D. D., & Gilliland, S. W. (2001). Procedural justice in personnel selection: International and cross-cultural perspectives. *International Journal of Selection and Assessment, 8*, 124–133..

Te Nijenhuis, J. (1997). *Comparability of tests scores for immigrants and majority group members in The Netherlands*. Unpublished doctoral dissertation, University of Amsterdam.

Te Nijenhuis, J., & van der Flier, H. (1997). Comparability of GATB scores for immigrants and majority group members: Some Dutch findings. *Journal of Applied Psychology, 82*, 675–687.

Viswesvaran, C., Ones, D. S., & Schmidt, F. L. (1996). Comparative analysis of the reliability of job performance ratings. *Journal of Applied Psychology, 81*, 557–574.

Viteles, M. (1932). *Industrial psychology*. New York: Norton.

HUMAN PERFORMANCE, *15*(1/2), 97–106

General Mental Ability and Selection in Private Sector Organizations: A Commentary

Jerard F. Kehoe
AT&T
Basking Ridge, NJ

Key considerations are summarized relating to the design of cognitively oriented selection procedures for the purpose of minimizing group differences and maximizing
selection effectiveness. It is concluded that selection effectiveness and selection rate
equality trade off within the cognitive domain and that design efforts to minimize
group differences are likely to result in differential prediction where it was previously
absent. It is also suggested that the frequently cited premise that selection procedures
of equal validity are substitutable is not, in general, true. Equal validity does not imply equal value for the organization. Finally, it is argued that additional research and
discussion is necessary to clarify and reach professional consensus regarding two
competing perspectives about the meaning of differential prediction. One perspective
views differential prediction as an extension of validation requiring the criterion to be
theoretically construct-relevant to the predictor. The other views differential prediction as analysis of valued outcomes requiring the criterion to be an encompassing
measurement of valued outcomes created by employees.

At the Department of Labor's National Skills Summit in April 2000, Ray Marshall,
former Secretary of Labor in the Carter administration, and Alan Greenspan,
Chairman of the Federal Reserve, cited two dramatic statistics about the link between skills and our current economic growth. (Marshall, 2000; Greenspan, 2000).
Marshall reported that approximately one third of our current high productivity
growth rate is driven directly by skill and knowledge growth—human capital. This
impact is higher than ever before. Perhaps more significant, both reported that now
the return on human capital investment is approximately three times greater than
the return on physical capital investment. That is, $1 invested in worker learning

---

Requests for reprints should be sent to Jerard F. Kehoe, Box 287, Pottersville, NJ 07979.

and knowledge leads to productivity increases approximately three times greater than that produced by $1 invested in physical capital. In our increasingly knowledge-based economy, the importance of thinking and learning for productivity is demonstrably increasing.

Certainly, our accumulating research base on abilities and work performance helps to understand this phenomenon. Tests of general mental ability (GMA) and cognitively loaded skill and knowledge measures, such as work samples, are the selection procedures most predictive of performance in complex work (Schmidt & Hunter, 1998). However, organizations face a significant dilemma when considering the role of GMA in their selection systems. The dilemma stems primarily from three key findings about GMA and work performance:

1. GMA tests are at least as predictive of work performance as other more job-specific tests in the cognitive domain and other assessments outside the cognitive domain, such as personality (Schmidt & Hunter, 1998).

2. Tailored combinations of tests assessing less general, more specific cognitive aptitudes are generally not more predictive of work performance than a representative GMA test (Hunter, 1986). In all probability, this is because the incremental predictive value of specific cognitive aptitudes is a function of improvement in the representation of GMA rather than incremental variance due to a specific, unique factor (Lubinski & Dawis, 1992).

3. There are substantial group differences on GMA tests that are not due to bias in the measurement (Wigdor & Garner, 1982).

The first two conclusions suggest efficient and effective selection strategies in which GMA is a primary component, but the third suggests undesirable social consequences.

This commentary discusses the factors that influence the design of private sector selection programs in an effort to achieve a balance between these competing considerations. These comments do not challenge the conclusion that GMA tests have broad and relatively unvarying predictive power for appropriate, or relevant, performance criteria. Also, because this "debate" deliberately chose to focus on issues relating to general mental ability, this commentary does not address selection issues relating to noncognitive selection procedures. Rather, the focus of this commentary is on the range of selection program design options within the cognitive domain.

CONSIDERATIONS IN THE DESIGN
OF SELECTION STRATEGIES

In designing selection strategies, organizations have many reasons to give primary consideration to GMA. Not only is validity relatively high, particularly with respect to performance and job knowledge in the current job, but higher ability employees are generally viewed as more likely to progress to positions of greater importance and value and more likely to avoid workplace problems including health and safety. Also, GMA-based assessment tools, such as tests, are readily available in the marketplace and relatively inexpensive. As a result, where selection strategies are professionally designed, GMA is frequently a primary focus. In designing the process, selection managers will typically evaluate a variety of local considerations to determine if some approach other than standardized GMA tests will ensure the desired level of cognitive ability in the workforce and enhance the social desirability of the selection outcomes. There are at least four common considerations that determine the manner in which cognitive ability is incorporated into a selection strategy:

1. Does the target work require specific knowledge or skills that are best measured by job-specific assessments?
2. Can group differences typically produced by GMA-based tests be reduced by modifying the content while retaining the original construct representation?
3. Are tests containing relatively more job-specific content more likely to satisfy regulatory requirements for validity than GMA-based tests?
4. Can recruiting strategies substitute for cognitively oriented selection procedures?

Assessments of Job-Specific Knowledge and Skill

Certainly many jobs require some minimum level of specific job knowledge to ensure a capacity to perform the work. For example, technical repair jobs in telecommunications frequently require specialized knowledge of electronics. For such jobs, the compelling reason for the use of the job-specific knowledge test is that performance, training, or both, require a certain minimum amount of a specific knowledge. This requirement does not necessarily correspond to a high operational validity coefficient, and it does not imply a nonlinear relation between the knowledge and performance. A selection test measuring a required knowledge may have lower validity than GMA because the applicant pools may be restricted, including only candidates who have some indication of having achieved a substantial amount of the knowledge in question. For this and other reasons, the decision to use a job knowledge assessment rather than a GMA test is usually not based on criterion-based validity correlation coefficients. It is the other decision—whether to use GMA-based screening in addition to the job knowledge requirements—that is usually an issue of incremental validity or, at least, incremental value. And the GMA research on this point, as exemplified by Hunter's (1986) analysis showing an effect of GMA on performance independent of job knowledge, argues in favor of a GMA component where the job knowledge requirement or associated recruiting strategies have not limited the range of applicant GMA too much. Where the job knowledge requirement corresponds to a restricted applicant pool, organizations may be willing to forego the smaller incremental benefit of GMA-based screening in favor of lower recruiting and employment administration costs.

Impact of Test Content on Group Differences

The second salient consideration, closely related to the first, is the matter of group differences and test content. It appears to be increasingly common that selection program designers and researchers explore methods for modifying cognitive tests specifically to reduce group differences. Within the cognitive domain, there appear to be two types of approaches—one that eliminates from the test certain cognitive components such as reading, and the other that builds job content or context into the cognitive test. High and low fidelity work samples, situational judgment tests, and general cognitive tests in a job context are common examples. Because g does not imply that group differences are invariant across specific abilities, the possibility exists that changes in ability-specific content can affect group differences. For example, reducing spatial ability and increasing verbal comprehension in a cognitive test is likely to reduce male–female differences.

Building job specificity into a cognitive test may impact group differences in at least two ways. First, job-specificity is likely to increase the salience of job-specific knowledge. Factors that impact the development of job knowledge such as level and type of education and job experience may affect group differences in ways that are independent of cognitive ability. Second, job-specific content may alter the salience of specific abilities. Lubinski and Dawis (1992) reported that group differences tend to be largest on cognitive abilities more central to g. So, to the extent that job-specific content gives greater weight to more specific abilities, group differences may be smaller.

Conversely, for well-designed cognitive tests in which group differences are not due to measurement bias, this means that changes in content within the cognitive domain that significantly alter group differences are likely to also significantly alter the abilities being measured. And the modification will likely change the extent to which g is well-represented by the now-tailored set of constructs underlying the modified test. If the change in specific ability constructs does not significantly reduce the representation of the general ability factor in the test, then validity with respect to a given criterion may change very little, if at all.

However, there is a subtle, ironic risk in this scenario. Changes to a cognitive test that succeed in reducing group differences without reducing predictive validity may well introduce differential prediction without eliminating the legal obligation to conduct such analyses. Indeed, test design decisions with the cognitive domain that reduce group differences may be likely to cause differential prediction to appear where it was previously absent in the original, unmodified GMA test.

This effect on differential prediction results is due to the relationship between the validity coefficient and the ratio of standardized group mean differences on the criterion and predictor measures. (This discussion only applies where differential prediction is based on group differences in slopes and intercepts.) Where differential prediction is absent, the true validity coefficient is equal to the ratio of the criterion and predictor standardized group differences. For example, a commonly reported conclusion about GMA tests is that they do not demonstrate substantial differential prediction for Blacks and Whites. This conclusion is consistent with the empirical findings that the estimated true validity of GMA tests (for relevant criteria) is approximately .50, and the standardized group mean differences on the criteria and predictors are approximately .50 and 1.00, respectively. Changes to the predictor that reduce group differences but do not proportionately increase validity will change the outcome of differential prediction analyses, statistical factors such as sample size, power, and distribution properties notwithstanding. This pattern of change might be expected where GMA tests are modified within the cognitive domain for the purpose of reducing group differences. For example, if modifications reduced the typical test difference from one standard deviation to, say, three quarters of a standard deviation, then differential prediction would be introduced where it was previously absent if the true validity did not correspondingly increase from .50 to .67 (i.e., .50:.75).

This would not be a significant problem, legally speaking, if such modifications eliminated adverse impact. Where adverse impact has been eliminated, an organization would presumably not be required to satisfy the differential prediction "test" imposed by the Uniform Guidelines on Employee Selection Procedures (U.S. Equal Employment Opportunity Commission, 1978). However, modifications within the cognitive domain alone are unlikely to eliminate adverse impact in most cases just as modifications that incorporate measures outside the cognitive domain have been shown to not eliminate adverse impact (Sackett & Ellingson, 1997; Schmitt, Rogers, Chan, Sheppard, & Jennings, 1997). As a result, modifications of GMA tests that successfully reduce group differences may lead to a failure of the differential prediction requirement.

At least one possible resolution of this dilemma warrants research. This possible resolution rests on the assumption that differential prediction analysis is a meaningful assessment of bias only when the predictor composite is theoretically relevant to the criterion composite. For example, by this assumption it is unlikely that we would consider the analysis of the differential prediction of, say, workplace helping behavior by a spatial ability test to be a meaningful evaluation of bias in the use of the spatial ability test. From this perspective, if predictor constructs are changed to reduce group differences, then the components of the criterion should be changed similarly for differential prediction analysis to be a meaningful assessment of bias. The empirical question is whether such concomitant criterion changes would increase the likelihood of avoiding differential prediction.

Considerations of Legal Defense

The third consideration is of a different sort. The legal defense of tests with job-specific content is more likely to be based on content validation than criterion validation, as would a GMA test, typically. However, unlike criterion validation, content validation success is directly and knowingly determined by the decisions of the test developer. As long as regulatory and professional standards emphasize the primacy of local validation studies over professionally responsible generalized conclusions, the validation rationale of GMA tests is risky because it is subject to the problems of local studies. As a result, where jobs have special content requirements in the cognitive domain, there is a compelling incentive to substitute job-specific, content-oriented selection procedures for GMA-based selection procedures.

Recruiting Alternatives

A consequence of low unemployment is that selection program managers have had to give increasing consideration to the relation between selection and recruiting. Although recruiting strategies can affect selection results in a variety of ways, the focus of this discussion is on effects relating to group differences caused by a reliance on cognitive ability in the selection process.

The primary consideration is that recruiting strategies can impact the effects of selection by changing the average ability level of the applicant pool. For example, suppose a GMA-based selection strategy has a passing rate equal to .50 and a criterion validity equal to .40 in an applicant pool created by a recruiting strategy that does not target any particular level of education. If, in contrast, only college educated applicants were recruited, the same selection strategy would likely yield a higher passing rate and lower validity. Also, increases to the average ability of the applicant pool will itself increase the average ability of hired applicants. In the previous example, for instance, a recruiting change that increased the average ability of the applicant pool by one standard deviation would increase the average ability of applicants selected by the original cutscore by approximately one half of a standard deviation.

Such a change can significantly alter the balance between the benefits of the selection strategy and the social consequences. First, all else the same, the higher passing rate in the higher ability pool implies that the difference between group passing rates would be reduced. The degree of adverse impact would likely be reduced. This improvement in social consequences could then be weighed against the additional costs of changes to the GMA tests to further reduce group differences. Second, under some conditions, organizations might consider the option of discontinuing GMA-based selection altogether if improved recruiting ensures a satisfactory level of average ability without any GMA-based selection. For example, random selection from the improved applicant pool discussed previously would yield an average ability level among new hires approximately equal to that produced by the original selection and recruiting strategy. Of course, as a practical matter there are many other significant trade-offs in redesigning recruiting strategies. The hypothetical improvement described previously that increased average applicant ability by one standard deviation would presumably be more expensive and slower than the original. In general, however, changes in recruiting strategies can impact both the selection benefits and the social consequences, which define the trade-off in question. As a result, the design of a selection strategy to achieve the intended balance should consider the role of recruiting strategy design as well.

EQUAL VALIDITY AND EQUAL VALUE

In the discussion of group differences and cognitive ability, a frequent assumption is that selection procedures of equal validity (defined, for this point, as equal correlation coefficients with either the same criterion or two different criteria) are of equal value to an organization. By this assumption, organizations should be indifferent between selection procedures of equal validity correlations. In this case, the selection procedure producing smaller group differences would be preferred. This assumption underlies, for example, the Uniform Guidelines on Employee Selection Procedures (U.S. Equal Employment Opportunity Commission, 1978) prescription regarding the evaluation of alternative selection procedures. This assumption also underlies the similar intention of selection program designers to modify cognitive selection procedures in ways that reduce group differences but leave validity coefficients unchanged. This assumption also underlies the common use and understanding of classic utility analysis in which two selection procedures of equal validity will have equal utility, all else the same.

However, this assumption is not true in general. A correlation coefficient of .25 between a personality composite and a measure of overall performance does not necessarily reflect the same value for an organization as a .25 correlation between GMA and the same measure of overall performance. The people chosen based on the personality measure would not be the same, and they would not have the same attribute profile, as the people chosen based on GMA. The two equal correlations would reflect different construct mappings of predictors onto the criterion, although the variance accounted for is the same. Operationally, the organization might experience the differences in a variety of tangible ways. For example, the "personality" employees might achieve their overall performance by being relatively more dependable, persistent, attentive, helpful, and so on. The "cognitive" employees might achieve their overall performance by being relatively more accurate, faster, effective problem solvers, and the like.

Although this point is relevant to the general matter of validity estimation, meaning, and interpretation, it also deserves some attention in this much narrower discussion of GMA, group differences, and selection. Changes to GMA tests that are explored to reduce group differences, such as the reduction or elimination of written content, may also impact the organization value of the selection procedure even if the validity coefficient is not changed. Practitioners should take care to understand the impact on organizational value of predictor construct changes designed to reduce group differences. One way in which this "care" might be manifest is by specifying the criteria constructs that are relevant to the predictor changes.

CONCLUSION

This commentary has summarized a variety of considerations within the domain of cognitive ability for the design of selection strategies to balance the benefits of selection and desired social consequences. The overall conclusion is that, for design decisions within the cognitive domain, the values of selection effectiveness and equal group selection rates compete with one another. That is, there is little reason to expect that any design decision will increase both selection effectiveness and equality of group selection rates. (It is worth noting that for selection design decisions that go beyond the cognitive domain, these factors may be complementary rather than competitive. That is, the optimal combination of cognitive and noncognitive selection has the potential to improve both validity and the equality of selection rates.)

Underlying this dilemma is a subtle assumption that deserves comment and continued research. The problem is not simply that selection effectiveness and selection rate equality trade off. A critical part of the dilemma is that GMA-based tests are generally regarded as unbiased based on the differential prediction definition of bias. This commentary suggests that changes designed to reduce group differences in the predictor may have the unintended consequence of introducing differential prediction. The fundamental cause of this problem is that construct changes in a test can affect group differences, but where those changes are within the cognitive domain, they are unlikely to affect validity.

On closer inspection, what we mean by this conclusion is that such changes are unlikely to affect validity with respect to the same criterion. We do not make the assumption in this conclusion that criteria are similarly modified when evaluating the differential prediction properties of a modified GMA test. Nevertheless, the commonly accepted definition of validity (Standards for Educational and Psychological Testing; American Educational Research Association, 1999) requires that validity evidence support the intended uses and interpretations of a test. This definition of validity would argue in favor of validity analyses between predictors and criteria that are theoretically construct-relevant. Presumably, then, if the predictor constructs are changed to reduce group differences, the intended criterion should change accordingly. In this case the changes to the criterion necessary to retain its theoretical construct-relevance to the revised predictor would impact group differences on the criterion commensurate with the impact on the predictor and may leave the differential prediction results unchanged.

However, this possibility depends on an unspoken assumption made by our profession, although perhaps not by the regulations governing selection procedures. It is that differential prediction is a subset of validation research. Based on this assumption, differential prediction should be conducted using the same theoretically relevant criterion as is used appropriate for the validation of that selection procedure. This assumption provides the foundation for regarding differential prediction as a method for detecting bias. Research is needed to determine how differential prediction results are affected by changes to criteria necessary to be theoretically consistent with the changes to predictors that reduced group differences.

An alternative perspective, however, is the "bottom line" point of view about predictive bias. This perspective argues that the most appropriate criterion for differential prediction is a measure of overall worth or merit that encompasses all the dimensions of employee value for an organization. In general, the criteria used in validation studies would not be the criteria appropriate for differential prediction analyses. Although a comprehensive measure might be an unattainable ideal, this perspective nevertheless defines the appropriate criterion in terms of valued outcomes rather than in terms of construct relevance to the predictor. This perspective removes differential prediction from the validation context and places it in the context of organizational values. The implication of this perspective for the points about differential prediction made in this commentary is that the research on g and its relations to other variables and much of the selection validity research is not sufficient to derive expectations about differential prediction. This point of view would argue that once a type of selection procedure, such as GMA tests, has been shown to relate to certain theoretically construct-relevant aspects of work behavior, then additional research would be necessary to complete an analysis of differential prediction. The needed additional research would evaluate the relationships between those selection procedures and other valued work behaviors such as retention, safety, progression, and so forth, to complete comprehensive differential prediction analyses.

These two perspectives about differential prediction are quite different and have very different implications for evaluating the types of selection design issues described here, not just for GMA-based selection, but for all types of selection procedures and valued outcomes. Considerably more research and professional discussion is necessary to clarify and reach consensus about the scientific evidence and the social considerations that should influence such design issues.

REFERENCES

American Educational Research Association, American Psychological Association, & National Council on Measurement in Education. (1999). *Standards for educational and psychological testing.* Washington, DC: American Educational Research Association.

Greenspan, A., (2000). The Evolving Demand for Skills. *National Skills Summit.* Washington, DC: U.S. Department of Labor.

Hunter, J. E. (1986). Cognitive ability, cognitive aptitudes, job knowledge, and job performance. *Journal of Vocational Behavior, 29,* 340–362.

Lubinski, D., & Dawis, R. V. (1992). Aptitudes, skills and proficiencies. In M. D. Dunnette & L. M. Hough (Eds.), *Handbook of I/O psychology* (Vol. 3, 1–59). Palo Alto, CA: Consulting Psychologists Press.

Marshall, R., (2000). Remarks by Ray Marshall. *National Skills Summit.* Washington, DC: U.S. Department of Labor.

Sackett, P. R., & Ellingson, J. E. (1997). The effects of forming multi-predictor composites on group differences and adverse impact. *Personnel Psychology, 50,* 707–721.

Schmidt, F. L., & Hunter, J. E. (1998). The validity and utility of selection methods in personnel psychology: Practical and theoretical implications of 85 years of research findings. *Psychological Bulletin, 124,* 262–274.

Schmitt, N., Rogers, W., Chan, D., Sheppard, L., & Jennings, D. (1997). Adverse impact and predictive efficiency of various predictor combinations. *Journal of Applied Psychology, 82,* 719–730.

U.S. Equal Employment Opportunity Commission, Civil Service Commission, Department of Labor, & Department of Justice. (1978). Uniform guidelines on employee selection procedures. *Federal Register, 43,* 38290–38315.

Wigdor, A. K., & Garner, W. R. (Eds.). (1982). *Ability testing: Uses, consequences, and controversies. Part 1: Report of the committee.* Washington, DC: National Academy Press.

HUMAN PERFORMANCE, *15*(1/2), 107–122

Theory Versus Reality:
Evaluation of *g* in the Workplace

Mary L. Tenopyr
Consultant
Bridgewater, New Jersey

Although it is recognized that *g* is important for success in the workplace, it is suggested that further research is necessary to understand the nature of *g* and to determine how prediction of job performance may be enhanced. Major relevant theories of intelligence are discussed and criticized. Questions about the roles of measures of knowledge, interests, and personality in providing incremental validity to that afforded by *g* are discussed. Difficulties in criterion definition and measurement are assessed. Additions to utility analysis are recommended. New findings relevant to group differences are discussed. The future of the prediction of workplace performance is discussed, and recommendations regarding the roles of both theoretical concepts and practical innovations are made.

Throughout the history of psychology, understanding of mental ability has been a major venue for endeavor. The philosophers and the early biologists, applying armchair methods and deductive logic, provided the early thinking that led to the faculty psychologists and their attempts to provide some semblance of the scientific method to defining mental abilities. The faculty psychologists' thinking was replaced by modern mental testing by the early 20th century, and, over the last 100 years, numerous theories of mental functioning have emerged, and many have been discarded.

By about 1900, it had been generally recognized that most tests of mental ability were positively correlated. Spearman in 1904 first put forth his theory that the common element underlying mental test performance was a general factor called *g* and a factor specific to the test. A variation of this theory is the basis for much modern test theory and the widespread application of *g* to workplace activities.

The importance of general mental ability or *g* for performance in a wide range of jobs is generally acknowledged (Schmidt & Hunter, 1998). However, more re-

---

Requests for reprints should be sent to Mary L. Tenopyr, 557 Lyme Rock Road, Bridgewater, NJ 08807–1604.

cent theoretical and practical developments suggest that new avenues of research are warranted and the possibility of the development of new theories of human ability cannot be dismissed.

RECENT THEORIES

For discussion of the history of mental testing, one should refer to Ackerman and Heggestad (1997). Among the more recent developments that deserve attention is Carroll's (1993) massive factor analysis of almost all of the credible data that have informed theories of intelligence over the years. His conclusion that a hierarchal organization of human abilities is the most explanatory has gained considerable acceptance in psychology. Although there are competing theories that also incorporate hierarchical arrangements, Carroll's is the one that is most supported by data. What is needed now is programmatic research to relate Carroll's theory to performance of individuals in the workplace.

Another recent development is the increased emphasis on more inclusive theories, incorporating intelligence, personality, and interests (Ackerman & Heggestad, 1997). These authors identified four major trait complexes. Following Carroll's (1993) basic information, the investigators then incorporated Ackerman's (1994) concept of intelligence as typical performance. His typical intellectual engagement (TIE) construct was developed in response to the potential problems of mental abilities being measured under conditions when maximum performance is called for and other variables of interest such as college grades reflect typical performance.

Another development based on Dawis and Lofquist's (1984) theory of work adjustment is the person–environment fit paradigm. This model was developed essentially within the field of career psychology and is consequently centered in the workplace. A special section of *Journal of Vocational Behavior* has been devoted to this model. The central article by Tinsley (2000a) was responded to by several others (Dawis, 2000; Gati, 2000; Hesketh, 2000; Prediger, 2000; Rounds, McKenna, Hubert, & Day, 2000; Tracey, Darcy, & Kovalski, 2000). In the following issue of the journal, Tinsley (2000b) wrote his rejoinder. Spokane, Meir, and Catalano (2000) made further observations on the theory.

Other theoretical developments of recent interest have been Sternberg's (1990) conception about the nature of intelligence. In particular, the status of his concept of a knowledge-based aspect intelligence has been influential in directing the debates on intelligence.

Also to be considered are the concepts put forth by Peterson, Mumford, Borman, Jeanneret, and Fleishman (1999) in the development of an occupational information network. This delineation of content includes specific knowledges in addition to cross-functional and occupation-specific skills. Contextual variables obviously have a major role in any theory relating to performance in the workplace. Tenopyr (1981) called for a merging of individual differences and organizational research. Gradually, the incorporation of variables from both areas in the same studies is being seen. As Katzell (1994) noted, personality is being brought into organizational research.

A summary of research on variables related to theories relating to aspects of individual job performance may be found in Guion (1998). All of the theories related to intellectual functioning have features that warrant their support; however, there are major controversies associated with all of them. There should be continued research to attempt to resolve a number of issues.

Ackerman and Heggestad (1997) had a massive amount of empirical support for their theoretical conclusions. They have filled a void in appropriate theorizing in which cognitive abilities, personality, and interests were studied separately and hence could not be easily included in a single theory. These researchers' model may well be the stepping stone to models of the future. However, it appears that there are opportunities for further refinement of the model.

Questions might be raised about the concept of TIE (Ackerman, 1994). Whether typical engagement has sufficient longitudinal stability should be the subject for future study. In the workplace, TIE could parallel what economists refer to as the hysteresis effect. It is possible that the early turn-of-the-century economy with its welfare-to-work programs may have had lasting effects by changing the work habits and skills of marginal workers. TIE could be conceived of as affected by this whole economic development. Also, changes in supervisory practices or organizational factors could affect TIE. Furthermore, it should be noted that upward changes in TIE would logically affect the lower part of the distribution most. Thus, differential positive changes in TIE could move the concept away from habitual performance and more toward maximum performance, and relations with other variables could change.

The treatment of interests in the work of Ackerman and Heggestad (1997) and the older person–environment fit model deserves consideration. The use of Holland's (1973) vocational interest theory within the environmental fit framework, as mentioned previously, was seriously scrutinized, for example, by Tinsley (2000a.) However, in the Ackerman and Heggestad (1997) work, the Holland themes are given prominence. Unfortunately, the construction of early major interest inventories rendered them generally unacceptable for use in meaningful correlational research. Hence, early opportunities for theory building were lost.

ROLES OF SPECIFIC VARIABLES

Findings (Schmidt & Hunter, 1998) about the low validities of interest inventories for predicting job performance suggest that the role of interests in theories of workplace mental functioning might better be accommodated by the Dawis and

Lofquist (1984) concepts satisfaction and satisfactoriness than those associated with more general theories. Interest measurement is essential in career theory. On a purely theoretical level, interests belong in general theories of mental functioning. However, as a practical matter within the workplace, interests have a much smaller role. Among incumbents in a given job, there often is considerable restriction of range in measured interests. Many incumbents, possibly with the aid of testing and counseling in the educational system, have already made career choices, more or less aligned with their interests. Another thought is that, for the most part, depending on economic and social circumstances, employers cannot guarantee employees work that is personally interesting to them. Research needs to be done with a hypothesis that many people who achieve career success do so not because of their interests, but because they work hard, regardless of whether they are interested in the task at hand. Certainly the relations between interest variables and measurements of conscientiousness that are figuring prominently in research on individual performance in the workplace (Mount & Barrick, 1995) warrant further study.

The role of knowledge in any theory that relates to individual performance in the workplace also merits some discussion. This is a difficult topic for research because knowledge can have many aspects. Even such an apparently simple concept like job knowledge can be defined in several ways. Job knowledge could well include task knowledge, organizational knowledge, political knowledge in the organization, knowledge of a body of information generally taught by the formal educational system, and knowledge of an industry, among others.

Definitions become even more difficult when less distinct knowledge is concerned. In particular, the concept of tacit knowledge central to Sternberg's (1990) theory of successful intelligence is subject to definitional problems. One of the reasons for this observation is that some of the research on this concept suggests that tacit knowledge cannot adequately be distinguished from job knowledge or other knowledge within a specific area. Although there appears to be some promise associated with Sternberg's work, some ambiguity remains.

Similar ambiguity is associated with what is being measured by the large number of situational judgment, mini-assessment, and other instruments designed to tap knowledge in largely social situations. Many of these instruments involve advanced technology, and certainly not all of these measures are probably lumped in one class as far as relations with other variables are concerned. One would expect, however, that purveyors of these methods should be obligated to show that what is being measured is not a concept that could be measured by simpler or more established means.

Schmidt and Hunter (1998) made the argument that many of the methods used in employee selection result in validity as a result of their relation to job knowledge, g, or both. For example, they pointed out that experience, up to a point, has value in predicting job success because experience is essentially a surrogate for job knowledge.

As was suggested in relation to the TIE concept, the effects of contextual variables should be studied in relation to theories regarding human performance. Certainly variables strongly related to job performance have been the subject of considerable study. Among these variables are compensation practices, job design, and leadership styles. However, further work is indicated on the numerous variables that can be expected to have more subtle effects on performance. Vicino and Bass (1978) provided an early tentative list of these variables; the list of pertinent organizational variables is expanding rapidly, and no attempt will be made to cover them here.

Personality variables figure prominently in the Ackerman and Heggestad (1997) model. The area of personality involves much more investigator disagreement than the area of mental ability. Furthermore, the problem is compounded by continual production of a host of new personality measures (American Psychological Association, 2000). Other factors clouding the use of personality variables in theory building are continuing concerns about the role of response styles in personality measurement.

The Five Factor Model (FFM; Digman, 1990) of personality has received considerable attention of late. However, various researchers are still exploring other models and are looking for refinements to the FFM. For example, Panter and Carroll (1999) applied hierarchical factor analyses to data and developed a model different from the FFM. Tellegen's Multidemensional Personality Questionnaire (MPQ), (1982) and Eysenck's (1994) three variables are also being studied by theory builders. However, from Schmidt and Hunter's (1998) meta-analytical study, it is evident that many personality variables derived from theory appear to have lower validity than might be desired. As was recently pointed out by an experienced researcher (L. R. Taylor, personal communication, September 19, 2000), the level of validity being found for personality inventories today is the same as that which made personnel researchers years ago decide that such inventories added little to prediction of performance. In addition, Hough and Oswald (2000) pointed out that the FFM validities are generally lower than those personality inventories reported by Ghiselli (1966). Also, Hough (1997) argued for a taxonomy more refined than FFM. Hogan (1998) also has a model that expands on the FFM.

It appears that special purpose inventories that are not totally tied to theory may still be needed to ensure better prediction of job performance variables in the workplace. It also seems that most theory-based personality variables have little to add to g in prediction of workplace variables.

The questions about the role of response styles on personality inventories used to predict workplace variables may never be satisfactorily resolved. The assumption that job incumbents are honest in their responses to personality tests given for research purposes may not be tenable. Particularly when job incumbents are concerned, it is highly unlikely that the researcher is trusted. This may be positive where maximum performance on research variables is desired, but problematic for variables for when typical performance is desired.

Another factor to be considered is the tendency in many business team development programs to require participants to reveal their life histories or share results of personality inventories (often homemade) with their supervisors and peers. More than one person has told the author of faking responses on such tests.

Still, it appears that applicant scores on personality inventories are inflated as compared with those of incumbents tested for research purposes only (Ones, Hough, & Viswesvaran, 2000). A question that has not been answered is whether there are different prediction equations for applicants who may have distorted results. Validity coefficients appear to be resilient to many influences including many group differences. A total differential prediction model would be more informative. It is recognized that research on the total predictive model is very difficult to do.

Another possibility explored long ago was that different test formats might ameliorate some of the problems associated with response styles. The forced choice format that yields ipsative scores has been criticized because of various properties of these scores (Anastasi & Urbina, 1997; Tenopyr, 1988). In particular, correlations with other variables are generally meaningless. The use of control scales to correct for distortion of responses is still subject to more research.

James (1998) developed a conditional reasoning theory that combines cognitive and personality variables and may indeed become a stepping stone to future theories of mental functioning.

INCREMENTAL VALIDITY

There are many difficulties in assessing the extent to which personality, interest, and other variables can provide incremental validity over that provided by measures of g. The research technique of using a personality or interest inventory involving multiples scales on a shotgun basis is to be deplored. Some investigators have concluded that the results of applying these inventories is low validity when, for example, for an inventory with 10 scales, only one or two scales can logically be expected to yield valid prediction. If investigators do not select conative predictors on a basis that has scientific or some other defensible merit, they cannot expect to obtain valid results. Ackerman's (1994) TIE variable was developed on the basis of an attempt to achieve construct validity. It is suggested that other efforts in personality and interest validation research should rely on specific hypotheses based on both knowledge of the literature and knowledge of the job.

A word should be said about the problem of mixing content and process in attempts to assess the degree of incremental validity afforded by adding predictors to cognitive ability measures. Schmidt and Hunter (1998) defended this practice; however, this author argues that the basic axiom from elementary factor analysis that validity depends on commonality of factor loadings of predictor and criterion variables should not be ignored. Process-based surrogates for construct-based variables may provide distorted information about the nature of relations among variables. Again, validity coefficients are relatively uninformative. Edwards and Bagozzi (2000) discussed in detail the relations between measures and constructs.

As indicated by Schmidt and Hunter (1998), the findings of incremental validity over that provided by g is not extraordinarily impressive. This fact begs this question about what psychologists can do to improve overall validity.

Certainly job performance can be predicted at a level that provides value to the employer. However, efforts to improve validity over the many years have not been that impressive. Emphasis on g appears to have been the most fruitful approach. However, there are few jobs for which Spearman's (1904) narrow definition of intelligence is appropriate. The broader theories of intelligence probably better represent the realities of the employment process. There are relatively few situations in private business in which selection on the basis of measures of g alone or g plus a single additional variable, such as results of an integrity inventory, would be acceptable to management. The more encompassing theories of intelligence probably better echo the prevailing folklore concerning employee selection and, hence, will be a better-accepted base for employee selection strategies. Despite the innovations in research by psychologists, the common folklore still cannot be ignored. Although scores on measures of g appear to gain in validity as job complexity increases (Schmidt & Hunter, 1998), the possibility that, in reality, g decreases in weight in an actual selection situation as job complexity rises should be studied. Restriction in range is possibly a major factor. It is well known, however, that most executives do not get training in selection. One effort to attempt to remedy this in executive development programs is that by the Center for Creative Leadership (Sessa & Taylor, 2000). Often when selection for high level positions is concerned, the best the company psychologist can hope for is to ensure that the non-g variables considered do not greatly detract from overall validity. Again, this is a subject for research. It should be noted that research data on some popular techniques, such as the assessment center, are based on use for one type of job. For example, validity data for assessment centers are largely for managerial jobs. Such validity may not generalize to other types of jobs such as those in marketing or engineering. Also, one must consider the cost-effectiveness of using supplements or alternatives to measures of g.

CRITERIA

Criteria have been discussed so much over the history of industrial psychology, it might seem that there is little more to be said. However, in an era with rapidly changing technology, the possibility of criteria becoming obsolescent must be considered. Merger and acquisition activity may also change criteria, particularly those associated with managerial jobs. Another complicating factor is that shorter term validation research is often in order, lest results be questioned regarding their applicability in a changed work situation. Certainly, the longitudinal research of the past no longer seems so feasible.

Seldom is any criterion variable free from criticism, and tomes have been devoted to the topic. However, there are new avenues for research that need exploring, particularly with respect to appraisals.

Validity may generally be considered at its measured highest at the time that the validation research is done (Harris, Smith, & Champagne, 1995). If the investigator has, for example, developed a supervisory rating form especially for the study and has designed and conducted a proper validation study, one can probably expect validity to be at its operational maximum. In situations in which a selection procedure must be used repeatedly as is typical in business, there is a possibility of validity decay (Tenopyr, 1999). This is particularly true in the case of techniques used with employees, amenable to content memorization, and sensitive to lack of standardized administration. Constant monitoring of standardization is necessary for techniques like structured interviews and assessment centers. Many companies require internal certification of interviewers and assessors. However, in the author's experience, training and certification must be accompanied by monitoring.

Another factor to be considered in evaluating criteria based on ratings is that it has become increasingly clear that performance appraisal done for administrative purposes is far more complicated to evaluate than was once assumed. A review by Arvey and Murphy (1998) clearly illustrates this contention. Study of the role of contextual factors in appraisal is increasing and is long overdue. Early studies in this area, for example (Michael & Tenopyr, 1963), showed this research area bore promise, but too much investigation over the years has focused on rating errors and design of forms. However, there are questions about whether contextual performance should be treated as a separate area for study. Every appraisal takes place within a context that may take on increasing relevance as job complexity increases, particularly within the managerial or high-level staff ranks. In evaluating contextual variables, the investigator must have in-depth understanding of the many variables in the organizational environment and even in the external environments that affect the organization.

A major problem, however, is that companies are often reluctant to share sensitive information with investigators, or some information given researchers is distorted. For example, in some companies, despite written policies to the contrary, employees not giving enough for savings bond drives or company-supported charities can expect poor performance ratings.

Unfortunately, possibly because only small N's are available for the populations for which contextual variables are probably most important, much of the research extant has been based on lower level jobs involving large groups such as factory workers. Also to be considered are the effects of the popular competency modeling programs that often take precedence over more rigorous job analysis. Many companies have developed core sets of values that include things such as integrity and innovation. Ratings on these values are often incorporated formally or informally into administrative performance appraisal processes.

There have been problems with some validation efforts because criteria and the job analyses supporting them have been based on either personality or ability variables that the typical rater probably could not understand or perhaps had not had the opportunity to observe. More research is needed to determine how useful various taxonomies of cognitive and conative variables will be in the workplace. This type of variable, despite its apparent potential for theory building, may in the long run prove impractical in most validation research. Thus, the potential for providing incremental validity over that afforded by g may be limited. Also to be considered are the amounts of time supervisors have to observe in the workplace the more narrow abilities and personality traits. Familiarity with the appraisee does have an effect on validity (Rothstein, 1990) and surely indirectly opportunities for theory building. Another factor to be considered is that g appears to affect many human activities and apparently is more subject to observation than many other variables. The processes by which observers ascertain an individual's level of g should be studied more. Interestingly enough, modern intelligence tests were developed because teachers and other school officials could not evaluate g very well. Now we use these same types of unstandardized observations as criteria for the validation of intelligence tests.

Another area for research involves the process by which appraisals are made. Although it is generally assumed that rating is essentially a dyadic process and it is usually studied as such, appraisal may well depend on group processes. Often a ratee may have no idea about how many persons have been involved in the appraisal received. As discussed by Tenopyr (2000), some appraisal programs should be conceptualized in terms of tournament theory, in which there are limited prizes for which the ratees compete. This could be said of ratings that are closely tied to compensation, promotion, or special status in the organization. Often competitors have different sponsors, each of whom tries to promote a particular candidate. Meetings to determine rewards are often held, and the dynamics of the process need to be studied and in many cases be a focus for improvement. When a performance appraisal is greatly affected by the relevant supervisor's bargaining prowess, it may well not be appropriate for use as a criterion in validation research. Also, appraisals and rewards should be studied together. The conditions under which the two are likely to be inconsistent need to be ascertained.

Rater source is another area that affects appraisal-based criteria. It has been known since the end of World War II that supervisor and peer ratings do not necessarily measure the same factors (Springer, 1953). This type of finding was recently confirmed by Ones et al. (2000). Furthermore, Schmidt and Hunter (1998) treat peer ratings as a predictor that is only moderately correlated with supervisors' ratings. Again, data from different rating sources should be considered in both validation research and associated theory development.

A new issue that affects criterion development has been raised in recent years. The newer technologies have made possible employee surveillance as never could be done before. Hawkins (2000) described it as "toiling in a fishbowl" (p. 62-68). The matter of employee privacy is being strongly debated; there are no easy answers. However, the new technology offers the opportunity to obtain more objective criterion data for certain types of jobs than was ever possible before and reduce dependence on subjective measures. However, there is the possibility that some objective data, for example, on employee political contributions, finances, and medical matters may be criterion contaminants.

UTILITY

Brogden (1949) provided the basic formula to determine the cost effectiveness of testing and other selection procedures. This formula lay dormant for years until it was resurrected by Schmidt, Hunter, McKenzie, and Muldrow (1979). Numerous investigators have embellished on the early work since that time. The major obstacle to applying the formula has been the need for an estimate of the standard deviation of the value of employee output. Such a value is hardly ever available. However, Hunter, Schmidt, and Judiesch (1990) developed ways of estimating this value, and many investigators have applied these methods in practice.

However, recent research has been concentrated on the credibility of results of utility analysis (Latham & Whyte, 1994). Overcoming the negative reactions to even conservative results of utility has been a major problem for practitioners. This author is one of the many who simply stopped doing the analyses because of the criticism of high utility estimates. There are a number of ways to show the value of a selection procedure other than a dollar-based utility estimate of the type envisioned by Brogden (1949), and these may very well be more effective in persuading decision makers that a selection procedure has value.

It is suggested that, in this area, a line of research harkening back to the early days of psychophysics be undertaken. Concepts such as the just noticeable difference (JND) should be revived. It is further suggested that, under ordinary circumstances, the JND is much larger than most psychologists would like to believe. The circumstances that affect the perception of difference in performance need to be understood. There is a possibility for both psychometric and laboratory research in this area. This line of research, of course, has implications for undertaking the performance appraisal process and for designing performance measurement systems.

Furthermore, the extent to which actual work and training procedures are changed as a result of selecting better employees should be studied. For example, when more trainable employees are selected, is the length of training really reduced? The organizational aspects of any intervention such as selection must be considered as part of a total system process.

Also, the research suggested has practical implications for those planning efforts to provide incremental validity over that afforded by measurers of g. The investigator must balance the theoretical value of increments against the possibility that decision makers may not be able to recognize the economic value of the effort. Also providing incremental validity and enhanced utility through self-report measures may be difficult because of the fact that self-report measures yield a different unit of measurement and zero point for each item for each examinee (Humphreys & Yao, 2000). This observation may, of course, have broader implications in research with self-report instruments.

GROUP DIFFERENCES

The fact that group differences and possible bias in cognitive test scores have been studied intensively for years to the point at which, from a psychometric viewpoint, many believed that there was little to be learned, Millsap (1995, 1997, 1998) brought some new perspectives to the subject. He used the conventional distinction between measurement bias and predictive bias. The former concerns systematic inaccuracies that the test provides about the latent variable to be measured. Predictive bias is concerned with systematic inaccuracies in predictions afforded by the test. He showed that if a predictor-criterion set is free of measurement bias, it will usually show predictive bias. He relatedly demonstrated that when predictive bias does not occur, the predictor-criterion set must be biased in the measurement sense. Millsap's work has important implications for attempts to eliminate bias in employment tests. Clearly there are limits to the extent bias can be removed. More applied research is needed to determine the practical effects of Millsap's theorems under a variety of circumstances. Millsap pointed out that the small samples typical in employment settings do not lend themselves to the application of his theorems. Millsap's proofs should be also studied in relation to Messick's (1989) widely quoted conception of validity. It would appear that there may be inconsistencies to be addressed.

The common problem of how to analyze data when the criterion is a dichotomous variable had been addressed by Ganzach, Saporta, and Weber (2000). In particular, they pointed out a difference in interactions depending on the model used in the research. Work of this sort and Millsap's needs to be extended to the problem of detecting predictive bias when a criterion is dichotomous.

In another methodological article related to differential prediction analysis, Oswald, Saad, and Sackett (2000) suggested that heterogeneity of variance should be considered more than it is in differential prediction research. The authors of the study briefly referred to a study by Dunbar and Novick (1988), in which it was concluded that tests yielded predictive bias against women in the U.S. Marine Corps. Unfortunately, the authors of this study evidently did not know that their sample data were from a period during which higher selection standards were applied to women than men. Consequently, the predictive bias found may essentially be artifactual. Again, the importance of knowing one's data and the realities of the workplace that affect it is supported.

One of the possible issues in using ratings as criteria for research purposes seems to have been largely resolved. Arvey and Murphy (1998), after an intensive review of the recent literature, concluded that many earlier suggested problems about rater and ratee race interactions were less serious than was believed.

Some group differences in mean scores on cognitive tests persist despite years of experimental programs and research. Questions about how to reduce these differences still appear to have no easy answers. Continued research is definitely needed in this area.

FUTURE THEORY BUILDING

There are many avenues for incorporating g into more comprehensive theories of intelligence. The wide generalizability of g should not preclude new research and theory building. Developmental psychologists, of course, have an important role. As Anastasi (1970) pointed out long ago, those things taught together tend to develop together. How this observation now relates to g still needs to be better understood. Researchers in the developmental psychology area still have much to offer.

Cognitive psychologists (Embretson, 1995) also have a place in theory building. For example, a cognitive test design system that would substitute spatial items that could be answered correctly through application of g with other items that minimize the role of g and require spatial ability has been developed by Embretson (1995). It remains to be seen how far this line of work can be extended beyond the spatial area.

What appears to be possible is to develop measures of ability variables other than g. The importance of g cannot be dismissed. Attempts to develop new general measures that reduce group differences associated with g have largely been unsuccessful. What is needed is to apply new developments in cognitive psychology to develop non-g measures.

However, it is clear that some of our traditional ways of thinking about cognitive abilities might need revising. For example, the division between verbal and quantitative ability as exemplified by the Scholastic Assessment Test was recognized long ago to be problematic. Guilford (1959) suggested that the ability to solve word problems in mathematics had a large verbal component. Humphreys, Lubinski, and Yao (1993) made a similar point regarding the need for spatial abilities in some of the sciences and professions. The emphasis on verbal and quantitative abilities with neglect of spatial abilities is a mistake in determining whether a student should enter the physical sciences or engineering.

Conative variables must have a place in any theory construction relating to intelligence. However, as has been indicated previously, there are many problems in using these variables. James's (1998) work may be the way such variables can be incorporated into a comprehensive theory.

Also to be considered are limitations of the linear model in providing answers in this area. Perhaps we have gone as far as we can with this model. The possibility of actions such as configural scoring and improved profile analysis should be entertained.

Another avenue to be explored is using workplace data to inform theory building. The variety of activities in the workplace far exceeds that in educational systems, which has been the major source of data for theory development. A practical obstacle is getting funds and cooperation for more basic research in the workplace.

A final question must be addressed regarding g and future research. Jensen (2000) indicated that research on g without consideration of physiological variables should cease. He deplored mind–body duality in theory and will do research to counter such a division in theory. Already he has data regarding g, brain size, and functioning variables.

The question of the amount of genetic involvement in the formation and application of g need not be reached here. It is clear that heredity and environment interact in determining behavior and that a relatively wide range of behavior can be expected within a genetically pure strain at some subhuman level (Sapolsky, 2000). This and other research data suggest that much more is to be learned about genetics and intelligence. Humphreys and Stark (2000) presented a detailed review of the subject.

DISCUSSION AND SUMMARY

It is suggested that, despite the fact that g apparently has strong relations with performance in many types of work, there should be further research that takes into account the realities of the workplace as well as theory.

Broader theories of intellectual functioning need to be evaluated and enhanced. Some older concepts need to be revised. Methods of assessing utility should be reviewed to take into account criticisms.

Both objective and subjective methods of job performance measurement need to be studied in relation to the conditions under which they were made, often too difficult to discern. The separate consideration of contextual variables in research needs to be examined.

The models normally used to study validity and generate theory should be scrutinized. In the first place, validity coefficients are relatively uninformative. Second, perhaps the research based on the linear model has afforded investigators as much as it can. The possibility of combining the clinical and the actuarial methods in the workplace should be considered. In view of the advances in technology, areas such as configural scoring should be studied anew.

Group differences and their consequences are still deserving of study. There are at this point in time many problems that need attention in this area.

Finally, the most important objective of this discussion was to convey the need for further research on *g* in the workplace. Researchers must resist the temptation of reductionism so prevalent today. Considering the advances in neuroscience, it is all too tempting to dismiss psychometric research, let alone its practical implications. This author believes that to strive only for physiological answers to psychological questions is premature at this time.

REFERENCES

Ackerman, P. L. (1994). Intelligence, attention and learning: Maximal and typical performance. In D. K. Ditterman (Ed.), *Current topics in human intelligence: Vol. 4: Theories of intelligence* (pp. 1–27). Norwood, NJ: Ablex.

Ackerman, P. L., & Heggestad, (1997). Intelligence, personality, and interests: Evidence for overlapping traits. *Psychological Bulletin, 121,* 219–245.

American Psychological Association (2000). *Convention program.* Washington, DC: Author.

Anastasi, A. (1970). On the formation of psychological traits. *American Psychologist, 25,* 899–910.

Anastasi, A., & Urbina, S. (1997). *Psychological testing* (7th ed.). Upper Saddle River, NJ: Prentice Hall.

Arvey, R. D., & Murphy, K. R. (1998). Performance evaluation in work settings. *Annual Review of Psychology, 49,* 141–168.

Brogden, H. E. (1949). When testing pays off. *Personnel Psychology, 2,* 171–183.

Carroll, J. B. (1993). *Human cognitive abilities: A survey of factor-analytic studies.* New York: Cambridge University Press.

Dawis, R. V. (2000). P–E fit as paradigm: Comment on Tinsley (2000). *Journal of Vocational Behavior, 56,* 180–183.

Dawis, R. V., & Lofquist, L. H. (1984). *A psychological theory of work adjustment.* Minneapolis: University of Minnesota Press.

Digman, J. M. (1990). Personality structure: Emergence of the five-factor model. *Annual Review of Psychology, 41,* 417–440.

Dunbar, S. B., & Novick, M. R. (1988). On predicting success in training for men and women: Examples from Marine Corps clerical specialties. *Journal of Applied Psychology, 73,* 545–550.

Edwards, J. R., & Bagozzi, R. P. (2000). On the nature and direction of relationships between constructs and measures. *Psychological Methods, 5,* 155–174.

Embretson, S. E. (1995). Development toward a cognitive design system for psychological tests. In D. J. Lubinsky & R. V. Dawis (Eds.), *Assessing individual differences in human behavior* (pp. 17–48). Palo Alto, CA: Davies-Black.

Eysenck, H. J. (1994). Personality and intelligence: Psychometric and experimental approaches. In R. J. Sternberg & P. Ruzgis (Eds.), *Personality and intelligence* (pp. 8–31). New York: Cambridge University Press.

Ganzach, Y., Saporta, I., & Weber, Y. (2000). Integration in linear versus logistic models: A substantive illustration using the relationship between motivation, ability and performance. *Organizational Research Methods. 3.* 237–253.

Gati, I. (2000). Pitfalls of congruence research: A comment on Tinsley's "The Consequence Myth". *Journal of Vocational Behavior, 56,* 184–189.

Ghiselli, E. E. (1966). *The validity of occupational aptitude tests.* New York: Wiley.

Guilford, J. P. (1959). *Personality.* New York: McGraw-Hill.

Guion, R. M. (1998). *Assessment, measurement, and predictions for personnel decisions.* Mahwah, NJ: Lawrence Erlbaum Associates, Inc.

Harris, M. M., Smith, D. E., & Champagne, D. (1995). A field study of performance appraisal purpose: Research versus administrative-based ratings. *Personnel Psychology, 48,* 151–160.

Hawkins, D. (2000). Privacy is under fire at work, at home, and online. *U.S. News & World Report, 129,* 62–68.

Hesketh, B. (2000). The next millennium of 'fit' research: Comments on "The Congruence Myth: An Analysis of the Efficiency of the Person–Environment Fit Model" by H.E.A. Tinsley. *Journal of Vocational Behavior, 56,* 190–196.

Hogan, R. (1973/1998). Reinventing personality. *Journal of Social and Clinical Psychology, 17,* 1–10.

Holland, J. L. (1973). *Making vocational choices: A theory of careers.* Englewood Cliffs, NJ: Prentice Hall.

Hough, L. M. (1997). The millennium for personality psychology: New horizons or good old daze. *Applied Psychology: International Review, 47,* 233–261.

Hough, L. M., & Oswald, F. L. (2000). Personnel selection: Looking toward the future—Remembering the past. *Annual Review of Psychology, 51,* 631–664.

Humphreys, L. G., Lubinski, D., & Yao. G. (1993). Utility of predicting group membership and the role of spatial visualization in becoming an engineer, physical scientist or artist. *Journal of Applied Psychology, 78,* 250–261.

Humphreys, L. G., & Stark, S. (2000). *Measurement, correlates, and interpretation of the cultural–genetic construct.* Manuscript submitted for publication.

Humphreys, L. G., & Yao. G. (2000). *Prediction of graduate major from cognitive and self-report test scores obtained during the high school years.* Manuscript submitted for publication.

Hunter, J. E., Schmidt, F. L., & Judiesch, M. K. (1990). Individual differences in output variability as a function of job complexity. *Journal of Applied Psychology, 75,* 28–42.

James, L. R. (1998). Measurement of personality via conditional reasoning. *Organizational Research Methods, 1,* 131–163.

Jensen, A. R. (2000, August). *g—The elephant in the classroom.* Address given at the meeting for the American Psychological Association, Washington, DC.

Katzell, R. A. (1994). Contemporary meta-trends in industrial and organizational psychology. In H. C. Triandis, M. D. Dunette, & L. M. Hough (Eds.), *Handbook of industrial and organizational psychology, 4* (1-89). Palo Alto, CA: Consulting Psychologists Press.

Latham, G. P., & Whyte, G. (1994). The futility of utility analysis. *Personnel Psychology, 47,* 31–46.

Messick, S. (1989). Validity. In R. L. Linn (Ed.), *Educational measurement* (3rd ed., pp. 13–103). New York: American Council on Education.

Michael, W. B., & Tenopyr, M. L. (1963). Comparability of the factored dimensions of personnel ratings obtained under two sets of instructions. *Personnel Psychology, 16,* 335–344.

Millsap, R. E. (1995). Measurement invariance, predictive invariance, and the duality paradox. *Multivariate Behavioral Research, 30,* 577–605.

Millsap, R. E. (1997). Invariance in measurement and prediction: Their relationship in the single factor case. *Psychological Methods, 2,* 248–260.

Millsap, R. E. (1998). Group differences in regression intercepts: Implications for factorial invariance. *Multivariate Behavioral Research, 33,* 403–424.

Mount, M. K., & Barrick, M. R. (1995). The big five personality dimensions: Implications for research and practice in human resources. In G. R. Ferris (Ed.), *Research in personnel and human resources management* (Vol. 13, pp. 153–200). Greenwich, CT: JAI.

Ones, D. S., Hough, L., & Viswesvaran, C. (2000, August). *Personality of managers: Mean differences and predictors of performance*. Paper presented at the meeting of the American Psychological Association, Washington, DC.

Oswald, F. L., Saad, S., & Sackett, P. (2000). The homogeneity assumption in differential prediction analysis: Does it really matter? *Journal of Applied Psychology, 85*, 526–535.

Panter, A. T., & Carroll, J. B. (1999, June). *Assessing hierarchical structure in the five-factor model*. Paper presented at the meeting of the Society of Multivariate Experimental Psychology, Riverside, CA.

Peterson, N. G., Mumford, M. D., Borman, W. C., Jeanneret, P. R., & Fleishman, E. A. (1999). *An occupational information system for the 21st1 century: The development of O*NET*. Washington, DC: American Psychological Association.

Prediger, D. J. (2000). Holland's hexagon is alive and well—Though somewhat out of shape: Response to Tinsley. *Journal of Vocational Behavior, 56*, 197–204.

Rounds, J., McKenna, M. C., Hubert, L., & Day, S. X. (2000). Tinsley on Holland: A misshapen argument. *Journal of Vocational Behavior, 56*, 205–215.

Rothstein, H. (1990). Interrater reliability of job performance rating: Growth to asymptote with increasing opportunity to observe. *Journal of Applied Psychology, 70*, 322–327.

Sapolsky, R. M. (2000). Anecdotal evidence. *The Sciences, 40*, 12–15.

Schmidt, F. L., & Hunter, J. E. (1998). The validity and utility of selection methods: Practical and theoretical implications of 85 years of research findings. *Psychological Bulletin, 124*, 262–274.

Schmidt, F. L., Hunter, J. E., McKenzie, R. C., & Muldrow, T. W. (1979). The impact of valid procedures on work-force productivity. *Journal of Applied Psychology, 71*, 432–439.

Sessa, V. I., & Taylor, J. (2000). *Executive selection: Strategies for success*. San Francisco: Jossey-Bass.

Spearmun, C. (1904). General intelligence, objectively determined and measured. *American Journal of Psychology, 15*, 201-293.

Spokane, A. R., Meir, E. I., & Catalano, M. (2000). Person–environmental congruence and Holland's theory: A review and reconstruction. *Journal of Vocational Behavior, 57*, 137–187.

Springer, D. Ratings of candidates for promotion by co-workers and supervisors. *Journal of Applied Psychology, 37*, 347-351.

Sternberg, R. J. (1990). *Metaphors of mind: Conceptions of the nature of intelligence*. Cambridge, England: Cambridge University Press.

Tellegen, A. T. (1982). *Brief manual for the Multidimensional Personality Questionnaire* (MPQ). Minneapolis, MN: Author.

Tenopyr, M. L. (1981). Trifling he stands. *Personnel Psychology, 34*, 1–17.

Tenopyr, M. L. (1988) Artificial reliability of forced choice scales. *Journal of Applied Psychology, 73*, 749-751.

Tenopyr, M. L. (1999). A scientist–practitioner's viewpoint on the admissibility of behavioral and social scientific information. *Psychology, Public Policy, and Law, 5*, 194–202.

Tenopyr, M. L. (2000). Individual differences: Time for a resurrection. *The Industrial–Organizational Psychologist, 38*, 29–30.

Tinsley, H. E. A. (2000a). The congruence myth: An analyses of the efficacy of the person–environment fit model. *Journal of Vocational Behavior, 56*, 147–179.

Tinsley, H. E. A. (2000b). The congruence myth revisited. *Journal of Vocational Behavior, 56*, 405–423.

Tracey, T. J. G., Darcy, M., & Kovalski, T. M. (2000). A closer look at person–environment fit. *Journal of Vocational Behavior, 56*, 216–224.

Vicino, F. L., & Bass, B. M. (1978). Lifespace variables and managerial success. *Journal of Applied Psychology, 63*, 81–88.

HUMAN PERFORMANCE, *15*(1/2), 123–142

g: Is This Your Final Answer?

Harold W. Goldstein
Department of Psychology
Baruch College

Sheldon Zedeck
Department of Psychology
University of California at Berkeley

Irwin L. Goldstein
Department of Psychology
University of Maryland

In many ways, it could be argued that the finding of a simple generalizable relation between cognitive ability and performance has inhibited progress in our attempts to understand the prediction of job performance. In this article, we focus on how the reliance on the cognitive ability–performance relation has yielded a flawed model of selection that is overly loaded on cognition. By pinpointing potential theoretical and empirical shortcomings in the relation between *g* and job performance, we hope to encourage and inspire further research on this important topic.

A basic question of research in Industrial and Organizational (I/O) psychology is how to predict job performance. Many researchers who propose *g* as the answer to this question see this issue as "case closed" (i.e., game over, final answer). This can be said of the broader discussion of the role of *g* in general life outcomes (e.g., economic success, quality of life, participation in illegal activities; Herrnstein & Murray, 1994a) as well as the focus within personnel selection on *g* as a predictor of job performance (Hunter & Schmidt, 1996; Schmidt & Hunter, 1998). *g* is considered by such researchers to be the single best predictor of both life and job per-

Requests for reprints should be sent to Harold W. Goldstein at Buruch College – The City University of New York, 1 Bernard Baruch Way, Box B8–215, New York, NY 10010–5518. E-mail: harold_goldstein@baruch.cuny.edu

formance outcomes. Interestingly enough, this conclusion tends to be stated as an indisputable fact and therefore a question that has been decided and resolved (Jensen, 1998; Schmidt, 1993). Some researchers profess it as an endpoint that does not beget additional research questions or a research agenda for the future.

The prediction of job performance, let alone life performance, is one of the most complex questions facing the field of I/O psychology. Yet g is presented as a final answer that solves this complicated question. Herrnstein and Murray's (1994a) *The Bell Curve* goes as far as to indicate that society is destined to become stratified based on intelligence, that factors other than intelligence play only a minimal role in overall success, and that interventions (e.g., Head Start) will do little to change the impact of intelligence. In terms of selection for jobs, Herrnstein and Murray (1994a) expressed the need for persons with less intelligence to identify lower level work positions more suited to their capabilities. The position of this article is that, just as with other simple relations that turn out to be more complex (e.g., goal setting and performance), g should be viewed as a starting point rather than an ending point.

Why has this not been the case? One reason presented by some researchers (Murphy, 1996; Wagner & Hollenbeck 1998) is that we are victims of our own success. They noted that the finding of a consistent simple generalizable relation between ability and performance has discouraged the creation of more comprehensive models. Although simple models should be encouraged, it is also critical that such models are complete. The amount of variance in performance not accounted for by g should be evidence enough that we do not have a comprehensive solution. Yet, as a field, we have been complacent in relying heavily on this simple finding regarding ability–performance. As stated by Murphy (1996), research in I/O psychology on individual differences can be categorized as (a) studies on the relation between cognitive ability and job performance and (b) other research, with the first category receiving the overwhelming majority of the focus. In part, this is because of the consistent finding of a correlation between tests of g and performance, and in part due to the claim of a lack of support for the incremental predictive power of noncognitive predictors (Herrnstein & Murray, 1994a; Jensen, 1998; Ree & Earles, 1992; Ree, Earles, & Teachout, 1994). Although it is unclear which noncognitive predictors are referred to (e.g., specific abilities, personality facets), the statement leans toward a "case closed" perspective.

Another reason may be that much of the discussion has played out against the political backdrop of discrimination and adverse impact against minorities and other groups. Research shows that Whites outperform Blacks by approximately one standard deviation on tests of general mental ability (Hunter & Hunter, 1984; Schmidt, 1988; Schmidt, Greenthal, Hunter, Berner, & Seaton, 1977). This finding has shifted the focus of the discussion to comparing g and alternative predictors in terms of validity and adverse impact as opposed to continuing the search for ways to capture job performance variance.

In fact, proponents of *g* state that there would be no issue except for the resulting Black–White differences. That is, if no Black–White differences existed, no one would be concerned with this issue at all. Is this the case? Would we be satisfied with the validity of *g* and our understanding of the prediction of job performance if significant differences did not exist between Blacks and Whites? Would we feel that the final answer has been identified? Or would we be asking more complex questions and examining more complicated models?

We argue that, in some ways, the issue of Black–White differences has distracted us from a primary objective—obtaining maximal prediction of performance on the job. Research has focused largely on comparing *g* and alternative tests, rather than delving more rigorously into identifying the set of best predictors of job performance. We argue that because *g* has served as a "final answer" in a political debate, this has diverted our attention from critical questions and generated an incomplete model of personnel selection.

This article first focuses on unresolved issues pertaining to the relation between *g* and job performance. Then, missing aspects of the model of personnel selection that has emerged are examined, and it is argued that this model is overly loaded on cognition. At this point, the implications of a cognitively overloaded model of personnel selection for adverse impact is briefly discussed. Last, a foundation is laid for future research questions that need to be addressed, rather than this issue being perceived as "case closed."

ISSUES WITH *g*

The primary focus of personnel selection research is to identify individuals who have the ability to perform particular jobs (Cascio, 1998; Gatewood & Field, 2001). A wide range of testing procedures has been developed for selection and promotion purposes, including cognitive ability tests, structured interviews, personality inventories, and work simulations. The literature demonstrates some solid support for the validity of many of these devices, although the capabilities of the instruments do vary in their ability to predict job performance (Schmidt & Hunter, 1998).

Currently, measures of cognitive ability are arguably the best available predictor of job performance (Hunter & Hunter, 1984; Ree & Earles, 1992; Schmidt & Hunter, 1998). In a recent review article, Schmidt and Hunter (1998) noted that cognitive ability is a strong predictor across a wide range of jobs and settings. They stated that measures of cognitive ability consistently demonstrate the highest validity for both entry-level and advanced positions. Based on a large meta-analytic study conducted for the U.S. Department of Labor, the validity of cognitive measures for predicting job performance has a value of .51 (Hunter, 1980).

Schmidt and Hunter (1998) claimed "special status" for cognitive ability tests as a selection predictor based on their strong theoretical and empirical foundation.

They stated that over the past 90 years, psychologists have developed and tested theories of intelligence, thus providing clarity with regard to the meaning of the intelligence construct and supportive evidence for its predictive powers in terms of job performance. They noted that thousands of studies have been conducted since the early 1900s that contribute quantitative support for the predictive validity of intelligence.

The success documented in the findings discussed earlier has emerged as a double-edged sword for I/O psychology as a field. On the one hand, cognitive ability tests have demonstrated the ability to predict job performance. On the other hand, there are omissions in this model from both a theoretical and empirical perspective that have long been ignored, in part because of the predictive success noted earlier.

Theoretical Foundations: Defining *g*

One proposed strength of the generalized intelligence construct as a selection device is the solid theoretical foundation that has been developed by researchers over the past century. Schmidt and Hunter (1998) noted that this provides a clear conceptualization of the construct that is not always found with other selection devices (e.g., structured interviews, work samples). Herrnstein and Murray (1994b) claimed that the definition and conceptualization of intelligence is a resolved issue. In their article for *The New Republic*, they stated the following:

> among the experts, it is now beyond much technical dispute that there is such a thing as a general factor of cognitive ability on which human beings differ and that this general factor is measured reasonably well by a variety of standardized tests, best of all by IQ tests designed for that purpose. (October 31, 1994, p. 35)

Echoing these sentiments, Gottfredson (December 13, 1994) published a letter in the *Wall Street Journal* that was signed by 53 fellow researchers concluding that a definition of intelligence was agreed on and that it could be measured and measured well.

Given these statements, it is interesting to note that the definition of intelligence varies depending on the researcher. For example, Spearman's (1927) defined intelligence as "a general capacity for inferring and applying relations drawn from experiences." Gottfredson's (1994) definition is stated as the following: "Intelligence is a very general mental capability that, among other things, involves the ability to reason, plan, solve problems, think abstractly, comprehend complex ideas, learn quickly, and learn from experience" (p. A18). In examining just these two definitions of the construct, there is clear overlap as well as differences. Both definitions refer to learning from experience; however, Gottfredson's adds a number of other additional skills that make up general intelligence. Thus, although *g* appears to be a well-established term, the operational definitions often vary.

In reaction to the claims of a single definition for g, Stephen Jay Gould (November 28, 1994) wrote in an article for *The New Yorker* that the definition of intelligence has only been agreed on by "experts" if "experts means that group of psychometricians working in the tradition of g" (p. 144). In fact, there are a number of schools of thought on the definition and conceptualization of the intelligence construct (Guion, 1997). For example, some organize theories on intelligence into three groups: classical, revisionist, and radical. The classicists view intelligence as a single factor (g) that has been defined and measured (e.g., Herrnstein & Murray, 1994a). The revisionists focus on process rather than the structure of g. They state that IQ is a summary score of multiple facets and ask what do we really learn by using a composite (e.g., Sternberg, 1985). The radicals completely reject the concept of g and make an argument for several distinct intelligences such as the following: linguistic, musical, logical–mathematical, spatial, bodily, interpersonal, and intrapersonal (e.g., Gardner, 1983, 1993). Guilford (1967) went as far as to posit the existence of 120 intelligences that lay within a three-dimensional structure that consisted of intellectual processes, stimuli, and products.

One thing that is clear on reviewing the literature on this issue is that the definition, structure, and conceptualization of intelligence is still being investigated and debated (Gould, 1994; Guion, 1997). Although the classicists state that the statistical evidence for a single factor is overwhelming, Gould argued that it is based on factor analysis and that the fact that a person's performance on various mental tests is positively correlated is not surprising and does not prove there is only one factor. He stated that rotating dimensions to different positions could yield multiple factors similar to what Gardner (1983, 1993) would predict in terms of his theory of multiple intelligences.

Aspects of the discussion mirror the search for structure in personality research and the multiple factor models that emerged from those investigations. For instance, existing 3-Factor (Eysenck, 1991), 5-Factor (Digman, 1990; Tupes & Cristal, 1961/1992), and 16-Factor (Cattell, Eber, & Tatsuoka, 1970) theories of personality are all viable models that capture the personality construct. Although these various models are debated by personality theorists, the question of interest for I/O psychology is which structural model predicts job performance. With regard to personality, the Five-Factor model is currently in favor based on positive research findings (e.g., Barrick & Mount, 1991; Tett, Jackson, & Rothstein, 1991). However, recent studies indicate that breaking the five factors into subfactors of greater specificity may increase the predictive power of personality (Gough, 1985; Hogan, Hogan, & Busch, 1984; Schmit, Ryan, Stierwalter, & Powell, 1995).

Thus, the analogous question for intelligence is which structural model of this construct best predicts job performance (e.g., Spearman's Single-Factor g (1927), Gardner's 7-Factor (1983, 1993), Guilford's 120-Factor (1967), etc.). Murphy (1996) stated that no existing structural model of cognitive ability is so superior to its competitors that it has become the standard for the field. He noted that any acceptable model should incorporate the single factor *g* as either a main facet or as an overarching hierarchical structure that subsumes other intelligence factors. However, he also wrote that it is as yet unclear what the structural model of intelligence should be, especially as it pertains to the prediction of job performance outcomes.

What is readily clear based on this discussion is that omissions exist in our theoretical conceptualization of the definition and structure of intelligence as it pertains to the prediction of job performance. Although this statement could be made in reference to many constructs (e.g., emotional intelligence, practical intelligence), the implications are particularly important with regard to *g* because it has impeded further theoretical and empirical research in that many view the issue as "case closed." There currently exist multiple definitions and various structural models of the intelligence construct that are unexplored in terms of their relation to the prediction of job performance. Although support has been found for a One-Factor approach (*g*), we have yet to fully investigate other theoretical models in terms of their predictive capabilities. In addition, what exactly is *g*? Do we truly understand what aspects of intelligence it refers to, and how it relates to other conceptualizations of intelligence? For example, what aspects of Guilford's (1967) 120 factors of intellect does *g* cover?

In addition, the use of a general composite score such as *g* does little to help us understand the relation between intelligence and job performance. Such an approach does not help explain the concept of human performance and the factors that contribute to it (Murphy, 1996). Just as with any composite score, it may be useful in terms of prediction, but it does not facilitate further understanding in terms of the processes and relations involved.

In summary, the successful findings using a One-Factor *g* solution are an adequate starting point for our investigation, but certainly not an endpoint. Further research and investigation is required to test the various models of intelligence that have been developed by intelligence theoreticians, so that the omissions in understanding the intelligence–job performance relation can be investigated and subsequently better understood.

Empirical Foundations: The Cognitive Ability–Performance Relation

Another proposed strength of the generalized intelligence construct as a selection device is the solid empirical foundation that exists. Schmidt and Hunter (1998) noted that literally thousands of studies have been conducted to explore the relation between cognitive ability and job performance. According to Jensen (1980, 1998), the research demonstrates that *g* accounts for most of the practical predictive validity of tests used for personnel selection in industry. He further stated that the incremental predictive power contributed by other factors independent of *g* is remarkably small. Although some support for this position can be found when looking across the research, a number of issues emerge that should be addressed in terms of these empirical findings.

The strength of the relation.   A critical issue involves the overall strength of the relation between cognitive ability and job performance. Although many note the consistent predictive validity of cognitive ability tests, they only account for approximately 25% of the variance in job performance (Schmidt & Hunter, 1998; Sternberg, Wagner, Williams, & Horvath, 1995). Therefore, intelligence can be thought of as a potent predictor; however, it must be noted that about 75% of variance is left unexplained (Mayer, Salovey, & Caruso, 2000). Also, this is using the corrected results for validity coefficients, which does not represent the use of these tests in the actual organizational settings.

One possible reaction to this finding is that human behavior is incredibly complex and influenced by chance events and unpredictable variables. This is a "case closed" approach to the topic of personnel selection and the valid prediction of job performance. Another possible reaction is to (a) search for better ways to measure intelligence and (b) to investigate other noncognitive factors that can contribute to the prediction of job performance. This latter reaction should be used to guide empirical research on this question.

In examining the empirical literature within the field of I/O psychology, there is little evidence of investigation of alternative techniques for measuring intelligence. Although many types of intelligence measures exist, studies in personnel selection tend to utilize standardized written paper-and-pencil tests. Thus, although some new techniques have emerged to measure intelligence (e.g., evoked brain potential), they have not been used to predict job performance in work settings. The low cost and thus increased utility of a written multiple-choice approach appears to drive the choice of measures of intelligence. However, the dominance of a single approach for measuring g creates the possibility of a potential method bias. In addition, the continued use of one methodology does not encourage the search for different and better measures of the intelligence construct. Instead, the field appears to be satisfied with its measurement of the intelligence construct, rather than exploring new and potentially more construct valid methods for capturing g. The question becomes, are there other ways to measure g other than using paper-and-pencil approaches, and would these methods be more construct valid?

As far as exploring noncognitive factors that add incrementally to the prediction of job performance, the literature shows more progress. Although Jensen (1998) claimed that only small amounts of incremental validity are contributed, the recent review article by Schmidt and Hunter (1998) showed that, depending on the type of alternative test used, significant variance can be accounted for above and beyond g. For example, their meta-analysis showed a validity value of .51 for tests of cognitive ability. However, adding a work sample test results in a validity of .63, adding an integrity test results in a validity of .65, and adding a structured interview results in a validity of .63. Other predictors such as biographical data and job experience faired less well (gain in validity of .01 and .03, respectively).

It should be noted that the cognitive and noncognitive distinction can be a bit arbitrary because few tasks are exclusively cognitive or exclusively motor or exclusively sensory, and so forth (Guion, 1997). Thus, some predictors referred to as "noncognitive" may contain a cognitive component. Although aspects of this cognitive component may be similar to what is captured using a standardized cognitive ability test, it is possible that other aspects of the cognitive component are fundamentally different than what is typically thought of as the cognition being captured using a standardized test of cognitive ability. Some support can be found for this argument in studies such as the one conducted by H. W. Goldstein, Yusko, Braverman, Smith, and Chung (1998), which found that when cognitive ability was partialed out of assessment center exercise scores, most exercises still significantly predicted job performance criterion. Based on these studies and others (e.g., McDaniel, Whetzel, Schmidt, & Mauer, 1994; Ones, Viswesvaran, & Schmidt, 1993), additional research on "noncognitive" predictors is certainly warranted.

To summarize, because of the large amount of variance unaccounted for in the cognitive ability–performance relation, we should be pursing avenues of research such as designing and testing alternative and better measures of the intelligence construct and further exploring the incremental validity of other noncognitive measures. However, in examining the personnel selection empirical literature, we seem to be ignoring the first suggestion. In terms of the second suggestion, research has been conducted on alternative noncognitive predictors, with some evidence emerging in support of incremental validity. This is a good start, but we argue that much more work needs to be done studying this issue. As noted by Schmidt and Hunter (1998), thousands of studies have been conducted on cognition, whereas only a handful have looked at other predictors (e.g., 89 validity studies have been conducted on the structured interview).

The predictor domain.   Building off this point, another troublesome issue regarding empirical work on the prediction of job performance is the narrow predictor domain that has been targeted and measured in personnel selection research (Murphy, 1996). Murphy (1996) pointed out that this is in part because of the success found in predicting performance using general cognitive ability and in part because of the poor quality research that was conducted on noncognitive facets. For example, early research on personality, a well-known noncognitive variable, as a predictor of job performance was of extremely poor quality. In the wake of Guion and Gottier's (1965) article that indicted previous personality research, the I/O psychology field reacted by halting further study of the personality–job performance relation.

As we have stated throughout this article, a more proper response may have been to continue research, but do so in a more rigorous manner (which was indeed what Guion and Gottier, 1965, intended, and what Guion, 1997, has continued to do with his work on personality-based job analysis research; Raymark, Schmit, & Guion, 1997). Eventually, work did continue, and continued successfully, on the personality–job performance relation (Barrick & Mount, 1991). The point of this article is that a research agenda that continues to expand the predictor domain could be useful for improving our ability to predict performance in the work place.

An expanded conceptualization of the predictor domain can involve both a cognitive and noncognitive initiative. From a cognitive perspective, new components of cognition can be posited and investigated. Current examples of this approach include concepts of practical intelligence (Sternberg, 1985), emotional intelligence (Mayer & Salovey, 1993; Salovey & Mayer, 1990), and multiple intelligences (Gardner, 1983, 1993). Research in these areas in terms of properly defining these concepts, developing valid measures, and conducting research on the relation to job performance could prove useful to the goals of personnel selection. It should be noted that subscribing to a unitary approach to cognition (i.e., g) and spending all efforts on protecting this conceptualization rather than exploring other possibilities inhibits the possibilities that may be found in such work.

In addition, as a field, we must recognize the effort required to properly research these concepts both theoretically and empirically. The research conducted on defining and researching g took place over nearly a century. Time and effort must be given to exploring these new concepts and measures to potentially approach the level of validity and reliability found in research on g. Expending all our effort on a "case closed" approach and noting the shortcomings of early research on these new concepts as compared to outcomes from the long-term work invested in g will not help the area of personnel selection progress.

From a noncognitive perspective, expanding the domain of constructs focused on in personnel selection may also prove useful. Some support for this is found in the research noted earlier that documents the incremental validity of many noncognitive predictors such as integrity and conscientiousness (Schmidt & Hunter, 1998). It is perplexing that although many jobs appear to involve far more skills than solely cognition and intelligence, the predictor domain remains restricted. An exception to this is the wider range of "noncognitive" skills often tapped by managerial assessment centers (e.g., stress resistance, interpersonal skills, teamwork skills). Why is it with so many other jobs that noncognitive skills are so often neglected? In part, the answer may be rooted in the job analyses that serve as the determinant of the predictor domain.

Raymark et al. (1997) claimed that the majority of job analysis inventories are most useful for developing hypotheses regarding aptitude and ability variables. However, they noted that they are less useful for developing hypotheses regarding alternative variables such as personality and other noncognitive factors. For example, Fleishman's F–JAS (Fleishman, 1992) job analysis inventory contains four main general ability categories (i.e., cognitive, psychomotor, physical, and sensory or perceptual), none of which focus on the noncognitive domain. Raymark et al. argued that the use of such job analysis inventories results in an emphasis on the cognitive and psychomotor elements of job performance. Thus, these elements will receive most of the attention in the development of selection systems, whereas noncognitive variables will be neglected. Raymark et al. noted that this is likely to happen regardless of how important other variables are to job performance. This lead H. W. Goldstein, Ruminson, Yusko, & Smith (2000) to posit that selection systems will be overloaded on cognition because of the heavy reliance on job analysis information to both develop tests components and weight test components. Therefore, it appears that the development of selection systems based on job analysis focused on cognitive KSAs (Knowledge, Skills, and Abilities) has the potential to be biased toward cognitive and psychomotor components, and against noncognitive components.

Another related potential reason that less attention is paid to noncognitive factors is the lack of adequate language to discuss these variables. For example, although we have an involved complex system of words that we use to describe cognitive concepts, this is not always the case when it comes to noncognitive facets. Thus, while noncognitive factors are often just labeled "interpersonal skills," description of cognitive factors are usually more involved and multidimensional (e.g., reasoning skills, problem solving, judgment, planning, thinking). Strong theoretical definitions do not exist for numerous noncognitive competencies. As noted by Murphy (1996), there is cognition, and then everything else is merely referred to as noncognitive. This does not build a proper theoretical, let alone empirical, foundation for the noncognitive domain.

Perhaps rich definitions and descriptors will evolve as we develop and expand our conceptualization of the noncognitive domain. Work in the area of personality-based job analysis (e.g., Raymark et al., 1997), as well as current research on concepts such as emotional intelligence (Mayer & Salovey, 1993; Salovey & Mayer, 1990), can be useful avenues for developing and expanding our conceptualization and terminology when it comes to noncognitive constructs. As a better understanding is gained of the noncognitive domain, it will increase the possibility of more accurately representing these aspects of job performance in job analysis and subsequently in the predictor domain.

The criterion domain.   In addition to the predictor issues noted earlier, another area to explore is the criterion side of the equation. The "criterion problem" has been discussed in many forums (e.g., Austin & Villanova, 1992; Thayer, 1992), so we will only touch on it as it pertains to this discussion. Similar to the narrow domain used in creating predictors, past empirical work often uses a narrow conceptualization of "job performance." We believe that this narrow view tends to focus on cognitive rather than noncognitive domains. Just as with the narrow predictor domain, this may in part be caused by job analyses that focus on cognitive and psychomotor aspects of job performance criteria as well as the lack of language to properly capture noncognitive performance factors.

Relatively recent work on contextual performance has helped to expand the criterion domain (Borman & Motowidlo, 1993). Contextual performance focuses on nontask aspects of the job such as teamwork, assisting others, and commitment. In addition, concepts such as organizational citizenship behavior (OCB) and prosocial organizational behaviors help to capture aspects of performance not typically considered (Borman & Motowidlo, 1997; Brief & Motowidlo, 1986). Interesting future research could focus on the validity of both g and noncognitive domains in terms of predicting contextual performance and OCBs in the workplace.

A number of other issues stand out in past empirical research with regard to criteria. When examining the literature, one cannot help but notice that often the criteria used in past research on the cognitive ability–performance relation is in the form of training performance data (Schmidt & Hunter, 1998). Because training performance is often assessed using tests (maybe even multiple-choice tests), there is the possibility that the validity relation observed in the literature is in part a matter of tests predicting tests (i.e., cognitive ability tests predicting performance on training tests). This potential common method bias may help inflate the validity observed in these research studies. An interesting question would be to examine how well cognitive ability predicts training performance when training performance is measured in ways other than with standard testing (e.g., work sample assessments).

A related issue centers on whether noncognitive variables are more important for predicting actual on-the-job performance rather than training performance. As noted by Hirsh, Northrop, and Schmidt (1986), cognitive ability may predict training criteria better than on-the-job performance data because other variables (e.g., personality or interpersonal skills) may play a larger role in on-the-job proficiency. They further noted that validity generalization results have shown a weaker than typical correlation between cognitive ability and job performance in more interactive occupations (e.g., police officer, sales clerk) where personality variables are hypothesized to be more important for job success (Hirsh et al., 1986).

Furthermore, the criteria that have been utilized in research on the predictive validity of g have been individual performance. That is, the criteria data collected have been at the individual level of analysis, with no attention paid to group or organizational level performance. This once again shows a limited narrow scope when it comes to the criterion domain. Although predicting individual performance is certainly important, most organizations use selection systems to improve the overall organization's performance (Schneider, Smith, & Sipe, 2000). There is likely a relation between individual and organizational performance, but as yet it is untested and there is no indicator of the strength of such a relation. Theoretically, we tend to assume the impact on organizational performance, yet there is a clear gap in the literature in terms of empirically testing this relation. It is also entirely possible that it is the noncognitive individual level variables (e.g., teamwork, organizational citizenship) that more strongly predict organizational relevant criteria.

A final criterion issue worth touching on focuses on the timing of data collection when it comes to gathering performance data. Guion (1997) noted that performance criteria are usually collected early on the job when conducting validation studies (e.g., a few months or perhaps a couple of years). Murphy (1989) stated that cognitive and noncognitive predictors could vary in the strength of their predictive validity depending on when the criteria data are collected. For example, cognitive predictors may predict better during initial learning stages on a job, whereas noncognitive predictors may predict better later in tenure when motivational issues become more important in terms of job performance. Helmreich, Sawin, and Carsrud (1986) documented just such an effect, which they labeled the "honeymoon period," when studying the validity of achievement motivation for predicting job performance. Thus, the time interval for collecting the criterion data is another issue that has not been extensively explored in the cognitive ability–performance relation research.

The nature of the relation.   A last empirical issue centers on the nature of the predictive relation that is tested when examining cognitive, noncognitive, and performance relations. Traditionally, performance has been conceptualized as a function of ability and motivation, $P = F (M \times A)$, a classic expression used to describe two important factors that have considerable influence on performance (Vroom, 1964). This relation has been posited and demonstrated in the literature (e.g., Hollenbeck, Brief, Whitener, & Pauli, 1988). However, our models of personnel selection tend to examine main effects of various predictors rather than interactions. The question becomes, do we now think that performance equals ability $(P = A)$, or should we be testing our validation models using interactions of both cognitive (e.g., A) and noncognitive (e.g., M) factors?

Summary

A number of unanswered questions exist from an empirical standpoint with regard to the relation between cognitive ability and job performance. We attempted to summarize a number of these issues earlier. Based on these omissions, we believe that an incomplete model of personnel selection has emerged that is overdependent on the relation between *g* and job performance. More specifically, we believe that the personnel selection model is overly cognitively loaded.

PERSONNEL SELECTION MODEL:
COGNITIVE OVERLOAD

As described in numerous texts of the I/O field (e.g., Gatewood & Field, 2001; Guion, 1997), the personnel selection model begins with determining which individual capabilities are required to be effective in a particular job position. Job analysis is performed to gather information on the critical competencies required to effectively perform the tasks of the job. The next step is to procure tests that measure these critical competencies. Validation studies are then performed to determine if the tests indeed predict performance on the job. Finally, the tests are administered, and candidate scores are used to make staffing decisions.

We believe that this model is overly loaded on cognition and thus does not capture reality when it comes to the primary goal of personnel selection, which is validly predicting job performance. We argue that this problem of cognitive overload infests the entire personnel selection process, as can be seen by tracing through the steps of the model:

• Job analysis. As discussed earlier, most job analysis inventories focus on cognitive and psychomotor competencies (H. W. Goldstein et al., 2000; Raymark et al., 1997). Because job analysis serves as the foundation of the personnel selection model, the model will tend to focus on cognition regardless of the importance of other competencies.

• Predictor. The cognitive load of the predictor is impacted by both content and method factors. The content of the predictor refers to what construct is being measured. As noted earlier, content tends to lean toward the cognitive domain. The method of the predictor refers to how the construct is being measured. Typical testing methods often involve a standardized, multiple-choice, written format, as found with most tests of cognitive ability.

This type of method has a strong cognitive load because of the cognitive demands made on the test-taker to complete such a format (e.g., reading, writing, time pressure; Sweller, 1988, 1989). Thus, in terms of the predictor, the domain space is focused primarily on cognitive constructs, and the very methodology used to collect the data imposes further cognitive demands on the test-taker (H. W. Goldstein, Braverman, & Chung, 1993; H. W. Goldstein et al., 1998).

• Criterion. Based on the "criterion problem," we should not assume that the criterion data we have are accurate, complete, and sufficient (Zedeck, Outtz, Cascio, & Goldstein, 1991). We believe that criteria tend to be multidimensional in terms of the cognitive aspects of performance, but narrow when it comes to the noncognitive aspects of performance.

• Implementation. The formation and use of test scores may have additional aspects that enhance the cognitive load of the system. For example, if multiple test scores are combined based on weights from job analysis (a common content validity-type approach to weighting test composites), the bias in job analyses toward cognition may lead to heavier weights for cognitive test components. As shown in a demonstration by Sackett and Ellingson (1997), when two predictors are combined, if the predictor with large subgroup differences is more heavily weighted than the predictor with small subgroup differences, the resulting composite will have larger subgroup differences. Thus, the resulting composite may have a higher cognitive load, although that is not truly representative of the target job (H. W. Goldstein et al., 2000).

Based on this analysis of the main structures of the personnel selection model, we believe that the cognitive load of the system does not properly reflect the nature of most target jobs. When considering the aforementioned factors in combination, you may have a system that targets mostly cognitive competencies, then generates cognitive predictors with cognitive methodologies, and validates them by targeting cognitively loaded criteria. To compound this, weighting systems used to form composites may subsequently more heavily weight the cognitive predictors.

In examining the well-known Binning and Barrett (1989) conceptualization of the validation model, we believe that current personnel selection practices fit appropriately in the model, but only capture half of the domain—the cognitive half. Our redesign of Binning and Barrett (see Figure 1) demonstrates our view of the cognitively loaded personnel selection model that has emerged. A study by Rothstein, Paunonen, Rush, and King (1994) provided support for this conceptualization. In a study of performance in graduate business school, they found that cognitive predictors were effective at predicting cognitive criteria (i.e., written class work), whereas noncognitive predictors (i.e., personality) were effective at predicting noncognitive criteria (i.e., in-class participative performance).

In a nutshell, the cognitively loaded model is correct; the problem is, it only tells half the story. To understand the rest of the story, we cannot treat this question as "case closed." That is, to understand the whole model, a future research agenda is required. However, first we must briefly address the issue that has distracted us from future research.

g AND BLACK–WHITE SUBGROUP DIFFERENCES

One major deterrent to progress on this issue appears to be the ramifications of the cognitive ability–performance relation for adverse impact and discrimination. Up until now, we have specifically avoided this topic so as to concentrate on the issue of the valid prediction of performance. We now briefly consider the implications of a cognitively loaded selection model on adverse impact. Because Whites typically outperform Blacks by one standard deviation on tests of cognitive ability (Hunter & Hunter, 1984), it is easy to infer that cognitive overload on each step in the selec-

Predictor Measure   Criterion Measure

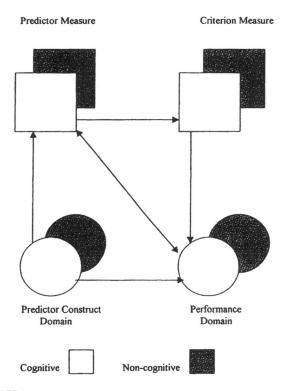

Predictor Construct   Performance
Domain   Domain

Cognitive [ ]   Non-cognitive [█]

FIGURE 1   Redesign of the Binning and Barrett (1989) Validation Model.

tion process (e.g., job analysis, predictor content, predictor method, criterion, implementation) will have a negative impact on minorities. Research conducted on various cognitive predictors (Hunter & Hunter, 1984), various methodologies used to measure variables (Reilly, 1996), and weighting systems to create composites (H. W. Goldstein et al., 2000; Sackett & Ellingson, 1997) have provided support for this conclusion.

Thus, the cognitive load of the selection model may not only have a limiting impact on our ability to increase the amount of explained job performance variance, but it may also have negative implications for minorities. As we explore more complete models of personnel selection, those that properly capture both cognitive and noncognitive components, we may not only increase validity in our ability to predict performance, but we may also reduce Black–White subgroup differences.

In fact, research on noncognitive based selection devices has shown considerable reduced subgroup differences (H. W. Goldstein et al., 1993; H. W. Goldstein et al., 1998; Ones & Viswesvaran, 1998; Pulakos & Schmitt, 1996; Schmitt,

Clause, & Pulakos, 1996). For example, personality measures demonstrate nonsignificant differences between Blacks and Whites (Hough, Eaton, Dunnette, Kamp, & McCloy, 1990). Similarly, research on interpersonal-based selection methods such as role-play work samples also show nonsignificant Black–White differences (H. W. Goldstein et al., 1998) while contributing incremental validity to the prediction of job performance. Because the noncognitive domain appears to have less Black–White differences, the addition of valid noncognitive facets to the selection model may work to both increase validity and reduce adverse impact. Thus, although validity and adverse impact often are perceived as competing goals, this may not be the case (Schmidt, 1993). That is, future research focused on boosting validity in the prediction of job performance may also identify answers for how to decrease adverse impact.

SEARCHING FOR THE "FINAL ANSWER": ESTABLISHING A RESEARCH AGENDA

The issue of g and performance has polarized various fields of research, including the area of personnel selection. Although debates have continued in articles, in courts of law, and at conferences, actual research on the topic has moved slowly. The main point of this article is that, with a question as complex as understanding performance in work organizations, we need to aggressively pursue new avenues of research and build more comprehensive models encompassing the relation between factors and variables. The focus of a future research agenda should include the following:

• Expansion of both the predictor and criterion domain to include multifaceted approaches that reflect noncognitive as well as cognitive components. In addition, the moderating effects of different contexts on predictor–criterion relations could be explored.
• Exploration of alternative predictors to determine what constructs they are measuring (e.g., structured interviews, work samples) and thus better understand why they predict performance.
• Broaden job analysis to properly capture noncognitive aspects of performance, including those required to operate effectively in the new world of work (e.g., technological skills, working with a diverse workforce, service orientation). Although some may note that future jobs will require more cognitive skills (e.g., information processing), a case can also be made for the growing criticality of noncognitive predictors, especially when it comes to predicting group and organizational level performance (I. L. Goldstein & Ford, 2001). Thus, properly capturing these competencies in job analysis is paramount.

- Generate new methodologies for testing competencies beyond the same types that have existed for decades (e.g., biodata, interview, work sample, cognitive ability test).
- Continue to conduct research on various combinations of predictors in the vein of Schmidt and Hunter's (1998) recent meta-analytic summary article.
- Conduct research that focuses beyond individual level performance to include group and organizational level criteria.
- Explore different ways that test scores can be used and implemented in organizations to meet various goals (e.g., valid prediction of job performance, adverse impact). Further research could be conducted on banding techniques, mixed decision models (e.g., hurdles combined with compensatory systems), and profile matching.

CONCLUSIONS

In summary, although research provides support for the relation between g and performance, our tendency to view this as "case closed" (and continuing arguments and debates over whether it is "case closed") has inhibited research in this area. The previous discussion was meant to raise unanswered questions regarding the nature and strength of the cognitive ability–performance relation in hopes of stimulating future research on the topic. A great deal of effort and work is required to begin to understand the complex question of predicting job performance, and, therefore, we cannot afford to perceive the question as already having a "final answer."

REFERENCES

Austin, J. T., & Villanova, P. (1992). The criterion problem: 1917–1992. *Journal of Applied Psychology, 77,* 836–874.

Barrick, M. R., & Mount, M. K. (1991). The Big Five personality dimensions and job performance: A meta-analysis. *Personnel Psychology, 44,* 1–26.

Binning, J. F., & Barrett, G. V. (1989). Validity of personnel decisions: A conceptual analysis of the inferential and evidential bases. *Journal of Applied Psychology, 74,* 478–494.

Borman, W. C., & Motowidlo, S. J. (1993). Expanding the criterion domain to include elements of contextual performance. In N. Schmitt, W. Borman, (Eds.), *Personnel selection in organizations* (pp. 71–98). San Francisco: Jossey-Bass.

Borman, W. C., & Motowidlo, S. J. (1997). Introduction: Organizational citizenship behavior and contextual performance. *Human Performance, 10,* 67-69.

Brief, A. P., & Motowidlo, S. J. (1986). Prosocial organizational behaviors. *Academy of Management Review, 11,* 710–725.

Cascio, W. F. (1998). *Applied psychology in human resource management* (5th ed.). Upper Saddle River. NJ: Prentice Hall.

Cattell, R. B., Eber, H. W., & Tatsuoka, M. M. (1970). *Handbook for The Sixteen Personality Factor Questionnaire (16 PF) in clinical, educational, industrial, and research psychology.* Champaign, IL: Institute for Personality and Ability Testing.

Digman, J. M. (1990). Personality structure: Emergence of the Five-Factor Model. *Annual Review of Psychology, 41,* 417–440.

Eysenck, H. J. (1991). Dimensions of personality: 16, 5, 3?—Criteria for a taxonomic paradigm. *Personality and Individual Differences, 12,* 773–790.

Fleishman, E. A. (1992). *Handbook of human abilities.* Palo Alto, CA: Consulting Psychologists Press.

Gardner, H. (1983). *Frames of the mind.* New York: Basic Books.

Gardner, H. (1993). *Multiple intelligences: The theory in practice.* New York: Basic Books.

Gatewood, R. D., & Field, H. S. (2001). *Human resource selection.* Chicago: Dryden.

Goldstein, H. W., Braverman, E. P., & Chung, B. (1993, April). *Method versus content: The effects of different testing methodologies on subgroup differences.* Paper presented at the eighth annual conference of the Society for Industrial and Organizational Psychology, Inc., San Francisco.

Goldstein, H. W., Ruminson, K. C., Yusko, K. P., & Smith, D. B. (2000, April). *The impact of test composite score weighting procedures on Black–White subgroup differences.* Paper presented at the conference for the Society for Industrial and Organizational Psychology, New Orleans, LA.

Goldstein, H. W., Yusko, K. P., Braverman, E. P., Smith, D. B., & Chung, B. (1998). The role of cognitive ability in the subgroup differences and incremental validity of assessment center exercises. *Personnel Psychology, 51,* 357–374.

Goldstein, I. L., & Ford, J. K. (2001). *Training in organizations.* Monterey, CA: Brooks/Cole.

Gottfredson, L. S. (1994, December 13). Mainstream science on intelligence. *The Wall Street Journal,* p. A18.

Gough, H. G. (1985). A work orientation scale for the California Psychological Inventory. *Journal of Applied Psychology, 70,* 505–513.

Gould, S. J. (1994, November 28). Curveball. *The New Yorker,* p. 139–149.

Guilford, J. P. (1967). *The nature of human intelligence.* New York: McGraw-Hill.

Guion, R. M. (1997). *Assessment, measurement, and prediction for personnel decisions.* Mahwah, NJ: Lawrence Erlbaum Associates, Inc.

Guion, R. M., & Gottier, R. F. (1965). Validity of personality measures in personnel selection. *Personnel Psychology, 18,* 135–164.

Helmreich, R. L., Sawin, L. L., & Carsrud, A. L. (1986). The honeymoon effect in job performance: Temporal increases in the predictive power of achievement motivation. *Journal of Applied Psychology, 71,* 185–188.

Herrnstein, R. J., & Murray, C. (1994a). *The bell curve: Intelligence and class structure in American life.* New York: Free Press.

Herrnstein, R. J., & Murray, C. (1994b, October 31). Race, genes, and IQ –an aplogia. *The New Republic,* p.35–37.

Hirsh, H. R., Northrop, L. C., & Schmidt, F. L. (1986). Validity generalization results for law enforcement occupations. *Personnel Psychology, 39,* 399–420.

Hogan, J., Hogan, R., & Busch, C. M. (1984). How to measure service orientation. *Journal of Applied Psychology, 69,* 167–173.

Hollenbeck, J. R., Brief, A. P., Whitener, E. M., & Pauli, K. E. (1988). An empirical note of the interaction of personality and aptitude in personnel selection. *Journal of Management, 14,* 441–451.

Hough, L. M., Eaton, N. E., Dunnette, M. D., Kamp, J. D., & McCloy, R. A. (1990). Criterion-related validities of personality constructs and the effect of response distortion on those validities. *Journal of Applied Psychology, 75,* 581–595.

Hunter, J. E. (1980). Validity generalization for 12,000 jobs: An application of synthetic validity and validity generalization to the General Aptitude Test Battery (GATB). Washington, DC: U.S. Department of Labor, Employment Service.

Hunter, J. E., & Hunter, R. F. (1984). Validity and utility of alternative predictors of job performance. *Psychological Bulletin, 96*, 72–98.

Hunter, J. E., & Schmidt, F. L. (1996). Intelligence and job performance: Economic and social implications. *Psychology, Public Policy, and Law, 2*, 447–472.

Jensen, A. R. (1980). *Bias in mental testing.* New York: Free Press.

Jensen, A. R. (1998). Jensen on "Jensenism". *Intelligence, 26*, 181–208.

Mayer, J. D., & Salovey, P. (1993). The intelligence of emotional intelligence. *Intelligence, 17*, 433–442.

Mayer, J. D., Salovey, P., & Caruso, D. (2000). Models of emotional intelligence. In R. Sternberg (Ed.), *Handbook of intelligence* (pp. 396–420). Cambridge, England: Cambridge University Press.

McDaniel, M. A., Whetzel, D. L., Schmidt, F. L., & Mauer, S. D. (1994). The validity of employment interviews: A comprehensive review and meta-analysis. *Journal of Applied Psychology, 79*, 599–616.

Murphy, K.R. (1989). Is the relationship between cognitive ability and job performance stable over time? *Human Performance, 2*, 183-200.

Murphy, K. R. (1996). Individual differences and behavior in organizations: Much more than *g*. In K. R. Murphy (Ed.), *Individual differences and behavior in organizations* (pp. 3–30). San Francisco: Jossey-Bass.

Ones, D. S., Viswesvaran, C., & Schmidt, F. L. (1993). Comprehensive meta-analysis of integrity test validities: Findings and implications for personnel selection and theories of job performance. *Journal of Applied Psychology Monograph, 78*, 679–703.

Pulakos, E. D., & Schmitt, N. (1996). An evaluation of two strategies for reducing adverse impact and their effects on criterion-related validity. *Human Performance, 9*, 241–258.

Raymark, P. H., Schmit, M. J., & Guion, R. M. (1997). Identifying potentially useful personality constructs for employee selection. *Personnel Psychology, 50*, 723–736.

Ree, M. J., & Earles, J. A. (1992). Intelligence is the best predictor of job performance. *Current Directions in Psychological Science, 1*, 86–89.

Ree, M. J., Earles, J. A., & Teachout, M. S. (1994). Predicting job performance: Not much more than *g*. *Journal of Applied Psychology, 79*, 518–524.

Reilly, R. R. (1996). Alternative selection procedures. In R. S. Barrett (Ed.), *Fair employment strategies in human resource management* (pp. 208–221). Westport, CT: Quorum.

Rothstein, M. G., Paunonen, S. V., Rush, J. C., & King, G. A. (1994). Personality and cognitive ability predictors of performance in graduate business school. *Journal of Educational Psychology, 86*, 516–530.

Sackett, P. R., & Ellingson, J. E. (1997). The effects of forming multi-predictor composites on group differences and adverse impact. *Personnel Psychology, 50*, 707–721.

Salovey, P., & Mayer, J. D. (1990). Emotional intelligence. *Imagination, Cognition, and Personality, 9*, 185–211.

Schmidt, F. L. (1988). The problem of group differences in ability test scores in employment selection. *Journal of Vocational Behavior, 33*, 272–292.

Schmidt, F. L. (1993). Personnel psychology at the cutting edge. In N. Schmitt & W. Borman (Eds.), *Personnel selection* (pp. 497–515). San Francisco: Jossey-Bass.

Schmidt, F. L., Greenthal, A. L., Hunter, J. E., Berner, J. G., & Seaton, F. W. (1977). Job sample vs. paper-and-pencil trades and technical tests: Adverse impact and examinee attitudes. *Personnel Psychology, 30*, 187–197.

Schmidt, F. L., & Hunter, J. E. (1998). The validity and utility of selection methods in personnel psychology: Practical and theoretical implications of 85 years of research findings. *Psychological Bulletin, 124*, 262–274.

Schmit, M. J., Ryan, A. M., Stierwalter, S. L., & Powell, A. B. (1995). Frame of reference effects on personality scale scores and criterion related validity. *Journal of Applied Psychology, 80*, 607–620.

Schmitt, N., Clause, C. S., & Pulakos, E. D. (1996). Subgroup differences associated with different measures of some common job-relevant constructs. In C. L. Cooper & I. T. Robertson (Eds.), *International review of industrial and organizational psychology* (Vol. 11, pp. 115–139). New York: Wiley.

Schneider, B., Smith, D. B., & Sipe, W. P. (2000). Personnel selection psychology: Multilevel considerations. In K. J. Klein & S. J. Kozlowski (Eds.), *Multilevel theory, research, and methods in organizations: Foundations, extensions, and new directions* (pp. 91-120). San Francisco: Jossey-Bass.

Spearman, C. (1927). *The abilities of man: Their nature and measurement.* New York: Macmillan.

Sternberg, R. J. (1985). *Beyond IQ: Practical intelligence and people skills.* New York: Cambridge University Press.

Sternberg, R. J., Wagner, R. K., Williams, W. M., & Horvath, J. A. (1995). Testing common sense. *American Psychologist, 50,* 912–927.

Sweller, J. (1988). Cognitive load during problem solving: Effects on learning. *Cognitive Science, 12,* 257–285.

Sweller, J. (1989). Cognitive technology: Some procedures for facilitating learning and problem solving in mathematics and science. *Journal of Educational Psychology, 81,* 457–466.

Tett, R. P., Jackson, D. N., & Rothstein, M. (1991). Personality measures as predictors of job performance: A meta-analytic review. *Personnel Psychology, 44,* 703–742.

Thayer, P. W. (1992). Construct validation: Do we understand our criteria? *Human Performance, 5,* 97–108.

Tupes, E. C., & Cristal, R. E. (1992). Recurrent personality factors based on trait ratings (USAF ASD Tech. Rep. No. 61–97). Lackland Air Force Base, TX: U.S. Air Force. (Original work published 1961)

Vroom, V. H. (1964). *Work and motivation.* New York: Wiley.

Wagner, J. A., & Hollenbeck, J. R. (1998). *Organizational behavior: Securing competitive advantage.* Upper Saddle River, NJ: Prentice Hall.

Zedeck, S., Outtz, J., Cascio, W. F., & Goldstein, I. L. (1991). Why do "testing experts" have such limited vision? *Human Performance, 4,* 297–308.

HUMAN PERFORMANCE, *15*(1/2), 143–160

Practical Intelligence, g, and Work Psychology

Robert J. Sternberg and Jennifer Hedlund
Department of Psychology
Yale University

Intelligence has been the most widely studied and controversial factor used to explain individual differences in job performance. The controversy stems not so much from the validity of some kind of g—the evidence in support of some kind of g is impressive—but from the perspective that g is the best or even the only indicator of human abilities. Although g is a fairly consistent predictor of performance, it is far from the sole determinant of performance. There are many other factors that influence performance, such as personality and motivational constructs, that should be considered in addition to g. But perhaps more important, g represents a limited conceptualization of intelligence. This article focuses on the concept of practical intelligence, which reflects a broader conceptualization of the abilities needed for real-world success. We review research on tacit knowledge as an aspect of practical intelligence and consider the implications that practical intelligence has for work psychology.

The concept of intelligence traditionally has been viewed as integral to successful performance because it represents the ability to adapt effectively to the environment and to learn from experience (Neisser et al., 1996). g is the most widely studied and validated predictor of performance in employment and educational settings (Brody, 2000; Schmidt & Hunter, 1998). It has been suggested that g becomes even more important to job performance as the nature of work becomes increasingly complex and unpredictable (Gottfredson, 1997; Snow & Snell, 1993). The important controversy surrounding g stems not from the evidence regarding its validity, but from the fact that there are different views about what intelligence is and how it should be measured. Rather than rehashing the familiar arguments surrounding g, we briefly summarize the main points before presenting an alternative approach to conceptualizing and measuring intelligence.

Requests for reprints should be sent to Robert J. Sternberg, Department of Psychology, Yale University, PO Box 208205, New Haven, CT 06520–8205.

The traditional view (Brand, 1996; Jensen, 1998; Ree & Earle, 1993; Schmidt & Hunter, 1998; Spearman, 1927) is that many of the competencies needed for success can be viewed as originating with one latent factor—general intelligence (or ability). Sometimes g is studied in its own right, and other times as a construct at the top of a hierarchy of ability constructs (e.g., Carroll, 1993; Cattell, 1971; Gustafsson, 1984; see also Sternberg & Grigorenko, in press). So-called general cognitive ability (g) is considered by many to be the best single basis for selecting individuals because it is well established as a valid predictor of performance and learning across a variety of jobs (Schmidt & Hunter, 1998). It is by far the most widely studied predictor used in personnel decisions.

Although g may be a valid predictor of performance in many jobs, there are several limitations and controversies surrounding g that warrant further efforts to understand job performance and how to predict it. First, validity estimates for so-called general mental ability (i.e., intelligence or g) indicate that (after correction for attenuation and restriction of range) g accounts for 20% to 25% of the variance in performance, leaving as much as 75% to 80% unexplained (Schmidt & Hunter, 1998). Second, intelligence tests often exhibit differences of more than one standard deviation between various subgroups, most notably, between blacks and whites (Hartigan & Wigdor, 1989; Neisser et al., 1996). Third, questions on intelligence tests often have little to do with the problems individuals encounter in real life (Neisser, 1976; Wagner & Sternberg, 1986). Therefore, intelligence tests may not accurately reflect all that an individual is capable of doing on the job. Fourth, intelligence tests are based on the assumption that g is a relatively stable trait that predicts performance fairly consistently over time and across domains. However, there is increasing evidence that performance on intelligence tests varies across contexts (e.g., Ceci & Roazzi, 1994; Serpell, 2000) and can be modified (e.g., Grotzer & Perkins, 2000; Nickerson et al., 1985; Perkins & Grotzer, 1997). Finally, Schmidt and Hunter (1998) argued that g has the strongest theoretical foundation and the clearest meaning of any predictor. Other researchers (e.g., Brody, 2000; Neisser et al., 1996; Sternberg, 1999) have argued, however, that there is no clear agreement on what intelligence tests measure psychologically or even on what g represents at a psychological level.

Many people—researchers and laypersons alike—agree that there is more to intelligent performance than what is measured by a standard IQ test (Sternberg, 1985; Sternberg, Conway, Ketron, & Bernstein, 1981; Sternberg & Kaufman, 1998; Yang & Sternberg, 1997). Recent theories reflect those views, identifying concepts such as interpersonal and intrapersonal intelligence (Gardner, 1983, 1993), emotional intelligence (Goleman, 1995, 1998; Mayer, Salovey, & Caruso, 2000), and creative and practical intelligence (Sternberg, 1985, 1997, 1999). These broader conceptualizations of intelligence recognize that individuals have different strengths and that these strengths may not be identified through traditional approaches to measuring intelligence. Practical intelligence provides the basis for one such approach.

Practical intelligence is defined as the ability that individuals use to find a more optimal fit between themselves and the demands of the environment through adapting to the environment, shaping (or modifying) the environment, or selecting a new environment in the pursuit of personally-valued goals (Sternberg, 1985, 1997, 1999). It can be characterized as "street smarts" or "common sense" and can be contrasted with academic intelligence or "book smarts." Practical intelligence encompasses the abilities one needs to succeed in everyday life, including in one's job or one's career. In this article, we review theoretical and empirical support for the construct of practical intelligence and consider its implications for work psychology.

PRACTICAL INTELLIGENCE AND TACIT KNOWLEDGE

Sternberg and his colleagues (see Sternberg et al., 2000; Sternberg & Wagner, 1993; Sternberg, Wagner, & Okagaki, 1993; Sternberg, Wagner, Williams, & Horvath, 1995; Wagner, 1987; Wagner & Sternberg, 1985) have taken a knowledge-based approach to understanding practical intelligence. Individuals draw on a broad base of knowledge in solving practical problems, some of which is acquired through formal training and some of which is derived from personal experience. Much of the knowledge associated with successful problem solving can be characterized as tacit. It is knowledge that typically is not openly expressed or stated—it is acquired largely through personal experience and guides action without being readily articulated.

The term *tacit knowledge* has roots in works on the philosophy of science (Polanyi, 1966), ecological psychology (Neisser, 1976), and organizational behavior (Schön, 1983) and has been used to characterize the knowledge gained from everyday experience that has an implicit, unarticulated quality. Such notions about the tacit quality of the knowledge associated with everyday problem solving also are reflected in the common language of the workplace as people attribute successful performance to "learning by doing" and to "professional intuition" or "instinct."

Research on expert knowledge is consistent with this conceptualization. Experts draw on a well-developed repertoire of knowledge in responding to problems in their respective domains (Scribner, 1986). This knowledge tends to be procedural in nature and to operate outside of focal awareness (see Chi, Glaser, & Farr, 1988). It also reflects the structure of the situation more closely than it does the structure of formal, disciplinary knowledge (Groen & Patel, 1988).

Sternberg and his colleagues (Sternberg, 1997; Sternberg et al., 2000; Sternberg & Horvath, 1999; Wagner & Sternberg, 1985) view tacit knowledge as an important aspect of practical intelligence that enables individuals to adapt to, select, and shape real-world environments. It is knowledge that reflects the practical ability to learn from experience and to apply that knowledge in pursuit of personally valued goals. Research by Sternberg and his colleagues (see, e.g., Sternberg et al., 2000;

Sternberg et al., 1993; Sternberg et al., 1995) showed that tacit knowledge has relevance for understanding successful performance in a variety of domains. The conceptualization and measurement of tacit knowledge are described later, followed by a review of the relevant research on tacit knowledge and practical intelligence.

The Conceptualization of Tacit Knowledge

Tacit knowledge is conceptualized by Sternberg and his colleagues (Sternberg, 1997; Sternberg et al., 2000; Sternberg & Horvath, 1999; Sternberg et al., 1995) according to three main features, which correspond to the conditions under which it is acquired, its structural representation, and the conditions of its use.

First, tacit knowledge is viewed as knowledge that generally is acquired with little support from other people or resources. In other words, the individual is not directly instructed as to what he or she should learn, but rather must extract the important lesson from the experience even when learning is not the primary objective. Formal training environments facilitate certain knowledge-acquisition processes. These processes include selective encoding (sorting relevant from irrelevant information in the environment), selective combination (integrating information into a meaningful interpretation of the situation), and selective comparison (relating new information to existing knowledge; Sternberg, 1988). When these processes are not well supported, as often is the case in learning from everyday experiences, the likelihood increases that some individuals will fail to acquire the knowledge. It also means that the knowledge will tend to remain unspoken, underemphasized, and poorly conveyed relative to its importance.

Second, tacit knowledge is viewed as procedural in nature. It is knowledge about how to perform various tasks in various situations. Drawing on Anderson's (1983) distinction between procedural and declarative knowledge, tacit knowledge can be considered a subset of procedural knowledge that is drawn from personal experience. And as is the case with much procedural knowledge, it tends to guide action without being easily articulated (Anderson, 1983). Part of the difficulty in articulating tacit knowledge is that it typically reflects a set of complex, multicondition rules (production systems) for how to pursue particular goals in particular situations (e.g., rules about how to judge people accurately for a variety of purposes and under a variety of circumstances). These complex rules can be represented in the form of condition–action pairings. For example, knowledge about confronting one's superior might be represented in a form with a compound condition:

IF <you are in a public forum>
   AND
   IF <the boss says something or does something that you perceive is wrong or inappropriate >
   AND

IF <the boss does not ask for questions or comments>

THEN <speak directly to the point of contention and do not make evaluative statements about your boss>

BECAUSE <this saves the boss from embarrassment and preserves your relationship with him.>

In other words, tacit knowledge is more than a set of abstract procedural rules. It is context-specific knowledge about what to do in a given situation or class of situations. As discussed later, this representation serves as the basis of our approach to measuring tacit knowledge.

The third characteristic feature of tacit knowledge is that it has direct relevance to the individual's goals. Knowledge that is based on one's own practical experience will likely be more instrumental to achieving one's goals than will be knowledge that is based on someone else's experience or that is overly generic. For example, leaders may be instructed on what leadership approach (e.g., authoritative vs. participative) is supposed to be most appropriate in a given situation, but they may learn from their own experiences that some other approach is more effective in that situation.

In describing tacit knowledge, it is also helpful to clarify that we do not equate tacit knowledge with job knowledge (see, e.g., Schmidt & Hunter, 1993). Rather, we view the two as overlapping concepts. Job knowledge includes both declarative and procedural knowledge, and only some procedural knowledge can be characterized as tacit. Tacit knowledge represents a component of procedural knowledge that is used to solve practical, everyday problems, but that is not readily articulated or openly conveyed.

The Measurement of Tacit Knowledge

Because people often find it difficult to articulate their tacit knowledge, we measure tacit knowledge in the responses individuals provide to practical situations or problems, particularly those situations in which experience-based tacit knowledge is expected to provide an advantage. The measurement instruments used to assess tacit knowledge typically consist of a series of situations and associated response options, which have been characterized in the literature as situational judgment tests (SJTs; Chan & Schmitt, 1998; Legree, 1995; Motowidlo, Dunnette, & Carter, 1990). These types of tests generally are used to measure interpersonal and problem-solving skills (Hanson & Ramos, 1996; Motowidlo et al., 1990) or behavioral intentions (Weekley & Jones, 1997). In a SJT or tacit-knowledge (TK) test, each question presents a problem relevant to the domain of interest (e.g., a manager intervening in a dispute between two subordinates) followed by a set of options (i.e., strategies) for solving the problem (e.g., meet with the two subordinates individually to find out their perspective on the problem; hold a meeting with both subordinates and have them air their grievances). Respondents are asked either to choose the best and worst alternatives from among a few options, or to rate on a Likert-type scale the quality or appropriateness of several potential responses to the situation.

The development of TK tests, like many SJTs, begins with the identification of critical incidents in the workplace (Flanagan, 1954). Individuals are asked to provide accounts of incidents from which they learned an important lesson about how to perform their job that was not something they had been taught in school or about which they had read in a textbook or manual. In other words, situations in which tacit knowledge is relevant are those for which the best response cannot be drawn from knowledge of explicit procedural rules. In fact, the best response may even contradict formal, explicit knowledge. The stories and the lessons learned from them are used to develop situational descriptions along with a set of possible responses. A TK test may consist of several situational descriptions, each followed by multiple response options, which vary in their appropriateness. A sample question from the Tacit Knowledge Inventory for Military Leaders (see Hedlund et al., 1998) is shown in the Appendix.

TK tests have been scored in one of four ways: (a) by correlating participants' ratings with an index of group membership (i.e., expert, intermediate, novice), (b) by judging the degree to which participants' responses conform to professional "rules of thumb," (c) by computing a profile match or difference score between participants' ratings and an expert prototype, or (d) on a theory-determined basis. Scores on TK tests have been evaluated relative to various indicators of performance, measures of g, experience, and other predictors (e.g., personality).

RESEARCH ON TACIT KNOWLEDGE

Sternberg and his colleagues (e.g., Sternberg et al., 2000; Sternberg et al., 1993; Sternberg et al., 1995; Wagner, 1987; Wagner & Sternberg, 1985; Wagner, Sujan, Sujan, Rashotte, & Sternberg, 1999) have used TK tests to study academic psychologists, salespersons, high school and college students, civilian managers, and military leaders, among people in other occupations. As yet unpublished research has also looked at elementary school teachers, principals, and individuals in roughly 50 varied occupations in the United States and Spain. We summarize here some of the findings from the research to date in regard to the relation of tacit knowledge with experience, g, personality, and performance.

Tacit Knowledge and Experience

The common phrase "experience is the best teacher" reflects the view that experience provides opportunities to develop important knowledge and skills related to performance. Several meta-analytic reviews indicate that the estimated mean population correlation between experience and job performance falls in the range of .18 to .32 (Hunter & Hunter, 1984; McDaniel, Schmidt, & Hunter, 1988; Quinones, Ford, & Teachout, 1995). Additional research suggests that this relation is mediated largely by the direct effect of experience on the acquisition of job knowledge (Borman, Hanson, Oppler, & Pulakos, 1993; Schmidt, Hunter, & Outerbridge, 1986).

Consistent with this research, Sternberg and his colleagues (Sternberg et al., 2000; Wagner, 1987; Wagner & Sternberg, 1985; Wagner et al., 1999) have found that tacit knowledge generally increases with experience. Wagner and Sternberg (1985) found a significant correlation between tacit knowledge scores of 54 business managers and the manager's level within the company, $r(54) = .34$, $p < .05$, and years of schooling, $r(54) = .41$, $p < .01$. In a follow-up study with 49 business professionals, Wagner (1987) found significant correlations between tacit knowledge scores and years of management experience, $r(49) = .30$, $p < .05$. He also found mean differences in tacit knowledge scores for groups of business managers, business graduate students, and general undergraduates, with the managers exhibiting the highest mean score. Comparable results were found for a TK test for academic psychologists when comparing psychology professors, psychology graduate students, and undergraduates.

In another study involving managers, Grigorenka and Sternberg (2001) studied predictors of adult physical and mental health among adults in Russia. In particular, they looked at the predictor power of analytical and practical intelligence. They found that, although both analytical and practical intelligence were predictive of both physical and mental health, practical intelligence was the better predictor. In a study with salespeople, however, tacit knowledge scores correlated significantly both with the number of years of sales experience, $r(45) = .31$, $p < .01$, and the number of years with the company, $r(45) = .37$, $p < .01$ (Wagner et al., 1999). Finally, research with three levels of military leaders found that tacit knowledge scores did not correlate with the number of months leaders had served in their current positions (see Sternberg et al., 2000), but did correlate significantly with leadership rank for two versions of the TK test for military leaders, $r(42) = .44$, $p < .01$, and $r(37) = .41$, $p < .05$, with leaders at higher levels of command exhibiting better scores than those at lower ranks (Hedlund, Sternberg, & Psotka, 2000). These findings suggest that rank may be a better indicator of experience than the time spent in any given position. In fact, a number of researchers (e.g., Tesluk & Jacobs, 1998) have begun to question the value of purely quantitative measures of experience. What matters is not so much experience, but rather what one learns from that experience.

The research evidence to date generally supports the claim that tacit knowledge is related to experience. The correlations, however, tend to be moderate, falling in the range of .20 to .40, and suggest that although tacit knowledge has some basis in experience, it is not simply a proxy for experience.

Tacit Knowledge and *g*

g is considered by many to be the best single predictor of job performance (e.g., Hunter, 1986; Ree, Earle, & Teachout, 1994; Schmidt & Hunter, 1998). The relation between *g* and performance is attributed largely to the direct influence of *g* on the acquisition of job-related knowledge (Borman et al., 1993; Hunter, 1986; Schmidt et al., 1986). Many job-knowledge tests, however, assess primarily declarative knowledge of facts and rules (McCloy, Campbell, & Cudneck, 1994). They consist of abstract, well-defined problems that are similar to the types of problems found on traditional intelligence tests, thus explaining the observed correlations between measures of job knowledge and cognitive ability tests. TK tests, however, consist of problems that are poorly defined and context-rich. We consider performance on these tests to be a function of practical rather than of abstract, general intelligence.

In the research reviewed here, TK tests exhibit trivial to moderate correlations with measures of *g*. In a sample of undergraduate students, scores on a test of verbal reasoning correlated nonsignificantly with scores on TK tests for academic psychologists, $r(29) = -.04, p > .05$, and a TK test for managers, $r(22) = .16, p > .05$ (Wagner, 1987; Wagner & Sternberg, 1985). Similarly, in a sample of business executives, scores on a TK test for managers exhibited a nonsignificant correlation, $r(45) = .14, p > .05$, with scores on a verbal reasoning test (Wagner & Sternberg, 1990). Scores on the verbal reasoning test also did not correlate with scores on a TK test for sales in samples of undergraduates and salespeople (Wagner et al., 1999). Further support comes from a study by Eddy (1988), in which the Armed Services Vocational Aptitude Battery (ASVAB) was administered along with a TK test for managers to a sample of 631 Air Force recruits. Scores on the TK test exhibited near-zero correlations (.00 to .10) with four factors on the ASVAB (vocational–technical information, clerical and speed, verbal ability, and mathematics).

Some studies have found significant correlations between *g* and tacit knowledge, but these relations are not always in the positive direction. In research with military leaders, leaders at three levels of command completed Terman's (1950) Concept Mastery Test along with a TK test for their respective level. Tacit knowledge scores exhibited correlations ranging from trivial and nonsignificant, $r(344) = .02, p > .05$, to moderate and significant, $r(157) = .25, p < .01$, with verbal reasoning ability (Sternberg et al., 2000). However, in one study conducted in Kenya, tacit knowledge scores actually correlated negatively with scores on tests of *g*, suggesting that, in certain environments, development of practical skills may be emphasized at the expense of development of academic skills (Sternberg, Nokes et al., 2001). Such environments are not limited to rural Kenya: Artists, musicians, athletes, and craftsmen all may decide that development of skills other than those taught in school may hold more value to them than do the more academic skills.

Over several studies, the evidence suggests that TK tests measure abilities that are distinct from those assessed by traditional intelligence tests. Even when significant correlations are observed, they tend only to be moderate. Additional research, which we discuss later, shows that TK tests measure something unique beyond g.

Tacit Knowledge and Criteria

In general, job knowledge tests have been found to predict performance fairly consistently, with an average corrected validity of .48 (Schmidt & Hunter, 1998). As indicated earlier, much of this prediction is attributed to the relation between job knowledge and g (Borman et al., 1993; Hunter, 1986). In other words, people with high g are expected to gain more knowledge and thus perform more effectively. TK tests also are expected to predict performance. Simply put, individuals who learn the important lessons of experience are more likely to be successful. However, because tacit knowledge is a form of practical intelligence, it is expected to explain aspects of performance that are not accounted for by tests of g.

TK tests have been found to predict performance in a number of domains and using a number of criteria. In studies with business managers, tacit knowledge scores correlated with criteria such as salary, $r(54) = .46, p < .01$, and whether the manager worked for a company at the top of the Fortune 500 list, $r(54) = .34, p < .05$ (Wagner & Sternberg, 1985; see also Wagner, 1987). These correlations, unlike those reported by Schmidt and Hunter (1998), are uncorrected for either attenuation or restriction of range. In a study with bank managers, Wagner and Sternberg (1985) obtained significant correlations between tacit knowledge scores and average percentage of merit-based salary increase, $r(22) = .48, p < .05.$, and average performance rating for the category of generating new business for the bank, $r(13) = .56, p < .05$. We are not the only ones to have found correlations between practical intelligence and measure of job success. A study in Brazil yielded similar findings. Colonia-Willner (1998) administered the Tacit Knowledge Inventory for Managers (TKIM; Wagner & Sternberg, 1991) to bank managers along with measures of psychometric and verbal reasoning. She found that scores on the TKIM significantly predicted an index of managerial skill, whereas psychometric and verbal reasoning did not.

Although much of the tacit knowledge research has involved business managers, there is evidence that tacit knowledge explains performance in other domains. In the field of academic psychology, correlations were found between tacit knowledge scores and criterion measures such as citation rate, $r(59) = .44, p < .01$; number of publications, $r(59) = .28, p < .05$; and quality of department, $r(77) = .48, p < .01$ (Wagner, 1987; see also Wagner & Sternberg, 1985). Sternberg, Wagner, and Okagaki (1993) found that the tacit knowledge of salespeople correlated with criteria such as sales volume, $r(39) = .28, p < .05$, and sales awards received, $r(45) = .32, p < .01$. In parallel studies conducted in the United States and Spain using a single measure of general tacit knowledge for people in roughly 50 diverse occupations, correlations with various ratings of job performance were at the .2 level in Spain ($N = 227$) and at the .4 level in the United States ($N = 230$; Grigorenko, Gil, Jarvin, & Sternberg, 2000).

Two studies showed the incremental validity of TK tests over traditional intelligence tests in predicting performance. In a study with business executives attending a Leadership Development Program at the Center for Creative Leadership, Wagner and Sternberg (1990) found that scores on a TK test for managers correlated significantly with performance on a managerial simulation, $r(45) = .61, p < .01$. Furthermore, tacit knowledge scores explained 32% of the variance in performance beyond scores on a traditional IQ test and also explained variance beyond measures of personality and cognitive style. In a study with military leaders, scores on a TK test for military leaders correlated significantly with ratings of leadership effectiveness made by subordinates, peers, or superiors. The correlations ranged from $r(353) = .14, p < .05$, for platoon leaders; to $r(163) = .19, p < .05$, for company commanders; to $r(31) = .42, p < .05$, for battalion commanders (see Sternberg et al., 2000). More important, tacit knowledge scores accounted for small (4%–6%) but significant variance in leadership effectiveness beyond scores on tests of general verbal intelligence and tacit knowledge for managers. These studies provide evidence that tacit knowledge accounts for variance in performance that is not accounted for by traditional tests of abstract, academic intelligence.

There is fairly strong evidence to suggest that TK tests not only explain individual differences in performance, but also measure an aspect of performance that is not explained by measures of general intelligence. We consider that aspect to represent practical intelligence.

Additional Findings Regarding Tacit Knowledge

Research on tacit knowledge has also addressed the relation between tacit knowledge and personality, the relations among different tests of tacit knowledge, differences in tacit knowledge scores across cultures, and differences in tacit knowledge scores across gender and racial groups. We briefly address those findings here.

First, Wagner and Sternberg (1990) found that tacit knowledge scores generally exhibited nonsignificant correlations with several personality-type tests, including the California Psychological Inventory, the Myers-Briggs Type Indicator, and the Fundamental Interpersonal Relations Orientation–Behavior (FIRO–B) given to a sample of business executives. The exceptions were that tacit knowledge scores correlated with the Social Presence factor of the California Psychological Inventory, $r(45) = .29, p < .05$, and the Control Expressed factor of the FIRO–B, $r(45) = .25, p < .05$. In hierarchical regression analyses, tacit knowledge scores consistently accounted for significant increments in variance beyond the personality measures. These findings suggest that measures of tacit knowledge are distinct from personality measures.

Second, tacit knowledge measures tend to correlate among themselves and to show a general factor among themselves (Grigorenko, Jarvin , & Sternberg,in press; Sternberg et al., 2000; Wagner, 1987) that is distinct from the general factor of tests of general ability. In one study, 60 undergraduates completed both a TK test for academic psychologists and a TK test for business managers; their scores on the two tests correlated .58 ($p < .01$; Wagner, 1987).

Third, tacit knowledge measures have been found, in at least one instance, to yield similar results across cultures. Patterns of preferences for the quality of responses to a tacit knowledge measure for the workplace were compared between workers in the United States and Spain. The correlation between the mean profiles for the two groups across 240 responses was .91 (Grigorenko, Gil, Jarvin & Sternberg, 2000).

Finally, traditional intelligence tests often are found to exhibit group differences in scores as a function of gender and race (for reviews, see Loehlin, 2000; Neisser et al., 1996). TK tests, because they are not restricted to knowledge or abilities developed in school, may be less susceptible to these differences. In Eddy's (1988) study of Air Force recruits, comparable levels of performance on the TK test were found among majority and minority group members and among men and women as indicated by nonsignificant correlations between tacit knowledge and dummy coded variables representing race (.03) and gender (.02). Significant correlations were found between scores on the ASVAB subtests and dummy variables for race and gender, ranging from .2 to .4. Therefore, there is some indication that TK tests do not exhibit the same group differences found on traditional intelligence tests.

The research reviewed earlier spans more than 15 years and lends support to several assertions regarding tacit knowledge. First, tacit knowledge generally increases with experience. Second, tacit knowledge is distinct from general intelligence and personality traits. Third, TK tests predict performance in several domains and do so beyond tests of general intelligence. Fourth, practical intelligence may have a substantial amount of generality that is distinct from the generality of psychometric g. Finally, scores on TK tests appear to be comparable across racial and gender groups. Thus, TK tests have the potential to contribute to our understanding of the competencies needed for real-world success and to address some of the limitations associated with traditional intelligence tests. TK tests represent one approach to measuring practical intelligence. Additional approaches to measuring practical intelligence, which we briefly review later, generally have met with similar success.

ADDITIONAL APPROACHES
TO MEASURING PRACTICAL ABILITIES

Efforts to measure practical abilities in the workplace date back nearly 50 years (Frederiksen, Saunders, & Wand, 1957). In-basket tests were designed to assess an individual's ability to deal with job-related tasks under some of the same constraints (e.g., deadlines) found on the actual job (Frederiksen, 1966; Frederiksen et al., 1957). Assessment centers also are used to observe an individual's performance in situations that have been created to represent aspects of the actual job situation. Assessment centers typically present small groups of individuals with a variety of tasks, including in-basket tests, simulated interviews, and simulated group discussions (Bray, 1982; Thornton & Byham, 1982). Responses to these simulations are considered to represent the actual, or close approximations of, responses that individuals would exhibit in real situations. Although it is difficult to evaluate the validity of assessment centers because they represent a combination of factors, Schmidt and Hunter (1998) reported that work sample tests, in general, actually have higher average validities than do general ability tests. In other words, there is evidence to suggest that measures intended to reflect actual job performance more closely may be more valid than measures of *g*.

Several researchers have explicitly used SJTs as measures of practical intelligence (e.g., Chan & Schmitt, 1998; Fox & Spector, 2000; Pulakos, Schmitt, & Chan, 1996). SJTs, as mentioned earlier, present written descriptions of situations that represent actual situations or approximations of actual situations in the domain of interest (e.g., a salesperson making a phone solicitation). Respondents are asked to indicate their endorsement of the options, either by selecting the best and possibly the worst from among a few strategies, or rating the effectiveness of each alternative.

Fox and Spector (2000) administered a SJT to undergraduate students participating in a simulated interview. The students were asked to select the response they would most likely or least likely take to several work-related situations. They found that practical intelligence significantly predicted evaluations of the interviewee's qualifications. They also found that scores on the practical-intelligence test exhibited a moderate, significant correlation (.25) with a measure of general intelligence. Pulakos et al. (1996), using a SJT specifically designed for entry-level professionals in a federal investigative agency, found that practical intelligence predicted both peer and supervisory ratings of performance. Furthermore, the effects of practical intelligence were not accounted for by *g*. Overall, Chan and Schmitt (1998) reported that SJTs tend to correlate with performance ratings for various jobs in the range of .13 to .37.

Another promising direction in measuring practical intelligence involves the assessment of an individual's potential for acquiring tacit knowledge. In a study by Okagaki, Sternberg, and Wagner (cited in Sternberg et al., 1993), participants were given different cues to help them acquire tacit knowledge. The participants were assigned to one of five conditions—two control and three experimental conditions. In all conditions, the participants were given a pretest and posttest of a TK test for salespeople. In addition, in some conditions participants completed a tacit knowledge acquisition task in which they took the role of a human resources manager whose job was to read the transcripts of three job interviews and evaluate the candidates for a sales position in the company.

In the first control group, participants completed the pretests and posttests without intervention. In the second control group, participants were given a tacit knowledge acquisition task without any cues. In the first experimental group, participants were given the task with cues to help them to selectively encode. Specifically, relevant information was highlighted and a relevant rule of thumb provided. In the second experimental group, participants were given the task with cues to aid selective combination. Relevant information was highlighted, a rule of thumb was provided, and a note-taking sheet was given to help participants combine the information. In the third experimental group, participants were given the acquisition task with selective comparison cues. Again, relevant information was highlighted and a rule of thumb provided, but, in addition, participants were given an evaluation of the situation made by a previous salesperson.

Sternberg, Wagner, & Okagaki, (1993) found that for participants who completed the acquisition task, those in the control group (with no cues) performed the worst in terms of their accuracy in identifying relevant information from the transcripts. Among the experimental groups, the selective-combination group performed the best. In terms of pretest–posttest difference scores on the TK test, the control group with no task performed the worst. In the groups with the knowledge-acquisition task, the selective-encoding and selective-combination groups showed the most gain in test scores. The selective-comparison cueing did not have an effect on scores. These findings suggest that prompting individuals to selectively encode and selectively combine information can enhance the acquisition of tacit knowledge, and that effective use of these processes may provide valuable insight into an individual's practical abilities.

DIRECTIONS FOR FUTURE RESEARCH

There is substantial evidence so far to suggest that practical intelligence provides a valuable direction for research. There are many issues that deserve further attention. Research is needed to help clarify the relation between experience and tacit knowledge. Following from emerging research on the developmental challenges provided by jobs (McCauley, Ruderman, Ohlott, & Morrow, 1994; Tesluk & Jacobs, 1998), efforts might be aimed at identifying the types of experiences that lead to the acquisition of tacit knowledge. Research might also seek to better understand how individuals learn from their experiences and what factors predict how well an individual will learn on the job. We currently are working with MBA business students and military leaders to identify and measure the processes underlying the effective acquisition of tacit knowledge. Additional evidence regarding the incremental validity of tacit knowledge over existing selection tools, including *g*, personality, and general job knowledge, is needed to lend further support to the importance of tacit knowledge. Finally, direct comparisons of work sample, situational judgment, and TK tests would provide insight into what constructs these tests measure.

CONCLUSION

We believe that researchers interested in the field of work psychology may, at some level, be persisting in attempting to answer—over and over again—a question that already has been answered. The so-called general factor (*g*) successfully predicts performance in virtually all jobs (Schmidt & Hunter, 1998). We do not believe there are any dissenters to this view. The general factor is relevant to success in the real world, but it is not the only cognitive index that is relevant to such success. The issue is resolved, and it is not clear that further research will do anything more than to replicate what has already been replicated many times over. The issue of today is how psychologists can improve on the prediction provided by general ability. Are there measures that provide significant incremental validity over the measures of *g* and that provide additional theoretical insights as well? Evidence reviewed here from our own research program as well as research by others indicates that the answer is affirmative and can be found considering alternative constructs such as practical intelligence and the tacit knowledge underlying it.

ACKNOWLEDGMENTS

Preparation of this article was supported by the U.S. Army Research Institute (contracts MDA903–92–K and DASW01–98–M–2036). Although we are grateful to these agencies for their support, the ideas expressed in this paper are solely those of the authors and do not represent any official position or policy on the part of these agencies.

REFERENCES

Anderson, J. R. (1983). *The architecture of cognition.* Cambridge, MA: Harvard University Press.

Borman, W. C., Hanson, M. A., Oppler, S. H., & Pulakos, E. D. (1993). Role of supervisory experience in supervisory performance. *Journal of Applied Psychology, 78*, 443–449.

Brand, C. (1996). *The g factor: General intelligence and its implications.* Chichester, England: Wiley.

Bray, D. W. (1982). The Assessment Center and the study of lives. *American Psychologist, 37,* 180–189.

Brody, N. (2000). History of theories and measurements of intelligence. In R. J. Sternberg (Ed.), *Handbook of intelligence* (pp. 16–33). New York: Cambridge University Press.

Carroll, J. B. (1993). *Human cognitive abilities: A survey of factor-analytic studies.* New York: Cambridge University Press.

Cattell, R. B. (1971). *Abilities: Their structure, growth and action.* Boston: Houghton Mifflin.

Ceci, S. J., & Roazzi, A. (1994). The effects of context on cognition: Postcards from Brazil. In R. J. Sternberg & R. K. Wagner (Eds.), *Mind in context: Interactionist perspectives on human intelligence* (pp. 74–101). New York: Cambridge University Press.

Chan, D., & Schmitt, N. (1998). Video-based versus paper-and-pencil method of assessment in situational judgment tests: Subgroup differences in test performance and face validity perceptions. *Journal of Applied Psychology, 82,* 143–159.

Chi, M. T. H., Glaser, R., & Farr, M. J. (Eds.). (1988). *The nature of expertise.* Hillsdale, NJ: Lawrence Erlbaum Associates, Inc.

Colonia-Willner, R. (1998). Practical intelligence at work: Relationship between aging and cognitive efficiency among managers in a bank environment. *Psychology and Aging, 13,* 45–57.

Eddy, A. S. (1988). *The relationship between the Tacit Knowledge Inventory for Managers and the Armed Services Vocational Aptitude Battery.* Unpublished master's thesis, St. Mary's University, San Antonio, TX.

Flanagan, J. C. (1954). The critical incident technique. *Psychological Bulletin, 51,* 327–358.

Fox, S., & Spector, P. E. (2000). Relations of emotional intelligence, practical intelligence, general intelligence, and trait affectivity with interview outcomes: It's not all just 'G'. *Journal of Organizational Behavior, 21,* 203–220.

Frederiksen, N. (1966). Validation of a simulation technique. *Organizational Behavior and Human Performance, 1,* 87–109.

Frederiksen, N., Saunders, D. R., & Wand, B. (1957). The in-basket test. *Psychological Monographs, 71.*

Gardner, H. (1983). *Frames of mind: The theory of multiple intelligences.* New York: Basic Books.

Gardner, H. (1993). *Multiple intelligences: The theory in practice.* New York: Basic Books.

Goleman, D. (1995). *Emotional intelligence.* New York: Bantam.

Goleman, D. (1998). *Working with emotional intelligence.* New York: Bantam.

Gottfredson, L. S. (1997). Why g matters: The complexity of everyday life. *Intelligence, 24,* 79–132.

Grigorenko, E. L., Gil, G., Jarvin, L., & Sternberg, R. J. (2000). *Toward a validation of aspects of the theory of successful intelligence.* Manuscript submitted for publication.

Grigorenko, E. L., Jarvin, L., & Sternberg, R. J., (in press). *School-based tests of the triarchic theory of intelligence: Three settings, three samples, three syllabi.* Manuscript submitted for publication.

Grigorenko, E. L., & Sternberg, R. J. (2001). Analytical, creative and practical intelligence as predictors of self-reported adaptive functioning. A case study in Russia. *Intelligence, 79,* 7–72.

Groen, G. J., & Patel, V. L. (1988). The relationship between comprehension and reasoning in medical expertise. In M. T. H. Chi, R. Glaser, & M. Farr (Eds.), *The nature of expertise* (pp. 287–310). Hillsdale, NJ: Lawrence Erlbaum Associates, Inc.

Grotzer, T. A., & Perkins, D. A. (2000). Teaching of intelligence: A performance conception. In R. J. Sternberg (Ed.), *Handbook of intelligence* (pp. 492–515). New York: Cambridge University Press.

Gustafsson J. E. (1984). A unifying model for the structure of intellectual abilities. *Intelligence, 8,* 179–203.

Hanson, M. A., & Ramos, R. A. (1996). Situational judgment tests. In R. S. Barrett (Ed.), *Fair employment strategies in human resource management* (pp. 119–124). Westport, CT: Greenwood.

Hartigan, J. A., & Wigdor, A. K. (Eds.). (1989). *Fairness in employment testing: Validity generalization, minority issues, and the General Aptitude Test Battery.* Washington, DC: National Academy Press.

Hedlund, J., Horvath, J. A., Forsythe, G. B., Snook, S., Williams, W. M., Bullis, R. C., et al. (1998). *Tacit Knowledge in Military Leadership: Evidence of Construct Validity* (Tech. Rep. No. 1080). Alexandria, VA: U.S. Army Research Institute for the Behavioral and Social Sciences.

Hedlund, J., Sternberg, R. J., & Psotka, J. (2000). *Tacit knowledge for military leadership: Seeking insight into the acquisition and use of practical knowledge* (Tech. Rep. No. ARI TR 1105). Alexandria, VA: U.S. Army Research Institute.

Hunter, J. E. (1986). Cognitive ability, cognitive aptitudes, job knowledge, and job performance. *Journal of Vocational Behavior, 29,* 340–362.

Hunter, J. E., & Hunter, R. F. (1984). Validity and utility of alternative predictors of job performance. *Psychological Bulletin, 96,* 72–98.

Jensen, A. R. (1998). *The g factor: The science of mental ability.* Westport, CT: Greenwood.

Legree, P. J. (1995). Evidence for an oblique social intelligence factor established with a Likert-based testing procedure. *Intelligence, 21,* 247–266.

Loehlin, J. C. (2000). Group differences in intelligence. In R. J. Sternberg (Ed.), *Handbook of intelligence* (pp. 176–193). New York: Cambridge University Press.

Mayer, J. D., Salovey, P., & Caruso, D. (2000). Competing models of emotional intelligence. In R. J. Sternberg (Ed)., *Handbook of intelligence* (pp. 396–420). New York: Cambridge University Press.

McCauley, C. D., Ruderman, M. N., Ohlott, P. J., & Morrow, J. E. (1994). Assessing the developmental components of managerial jobs. *Journal of Applied Psychology, 79,* 544–560.

McCloy, R. A., Campbell, J. P., & Cudneck, R. (1994). A confirmatory test of a model of performance determinants. *Journal of Applied Psychology, 79,* 493–505.

McDaniel, M. A., Schmidt, F. L., & Hunter, J. E. (1988). Job experience correlates of job performance. *Journal of Applied Psychology, 73,* 327–330.

Motowidlo, S. J., Dunnette, M. D., & Carter, G. W. (1990). An alternative selection procedure: The low-fidelity simulation. *Journal of Applied Psychology, 75,* 640–647.

Neisser, U. (1976). *Cognition and reality.* San Francisco: Freeman.

Neisser, U., Boodo, G., Bouchard, T. J., Boykin, A. W., Brody, N., Ceci, S. J., et al. (1996). Intelligence: Knowns and unknowns. *American Psychologist, 51,* 77–101.

Nickerson, R. S., Perkins, D. N., & Smith, E. E. (1985). *The teaching of thinking.* Hillsdale, NJ: Lawrence Erlbaum Associates, Inc.

Perkins, D. N., & Grotzer, T. A. (1997). Teaching intelligence. *American Psychologist, 52,* 1125–1133.

Polanyi, M. (1966). *The tacit dimensions.* Garden City, NY: Doubleday.

Pulakos, E. D., Schmitt, N., & Chan, D. (1996). Models of job performance ratings: An examination of ratee race, ratee gender, and rater level effects. *Human Performance, 9,* 103–119.

Quinones, M. A., Ford, J. K., & Teachout, M. S. (1995). The relationship between work experience and job performance: A conceptual and meta-analytic review. *Personnel Psychology, 48,* 887–910.

Ree, M. J., & Earle, J. A. (1993). *g* is to psychology what carbon is to chemistry: A reply to Sternberg and Wagner, McClelland, and Calfee. *Current Directions in Psychological Science, 1,* 11–12.

Ree, M. J., Earle, J. A., & Teachout, M. S. (1994). Predicting job performance: Not much more than *g.* *Journal of Applied Psychology, 79,* 518–524.

Schmidt, F. L., & Hunter, J. E. (1993). Tacit knowledge, practical intelligence, general mental ability, and job knowledge. *Current Directions in Psychological Science, 2,* 8–9.

Schmidt, F. L., & Hunter, J. E. (1998). The validity and utility of selection methods in personnel psychology: Practical and theoretical implications of 85 years of research findings. *Psychological Bulletin, 124,* 262–274.

Schmidt, F. L., Hunter, J. E., & Outerbridge, A. N. (1986). The impact of job experience and ability on job knowledge, work sample performance, and supervisory ratings of job performance. *Journal of Applied Psychology, 71,* 432–439.

Schon, D. A. (1983). *The reflective practitioner: How professionals think in action.* New York: Basic Books.

Scribner, S. (1986). Thinking in action: Some characteristics of practical thought. In R. J. Sternberg & R. K. Wagner (Eds.), *Practical intelligence: Nature and origins of competence in the everyday world* (pp. 13–30). New York: Cambridge University Press.

Serpell, R. (2000). Intelligence and culture. In R. J. Sternberg (Ed.), *Handbook of intelligence* (pp. 549–580). New York: Cambridge University Press.

Snow, C. C., & Snell, S. A. (1993). Staffing as a strategy. In N. Schmitt & W. C. Borman (Eds.), *Personnel selection in organizations* (pp. 448–478). San Francisco: Jossey-Bass.

Spearman, C. (1927). *The abilities of man.* London: Macmillan.

Sternberg, R. J. (Ed.). (1985). *Beyond IQ: A triarchic theory of human intelligence.* New York: Cambridge University Press.

Sternberg, R. J. (1988). *The triarchic mind: A new theory of human intelligence.* New York: Penguin.

Sternberg, R. J. (1997). *Successful intelligence.* New York: Plume.

Sternberg, R. J. (1999). The theory of successful intelligence. *Review of General Psychology, 3,* 292–316.

Sternberg, R. J., Conway, B. E., Ketron, J. L., & Bernstein, M. (1981). People's conceptions of intelligence. *Journal of Personality and Social Psychology, 41,* 37–55.

Sternberg, R. J., Forsythe, G. B., Hedlund, J., Horvath, J. A., Wagner, R. K., Williams, W. M., et al. (2000). *Practical intelligence in everyday life.* New York: Cambridge University Press.

Sternberg, R. J., & Grigorenko, E. L. (Eds.). (in press). *How general is the general factor of intelligence.* Mahwah, NJ: Lawrence Erlbaum Associates, Inc.

Sternberg, R. J., & Horvath, J. A. (Eds.). (1999). *Tacit knowledge in professional practice.* Mahwah, NJ: Lawrence Erlbaum Associates, Inc.

Sternberg, R. J., & Kaufman, J. C. (1998). Human abilities. *Annual Review of Psychology, 49,* 479–502.

Sternberg, R. J., Nokes, K., Geissler, P. W., Prince, R., Okatcha, F., Bundy, D. A., & Grigorenko, E. L. (2001). The relationship between academic and practical intelligence: A case study in Kenya. *Intelligence, 29,* 401–404.

Sternberg, R. J., & Wagner, R. K. (1993). The *g*-ocentric view of intelligence and job performance is wrong. *Current Directions in Psychological Science, 2,* 1–4.

Sternberg, R. J., Wagner, R. K., & Okagaki, L. (1993). Practical intelligence: The nature and role of tacit knowledge in work and at school. In H. Reese & J. Puckett (Eds.), *Advances in lifespan development* (pp. 205–227). Hillsdale, NJ: Lawrence Erlbaum Associates, Inc.

Sternberg, R. J., Wagner, R. K., Williams, W. M., & Horvath, J. A. (1995). Testing common sense. *American Psychologist, 50,* 912–927.

Terman, L. M. (1950). *Concept Mastery Test.* New York: Psychological Corporation.

Tesluk, P. E., & Jacobs, R. R. (1998). Toward an integrated model of work experience. *Personnel Psychology, 51,* 321–355.

Thornton, G. C., & Byham, W. C. (1982). *Assessment centers and managerial performance.* New York: Academic.

Wagner, R. K. (1987). Tacit knowledge in everyday intelligent behavior. *Journal of Personality and Social Psychology, 52,* 1236–1247.

Wagner, R. K., & Sternberg, R. J. (1985). Practical intelligence in real-world pursuits: The role of tacit knowledge. *Journal of Personality and Social Psychology, 49,* 436–458.

Wagner, R. K., & Sternberg, R. J. (1986). Tacit knowledge and intelligence in the everyday world. In R. J. Sternberg & R. K. Wagner (Eds.), *Practical intelligence: Nature and origins of competence in the everyday world* (pp. 51–83). New York: Cambridge University Press.

Wagner, R. K., & Sternberg, R. J. (1990). Street smarts. In K. E. Clark & M. B. Clark (Eds.), *Measures of leadership* (pp. 493–504). West Orange, NJ: Leadership Library of America.

Wagner, R. K., & Sternberg, R. J. (1991). *Tacit knowledge inventory for managers.* San Antonio, TX: Psychological Corporation.

Wagner, R. K., Sujan, H., Sujan, M., Rashotte, C. A., & Sternberg, R. J. (1999). Tacit knowledge in sales. In R. J. Sternberg & J. A. Horvath (Eds.), *Tacit knowledge in professional practice* (pp. 155–182). Mahwah, NJ: Lawrence Erlbaum Associates, Inc.

Weekley, J. A., & Jones, C. (1997). Video-based situational testing. *Personnel Psychology, 50,* 25–49.

Williams, W. M., & Sternberg, R. J. (in press). *Success acts for managers.* Mahwah, NJ: Lawrence Erlbaum Associates, Inc.

Yang, S., & Sternberg, R. J. (1997). Taiwanese Chinese people's conceptions of intelligence. *Intelligence, 25,* 21–36.

APPENDIX
Sample Question From the Tacit Knowledge Inventory
for Military Leaders

1	2	3	4	5	6	7	8	9
Extremely Bad		Somewhat Bad		Neither Bad Nor Good		Somewhat Good		Extremely Good

You are a company commander, and your battalion commander is the type of person who seems always to "shoot the messenger"—he does not like to be surprised by bad news, and he tends to take his anger out on the person who brought him the bad news. You want to build a positive, professional relationship with your battalion commander. What should you do?

_____Speak to your battalion commander about his behavior and share your perception of it.

_____Attempt to keep the battalion commander "over-informed" by telling him what is occurring in your unit on a regular basis (e.g., daily or every other day).

_____Speak to the sergeant major and see if he or she is willing to try to influence the battalion commander.

_____Keep the battalion commander informed only on important issues, but don't bring up issues you don't have to discuss with him.

_____When you bring a problem to your battalion commander, bring a solution at the same time.

_____Disregard the battalion commander's behavior: continue to bring him news as you normally would.

_____Tell your battalion commander all of the good news you can, but try to shield him from hearing the bad news.

_____Tell the battalion commander as little as possible; deal with problems on your own if at all possible.

HUMAN PERFORMANCE, *15*(1/2), 161–171

The Role of Cognitive Ability Tests in Employment Selection

James L. Outtz
Outtz & Associates

Cognitive ability tests correlate with measures of job performance across many jobs. However, cognitive ability tests produce racial differences that are 3 to 5 times larger than other predictors—such as biodata, personality inventories, and the structured interview—that are valid predictors of job performance.

Given that (a) cognitive ability tests can be combined with other predictors such that adverse impact is reduced while overall validity is increased, and (b) alternative predictors with less adverse impact can produce validity coefficients comparable to those obtained with cognitive ability tests alone, sole reliance on cognitive ability tests when alternatives are available is unwarranted.

Tests designed to measure general mental ability have been used in employment selection for more than 80 years. Validation research over a similar period has shown that cognitive ability tests (CATs) correlate with measures of job performance across a large number of jobs. Meta-analytic estimates of the correlation between CATs and measures of job performance (usually supervisors' ratings) place the mean validity coefficient at .30 (Bobko, Roth, & Potosky, 1999; Schmitt, Rogers, Chan, Sheppard, & Jennings, 1997). Estimates of validity with corrections for attenuation result in a mean validity coefficient of .50. For purposes of this discussion, the uncorrected validity coefficient will be used because it reflects the operational use of the predictor.

The meta-analytic research clearly shows that CATs can be a useful tool in making employment decisions. There is little controversy on this point.

Requests for reprints should be sent to James L. Outtz, Outtz & Associates, 816 Connecticut Avenue, N. W., Washington, DC 20006.

THE CONTROVERSY SURROUNDING CATs

The controversy surrounding the use of CATs in employment selection arises from the fact that these tests produce large differences in the scores of racial groups (Hunter & Hunter, 1984; U.S. Employment Service, 1970).

As an example, CATs typically produce a standardized mean difference between African American and White applicants of one standard deviation (Hunter & Hunter, 1984). The mean difference between Hispanics and Whites is somewhat smaller, but nonetheless substantial (Pulakos & Schmitt, 1996). These differences typically result in substantial adverse impact.

Adverse impact is determined by comparing the selection ratio of minority applicants to that of nonminority applicants. Assume that an employer uses a CAT to make hiring decisions. Assume further that the test produces a 1 standard deviation difference between African American and White applicants. A subgroup difference of this magnitude would result in a selection ratio for African Americans that is approximately one-tenth of the selection ratio for Whites (Sackett & Ellingson, 1997). Put another way, if the employer hired 10 of every 100 White applicants, only one of every 100 African American applicants would be hired.

Let us limit the applicant pool to African Americans and Whites for purposes of illustration. Assume that there are 1,000 applicants, 30% of whom are African American. The selection ratios previously described would result in the hiring of 70 Whites, but only 3 African Americans.

This outcome produces controversy for a number of reasons. Before discussing them, it should be noted that adverse impact, even as severe as that previously described, does not, in and of itself, show that an employment test is "biased" or unfair. However, the severe adverse impact produced by CATs warrants close scrutiny of these tests to determine whether their use is justified or appropriate in a given employment situation. This is particularly true given that CATs produce much greater adverse impact than other selection devices—such as biodata, personality inventories, and structured interviews—that can reach comparable levels of validity (Huffcutt & Arthur, 1994; Schmitt et al., 1997).

The severe adverse impact produced by CATs makes them controversial because employers typically have multiple goals when making employment selection decisions (Pulakos & Schmitt, 1996). An employer obviously wants to hire the best applicants available. In addition, however, employers may want racial and gender diversity within their workforce. Furthermore, legal and regulatory statutes call for employers to provide racial, ethnic, and gender equity in terms of access to employment. Some employers believe that a diverse workforce can provide a competitive advantage, particularly in markets where the customer base is diverse.

The research literature regarding gains in utility associated with workforce diversity is sparse. The lack of research in this area is probably due to the fact that utility is typically defined in terms of worker productivity. This narrow conceptualization of utility does not address larger organizational goals and objectives that may go beyond the limited notion of worker productivity.

As an example, many public sector employers at both the state and federal levels give preference in hiring to applicants who are military veterans. That is, military veterans are given "extra points" in the selection process that typically put them ahead of other applicants in terms of the likelihood of being hired. Such policies are not based on the notion of increasing the utility of the selection process. In some instances, federal agencies have conducted studies that showed their veterans preference policies actually reduced the utility of valid selection devices. Nonetheless, public sector employers continue such policies because they serve the larger organizational goal of rewarding applicants who have given service to their country.

Similarly, it may be difficult to assess the utility of workforce diversity as long as the unit of measurement is limited to worker productivity. The dearth of empirical research regarding the utility of workforce diversity is likely to continue unless and until utility is defined more broadly. Use of the traditional definition of utility to assess workforce diversity also implies that an employer has the same discretion with regard to determining the diversity of its workforce as it has in choosing a selection device. This may not be the case.

Over a decade ago, researchers estimated that the number of racial and ethnic minority applicants entering the U.S. workforce would rise steadily throughout the 1990s (Offermann & Gowing, 1990). Johnson and Packer (1987) projected that a third of the new entrants into the workforce between the late 1980s and the year 2000 would be minority group members. These projections have been accurate. Therefore, workforce diversity is increasing, and will continue to increase, because minority groups make up an increasingly greater proportion of job applicants. Thus, the question of the utility of workforce diversity may be moot. That is, the critical question may be how to obtain the most productivity from a workforce that is and will become more diverse.

CATs have become even more controversial given the demographic changes in the applicant population that have taken place over the past two decades. Employers must find ways to meet their workforce needs by identifying a larger number of qualified workers from racial and ethnic minority groups. Sole reliance, or even substantial reliance, on CATs may not be the best method to achieve this goal.

Finally, CATs are controversial not just because they produce racial group differences, but because they produce racial differences that can be 10 times larger than racial group differences on measures of job performance. Schmitt et al. (1997) estimated that the effect size (i.e., standardized difference between subgroup means) for criterion performance for African Americans and Whites is .45. This is less than half the effect size of 1.0 for the difference between these same subgroups on CATs.

Moreover, Schmitt et al. (1997) may have overestimated the difference in criterion performance. Their estimate was based on a meta-analysis by Ford, Kraiger, and Schechtman (1986). Ford et al. found that the effect size depended to a large degree on what aspect of performance was being measured and the manner in which it was measured. Although objective and subjective criterion measures produced similar effect sizes overall, the largest effect sizes were produced by paper-and-pencil performance measures such as training tests and job knowledge tests. Smaller effect sizes were found for objective performance indicators such as units produced, shortages, accidents, and customer complaints.

Sackett and DuBois (1991) analyzed performance data from Kraiger and Ford (1985), together with data from a large-scale military study by Pulakos, Oppler, White, and Borman (1989), and a data set from a large-scale civilian study. The Pulakos et al. military data included ratings in three performance areas: technical skill and job effort, personal discipline, and military bearing. The civilian study was based on performance ratings for more than 36,000 individuals in 174 jobs representing 2,876 firms (Sackett & DuBois, 1991). Ratings from the civilian study were averaged across multiple performance dimensions to obtain ratings of overall performance.

One purpose of the Sackett and DuBois (1991) study was to address Black and White differences in performance ratings as a function of rater race. Table 1 shows the effect sizes for Black and White differences in performance ratings for all three data sets analyzed by Sackett and DuBois (1991). All of the effect sizes in Table 1 were corrected for unreliability of the ratings.

Table 1 shows that differences in the performance of Blacks and Whites were considerably smaller when the ratings were provided by Black raters. The direction of the difference was reversed for the Kraiger and Ford (1985) study indicating that Blacks received higher ratings than Whites when rated by Blacks. Sackett and DuBois (1991) offered an explanation for the inconsistency in the results from the

TABLE 1
Effect Sizes for Black and White Differences
in Job Performance as a Function of Rater Race

Study	White Rater	Black Rater
Kraiger and Ford (1985)[a]	.37	−.45
Sackett and DuBois (1991)[b]	.43	.16
Pulakos, Oppler, White, and Borman (1989)[c]		
Technical skill and job effort	.35	.14
Personal discipline	.11	.06
Military bearing	−.37	−.44

Note. Source: Sackett and DuBois (1991).
[a]White: $n = 17,159$; Black: $n = 2,428$. [b]White: $n = 17,994$; Black: $n = 1,771$. [c]White: $n = 24,039$; Black: $n = 12.091$.

Kraiger and Ford (1985) study and the other two studies. Their explanation was that the Kraiger and Ford (1985) meta-analysis included a relatively large percentage of ratings from laboratory studies using undergraduate students as raters and studies involving peer ratings (Sackett & DuBois, 1991).

Table 1 also shows that the effect sizes for the three performance criteria in the Pulakos et al. (1989) study differed in magnitude and direction. This indicates that subgroup differences in performance were influenced by the dimension of job performance assessed.

In a study designed to assess whether the relation between CAT scores and performance ratings is moderated by rater race, Rotundo and Sackett (1999) produced findings that bear directly on the issue of the magnitude of racial group differences in job performance relative to differences on CATs. The study used data collected by the U.S. Employment Service between 1972 and 1987. Scores on the General Aptitude Test Battery (GATB), along with performance ratings, were collected for more than 36,000 individuals as part of concurrent test validation studies. The database included test scores, performance ratings, and demographic data on 36,614 individuals in 171 different jobs representing 653 different employers (Rotundo & Sackett, 1999).

The researchers decided to focus on ratees who were either Black or White, thus excluding any other racial or ethnic groups. The study also focused solely on supervisory ratings as the criterion measure, thus excluding training scores or test scores. Establishing these criteria reduced the sample to approximately 26,000 individuals.

The primary purpose of the study was to assess the validity of the GATB in Black and White samples with different rater–ratee combinations. A byproduct of the data analysis, however, was an opportunity to compare Black and White differences on a CAT with Black and White differences on a measure of job performance.

The results of the study showed that Black and White effect sizes for the GATB ranged from .86 to .98. Black and White effect sizes on the performance measure ranged from 0.30 to 0.37 when all of the raters were White. These effect sizes fell to between .06 and .07 when the rater and ratee were matched on race.

The research literature showed clearly that the racial differences produced by CATs are substantially higher than racial differences on measures of job performance. This means that either (a) CATs measure constructs that are not required for successful job performance or (b) employees compensate for cognitive ability on the job. The imbalance between racial differences produced by the tests and racial differences in actual job performance also means that the use of CATs will typically result in a higher proportion of false negatives among minority applicants. Racial differences in job performance fluctuate substantially based on factors such as the job dimension assessed and the race of the rater and ratee. Thus, the imbalance cannot be explained as a statistical artifact (e.g., regression toward the mean) or as simply a function of less than perfect validity.

THE UTILITY OF CATs

Proponents of the use of CATs offer as the primary basis for their enthusiasm the ubiquitous and robust validity of these instruments across almost all jobs (Hunter & Hunter, 1984). Much is often made of the estimated loss in performance that can result when CATs are not used in making selection decisions. The core of this argument is a mean validity coefficient of .30. It is unclear to this writer how a validity coefficient of this magnitude establishes the gargantuan utility of CATs.

Researchers have begun to investigate taxonomies of job performance that may have implications for the kinds of selection devices that are useful selection tools. Borman and Motowidlo (1997), for example, distinguished between task performance and contextual performance. They presented evidence that supervisors weight task performance and contextual performance equally. Borman and Motowidlo also presented evidence that indicates contextual performance is best predicted by personality, whereas task performance is best predicted by general cognitive ability.

McHenry, Hough, Toquam, Hanson, and Ashworth (1990) used a predictor battery of cognitive ability, perceptual ability, temperament and personality, interest, and job outcome preference measures to predict performance in nine jobs. They found that scores from the cognitive and perceptual-motor ability tests provided the best prediction of task performance measures such as core technical proficiency. However, temperament and personality measures were the best predictors of contextual performance measures such as giving extra effort, supporting peers, and exhibiting personal discipline. Van Scotter, Cross, and Motowidlo (2000) presented evidence that contextual performance can affect career advancement and rewards over time.

The point is that accuracy in predicting job performance may be enhanced by finding links between different predictors and individual criterion elements (Borman & Motowidlo, 1997). Thus, predictor batteries that include noncognitive as well as cognitive ability measures will no doubt produce greater utility than cognitive ability measures alone. Similarly, predictors other than CATs may be just as important as cognitive ability measures in predicting job success.

Some proponents of the use of CATs in employment also argue that attempts to reduce the adverse impact of such tests by increasing minority hiring substantially degrades utility. However, on closer examination, this argument is not as credible as it appears. Silva and Jacobs (1993) examined the impact of increasing minority hiring on overall performance. They concluded that hiring minorities in proportion to their applicant representation results in a cumulative performance loss of between .017 and .041 standard deviation units.

Hunter, Rauschenberger, and Schmidt (1977) compared the effects of different methods of hiring on utility. Their analysis was based on the assumption that the job performance of minority employees is .50 standard deviations below that of

Whites. The hiring methods they compared included top-down selection (Cleary, 1968) and selection of minority applicants in proportion to their success on the job (Thorndike, 1971). Their analysis showed that with an applicant population that is 30% minority, a validity coefficient of .30, and a selection ratio of .10, the marginal increase in utility of top-down selection was .032 standard deviations.

Hunter et al. (1977) concluded that a marginal gain of .032 standard deviations would result in a substantial gain in utility. They determined, for example, that if the dollar value of the gain (measured in standard deviation units) in average employee performance based on strict rank order is $1,000, the dollar value of a marginal increase in utility of .032 standard deviations would be $32 per employee. This estimate is based on the assumption that the costs to the employer of strict rank order selection and of hiring on the basis of minority success on the job are equal.

These costs may not be equal for a number of reasons. First of all, the strict rank order method resulted in a minority selection ratio of .003 (Hunter et al., 1977) compared with a selection ratio of .048 for the Thorndike (1971) method. This may represent a substantial cost to the employer if a diverse workforce is an important goal. In addition, the extremely low minority selection ratio for the Cleary (1968) method would place the employer in a more precarious position in terms of legal defensibility. Finally, the assumption that minority performance is .50 standard deviations below that of nonminority employees oversimplifies the criterion problem. As pointed out earlier, the minority and nonminority difference in job performance is influenced by a number of factors including the particular aspect of performance that is measured. For supervisory ratings, the race of the rater may have a significant impact on the effect size.

Given the current state of our understanding of racial differences in criterion performance, estimates of the magnitude of such differences are probably exaggerated and speculative at best. Thus, estimates of the loss of utility associated with minority hiring also are speculative. However, the effect of relying on CATs in making selection decisions is quite real in terms of the level of adverse impact produced. It would seem inadvisable for an employer to rely primarily, or even substantially, on CATs based on the utility argument, given the level of adverse impact produced by these tests and the availability of alternatives.

ALTERNATIVES TO CATs

Meta-analytic research indicates that there are a number of employment selection devices that have demonstrated validity and substantially less adverse impact than CATs. These alternative devices include structured interviews, biodata, and the construct of conscientiousness measured via personality inventories. The mean validity coefficients for these alternatives are .30, .28, and .18, respectively (Bobko et al., 1999). However, the effect sizes for Black and White differences on these devices are .23, .33, and .09, respectively.

Schmitt et al. (1997) assessed the effects of combining low-adverse-impact predictors with a CAT. Their results showed that adverse impact was substantially reduced. Their analysis also showed that the validity of a predictor battery consisting of a CAT and low-adverse-impact predictors can be higher than the validity of the CAT alone.

DeCorte (1999) used controlled linear programming in lieu of regression weighting to establish the component weights of a predictor battery consisting of a CAT and a personality measure. The objective of controlled linear programming is to combine predictors into a composite in such a manner that adverse impact is minimized, the average performance of selected employees is maximized, and a given selection ratio is achieved. DeCorte's weighting system held adverse impact ratios constant at .80 while providing a method of estimating any loss in the expected average quality of the workforce. The work of DeCorte demonstrates the impact that weighting decisions can have on the adverse impact of a predictor battery.

Pulakos and Schmitt (1996) examined two strategies of reducing adverse impact and their effects on criterion-related validity. The first strategy involved assessing a broad range of cognitive and noncognitive abilities determined via job analysis to be important to job success. The second strategy involved the development of alternative ways of measuring verbal ability beyond the traditional multiple-choice test. Pulakos and Schmitt found that both strategies reduced adverse impact and that validity was substantially increased by expanding the array of abilities measured.

Hattrup, Rock, and Scalia (1997) used Monte Carlo simulation based on meta-analytic evidence of multiple predictor and criterion relations to illustrate methods of predicting multiple criterion dimensions. Using the task performance and contextual performance taxonomy of Borman and Motowidlo (1997), Hattrup et al. illustrated an approach that improved validity and reduced adverse impact.

Huffcutt and Arthur (1994) conducted a meta-analysis of 114 entry-level validity coefficients for the interview. They concluded that interviews, particularly structured interviews, can produce validity coefficients comparable to those produced by CATs.

Outtz (1998) pointed out a link between method of measurement and adverse impact. He proposed that the method of testing (e.g., multiple-choice test questions) may produce adverse impact independent of content. Chan and Schmitt (1997) investigated this question by assessing the adverse impact of a situational judgment test presented via a video and a paper-and-pencil format. The results showed that racial group differences were substantially smaller for the video-based form of the test.

It should be noted that the purpose of this discussion of alternatives is to present a case for greater use of combinations of selection devices that may be just as valid, if not more valid, than CATs alone and have less adverse impact. The alternatives discussed here are not intended to preclude the measurement of *g* when making selection decisions. The intent is not to present replacements for *g*.

The real issue centers around the questions of relative emphasis, method of measurement, and method of use. In this regard, questions such as the following become critical: (a) Should cognitive ability be the only or even primary construct of interest in making employment selection decisions?, (b) What should be the relative emphasis given to cognitive and noncognitive measures in a selection battery?, and (c) What measures in addition to measures of cognitive ability can be employed (given the multidimensional nature of job performance) to increase validity and reduce adverse impact?

CONCLUSIONS

The relationship between CATs and measures of job performance is well established. Meta-analytic research indicates that the mean validity coefficient for CATs is .30. However, a validity coefficient of this magnitude does not substantiate the conclusion that cognitive ability is the primary construct underlying successful job performance.

CATs are controversial because they produce severe adverse impact. As an example, the mean score for African Americans is one standard deviation below the mean for Whites (Hunter & Hunter, 1984). Minority and nonminority mean differences on CATs are much larger than differences between these subgroups on measures of job performance. Therefore, a disproportionate number of qualified minority applicants will be rejected when CATs alone are used in employment selection.

One explanation for the discrepancy between subgroup differences on CATs and subgroup differences on measures of job performance might be that CATs are not perfectly correlated with job performance. That is, if CATs were perfectly valid, the differences in subgroup performance on the predictor would be mirrored by subgroup differences of similar magnitude on measures of job performance. This hypothesis lacks credibility simply because non-cognitive predictors—such as biodata measures, work samples, and personality inventories—that, either individually or in combination, produce validity coefficients similar to those of CATs result in subgroup differences that are similar to those typically found on measures of actual job performance.

Alternative selection batteries that include CATs and low-adverse-impact predictors can reduce adverse impact and improve validity (Pulakos & Schmitt, 1996; Schmitt et al., 1997). Use of weighting systems other than regression weights can allow an employer to determine the most desirable balance between utility and increasing workforce diversity (DeCorte, 1999).

Given that the goals of employment selection may go beyond maximizing individual performance, methods of weighting predictor components other than regression weighting may be warranted. Guion (1998) noted that regression weighting is often assumed to be the most appropriate weighting procedure without justification. More research is needed on weighting systems that reduce adverse impact with minimal effect on utility.

Hunter and Hunter (1984) speculated that using other predictors in conjunction with CATs might improve validity and reduce adverse impact. They concluded, however, that at that time no database was available for studying this possibility. That database does exist today. The research evidence shows that combining low-adverse-impact predictors with CATs can improve validity and reduce adverse impact (Cortina, Goldstein, Payne, Davison, & Gilliland, 2000; Huffcutt & Roth, 1998; Pulakos & Schmitt, 1996; Schmitt et al., 1997).

Given the available alternatives, the use of CATs alone in making selection decisions should be carefully scrutinized. If CATs are used, adverse impact should be minimized.

REFERENCES

Bobko, P., Roth, P. L., & Potosky, D. (1999). Derivation and implications of a meta-analytic matrix incorporating cognitive ability, alternative predictors, and job performance. *Personnel Psychology, 52,* 561–589.

Borman, W. C., & Motowidlo, S. J. (1997). Task performance and contextual performance: The meaning for personnel selection research. *Human Performance, 10,* 99–109.

Chan, D., & Schmitt, N. (1997). Video-based versus paper-and-pencil method of assessment in situational judgment tests: Subgroup differences in test performance and face validity perceptions. *Journal of Applied Psychology, 42,* 143–159.

Cleary, T. A. (1968). Test bias: Prediction of grades of Negro and White students in integrated colleges. *Journal of Educational Measurement, 5,* 115–124.

Cortina, J. M., Goldstein, N. B., Payne, S. C., Davison, H. K., & Gilliland, S. W. (2000). The incremental validity of interview scores over and above cognitive ability and conscientiousness scores. *Personnel Psychology, 53,* 325–351.

DeCorte, W. (1999). Weighing job performance predictors to both maximize the quality of the selected workforce and control the level of adverse impact. *Journal of Applied Psychology, 84,* 695–702.

Ford, J. K., Kraiger, K., & Schechtman, S. L. (1986). Study of race effects in objective indices and subjective evaluations of performance: A meta-analysis of performance criteria. *Psychological Bulletin, 99,* 330–337.

Guion, R. M. (1998). *Assessment, measurement, and prediction for personnel decisions.* Mahwah, NJ: Lawrence Erlbaum Associates, Inc.

Hattrup, K., Rock, J., & Scalia, C. (1997). The effects of varying conceptualizations of job performance on adverse impact, minority hiring, and predicted performance. *Journal of Applied Psychology, 82,* 656–664.

Huffcutt, A. I., & Arthur, W., Jr. (1994). Hunter & Hunter (1984) revisited: Interview validity for entry-level jobs. *Journal of Applied Psychology, 79,* 184–190.

Huffcutt, A. I., & Roth, P. L. (1998). Racial group differences in employment interview evaluations. *Journal of Applied Psychology, 83,* 179–189.

Hunter, J. E., & Hunter, R. F. (1984). Validity and utility of alternative predictors of job performance. *Psychological Bulletin, 96*, 72–98.

Hunter, J. E., Rauschenberger, J. M., & Schmidt, F. L. (1977). Fairness of psychological tests: Implications of four definitions for selection utility and minority hiring. *Journal of Applied Psychology, 62*, 245–260.

Johnson, W. B., & Packer, A. H. (1987). *Workforce 2000: Work and workers for the twenty-first century.* Indianapolis, IN: Hudson Institute.

Kraiger, K., & Ford, J. K. (1985). A meta-analysis of ratee race effects in performance ratings. *Journal of Applied Psychology, 70*, 56–65.

McHenry, J. J., Hough, L. M., Toquam, J. L., Hanson, M. A., & Ashworth, S. (1990). Project A validity results: The relationship between predictor and criterion domains. *Personnel Psychology, 43*, 335–354.

Offermann, L. R., & Gowing, M. K. (1990). Organizations of the future: Changes and challenges. *American Psychologist, 45*, 95–108.

Outtz, J. L. (1998). *Testing medium, validity, and test performance. Beyond multiple choice.* Mahwah, NJ: Lawrence Erlbaum Associates, Inc.

Pulakos, E. D., Oppler, S. H., White, L. A., & Borman, W. C. (1989). Examination of race and sex effects on performance ratings. *Journal of Applied Psychology, 74*, 770–780.

Pulakos, E. D., & Schmitt, N. (1996). An evaluation of two strategies for reducing adverse impact and their effects on criterion-related validity. *Human Performance, 9*, 241–258.

Rotundo, M., & Sackett, P. R. (1999). Effect of rater race on conclusions regarding differential prediction in cognitive ability tests. *Journal of Applied Psychology, 84*, 815–822.

Sackett, P. R., & DuBois, C. L. Z. (1991). Rater–ratee race effects on performance evaluation: Challenging meta-analytic conclusions. *Journal of Applied Psychology, 76*, 873–877.

Sackett, P.R., & Ellingson, J.E. (1997). The effects of forming multi-predictor composites on group differences and adverse impact. *Personnel Psychology, 50*, 707- 721.

Schmitt, N., Rogers, W., Chan, D., Sheppard, L., & Jennings, D. (1997). Adverse impact and predictive efficiency of various predictor combinations. *Journal of Applied Psychology, 82*, 719–730.

Silva, J. M., & Jacobs, R. R. (1993). Performance as a function of increased minority hiring. *Journal of Applied Psychology, 78*, 591–601.

Thorndike, R. L. (1971). Concepts of culture—fairness. *Journal of Educational Measurement, 8*, 63–70.

U.S. Employment Service. (1970). *Manual for the USES General Aptitude Test Battery, Section III: Development.* Washington, DC: U.S. Department of Labor, Manpower Administration.

Van Scotter, J. R., Cross, T. C., & Motowidlo, S. J. (2000). Effects of task performance and contextual performance on systemic rewards. *Journal of Applied Psychology, 85*, 526–535.

HUMAN PERFORMANCE, 15(1/2), 173–186

Can Conflicting Perspectives on the Role of *g* in Personnel Selection Be Resolved?

Kevin R. Murphy
Department of Psychology
Pennsylvania State University

Cognitive ability tests represent the best single predictor of job performance, but also represent the predictor most likely to have substantial adverse impact on employment opportunities for members of several racial and ethnic minority groups. Debates over the use of these tests in selection often involve trade-offs between two criteria that are valued by decision makers—that is, efficiency and equity. Findings and methods from decision research can help us frame these trade-offs, but in most cases they cannot be avoided.

Debates about the fairness and appropriateness of different tests or methods of personnel selection often boil down to disagreements about which criteria should be emphasized in evaluating these tests (Gottfredson, 1988; Hunter & Schmidt, 1976). This is particularly true in debates over the use of measures of general cognitive ability in personnel selection. Researchers who emphasize criteria such as efficiency, performance, productivity, or profit tend to take a favorable view of using measures of general cognitive ability in making selection decisions. Researchers who emphasize criteria such as group parity, non-discrimination, equity, or social goals tend to view the use of general cognitive ability with considerable caution, if not outright hostility. Some scholars (e.g., Perloff & Bryant, 2000) have argued that increasing diversity can have direct payoffs to organizations, suggesting that economic criteria are not necessarily always in conflict with equity criteria. However, to date, there have been few convincing demonstrations of extensive economic payoffs resulting from efforts to increase workforce diversity, which suggests that emphasis of efficiency versus

Requests for reprints should be sent to Kevin R. Murphy, Department of Psychology, Pennsylvania State University, University Park, PA 16802–3104. E-mail: krmurphy@psu.edu equity criteria in hiring is likely to lead to conflicting choices among hiring methods, applicants, and so forth.

The debate between proponents of these two perspectives has generated a good deal of heat and occasionally some light. Because this debate boils down to differences in values (i.e., differences in the criteria that are seem as important or worth considering), it is not clear that it will ever be fully resolved. However, some progress can be made by framing this debate in terms of perspectives from decision theory (Edwards & Newman, 1983). In particular, it is possible to identify sets of circumstances under which selection systems that omitted any use of measures of cognitive ability measures might be preferred to selection systems that incorporated or relied on measures of general cognitive ability. If such circumstances can be defined, it becomes an empirical question whether they are likely to be encountered. Similarly, it is possible to identify circumstances under which selection systems that rely heavily on cognitive ability measures are almost certain to be preferred to selection systems that avoid these measures. Finally, it is possible to identify the range of circumstances under which the decision to use or avoid cognitive ability measures is impossible to resolve without defining the relative value of efficiency and equity criteria.

Before discussing potential frameworks for examining conflicting perspectives on the role of cognitive ability measures in personnel selection, it is useful to review (at least briefly) the two streams of evidence that have fueled this debate. First, there is a large body of research showing that cognitive ability is unique in terms of its relevance for predicting performance on a wide range of jobs. No other single measure appears to work so well, in such a wide range of circumstances, as a predictor of overall job performance as a good measure of general cognitive ability. From the perspective of an emphasis on efficiency, it seems hard to argue against using these measures in personnel selection.

Unfortunately, measures of cognitive ability also appear to be unique in the sense that there is no other widely used selection test or assessment that is more likely to produce adverse impact against members of racial and ethnic minority groups. Unscrupulous decision makers who intend to screen out Blacks, Hispanics, and so forth, when selecting for a highly competitive job could scarcely do better (without running seriously afoul of the law) than they would by relying heavily on measures of cognitive ability. Completely scrupulous decision makers who have no intention of discriminating on the basis of race will nevertheless do so if they rely on such tests as an important part of their selection decision. The decision to rely heavily on measures of cognitive ability necessarily implies a willingness to take measures that will have adverse impact on identifiable groups of applicants. From the perspective of an emphasis on equity, it seems hard to argue for these measures, especially if alternatives that accomplish the same productivity goals while having a lower adverse impact can be developed.

A COGNITIVE ABILITY TEST IS THE BEST SINGLE
PREDICTOR OF JOB PERFORMANCE

There is abundant evidence that general cognitive ability is highly relevant in a wide range of jobs and settings (Hough, Eaton, Dunnette, Kamp, & McCloy, 1991; Hunter, 1986; Hunter & Hunter, 1984; McHenry, Hough, Toquam, Hanson, & Ashworth, 1990; Ree & Earles, 1992; Schmidt & Hunter, 1998; Schmidt, Ones, & Hunter, 1992) and that measures of general cognitive ability represent perhaps the best predictors of performance (for dissenting views on the importance of general cognitive ability, see McClelland, 1993; Sternberg & Wagner, 1993). Ability–performance relations are essentially linear (Coward & Sackett, 1990), and the correlation between general cognitive ability and performance appears similar across jobs that differ considerably in content (Hunter & Hirsh, 1987). There is some evidence that ability–performance correlations tend to increase as jobs become more complex (Gutenberg, Arvey, Osburn, & Jenneret, 1983), but few other consistent moderators of the ability–performance correlation have been reported. Finally, the incremental contribution of specific abilities (defined as ability factors unrelated to the general factor) to the prediction of performance or training outcomes may very well be minimal (Ree & Earles, 1991a, 1991b, 1992; Ree, Earles, & Teachout, 1994).

Carroll's (1993) three-stratum model of cognitive ability (based on the results of a large number of factor-analytic studies) nicely illustrates the nature of modern hierarchical models of cognitive ability and helps explain why measures of general cognitive ability appear to be useful in such a wide range of settings. At the most general level, there is a g factor, which implies stable differences in performance on a wide range of cognitively demanding tasks. At the next level (the broad stratum), there are a number of areas of ability, which imply that the rank-ordering of individuals' task performance will not be exactly the same across all cognitive tasks, but rather will show some clustering. The broad abilities in Carroll's model include the following: (a) fluid intelligence, (b) crystallized intelligence, (c) general memory ability, (d) broad visual perception, (e) broad auditory perception, (f) broad retrieval ability, and (g) broad cognitive speediness. The implication of distinguishing these broad abilities from g is that some people will do well on a broad range of memory tasks, and these will not be exactly the same set of people who do well on a broad range of tasks tapping cognitive speed, visual perception, and so forth. However, these groups will overlap considerably. Finally, each of these broad ability areas can be characterized in terms of a number of more specific abilities (the narrow stratum) that are more homogeneous still than those at the next highest level. Examples corresponding to each of the broad spectrum abilities labeled earlier include the following: (a) induction, (b) language development, (c) memory span, (d) spatial relations, (e) sound discrimination, (f) word fluency, and

(g) perceptual speed. Once again, the implication of distinguishing specific narrow abilities from their broad parent abilities is that the individuals who do well on inductive reasoning tasks might not be exactly the same as those who do well on other fluid intelligence tasks (although the groups will once again overlap substantially and also overlap with those classified as high on g).

Because human cognitive abilities tend to be positively correlated (i.e., scores on cognitively demanding tasks exhibit positive manifold—see Ackerman & Humphreys, 1990; Allinger, 1988; Carroll, 1993; Guttman & Levy, 1991; Humphreys, 1979; Jensen, 1980; Ree & Earles, 1991b), it is somewhat difficult to sort out the roles of various abilities in influencing performance. That is, because general cognitive abilities subsume more specific ones, it is likely that measures of general cognitive ability will prove useful as predictors even if it is a more specific ability (e.g., verbal fluency) that influences performance on a specific task. There are theories of cognitive ability that give little emphasis to g (e.g., Sternberg, 1977; Sternberg & Wagner, 1993) or that deny the utility of a general factor (e.g., Guilford, 1988), but these have not been successful in accounting for patterns of performance on cognitively demanding tasks.

Three conclusions can be drawn from research on the correlations between measures of general cognitive ability and job performance. First, ability measures are likely to be correlated with performance in virtually any job, in part because all jobs call for some learning, judgment, and active information processing. Second, the question of which abilities are influencing performance on which tasks may not be crucially important if your goal is to find valid and useful predictors of performance. Third, all other things being equal, measures of cognitive ability are likely to be the most useful and valuable component of a personnel selection system. Unfortunately, all other things are not equal. The decision to use measures of general cognitive ability in making personnel selection decisions is also a decision to accept and allow some level of discrimination against members of several ethnic and racial groups (notably Black and Hispanic applicants). This discrimination is often legally defensible (e.g., if the test that produces this discrimination can be shown to be job related) and is "fair" from a number of perspectives (because scores on cognitive ability tests are usually related to job performance). Nevertheless, it is important to keep in mind that the decision to use this class of tests implies a conscious decision to live with the social consequences of these tests.

COGNITIVE ABILITY TESTS SHOW ADVERSE IMPACT

Since its inception, however, cognitive ability testing has been the focus of sustained public controversy (Cronbach, 1975). Although conflicts between test specialists sometimes revolve around technical or esoteric issues, the primary issue that has fueled the bitter public debate over IQ testing has been the fact that the average test scores for members of a number of minority groups tend to be lower than average test scores for White examinees. For example, the difference between the means ability test scores of White and Black examinees is generally about the same size as the standard deviation of the test (i.e., the standardized mean difference on ability tests is often in the range of .85–1.00). White–Hispanic differences in average scores are somewhat smaller, but still substantial. The difference in average test scores means that there will be relatively few Black or Hispanic applicants who receive high test scores and that Black and Hispanic applicants will be overrepresented among those receiving low scores on the test. As a result, if tests are used as the sole method of making decisions, fewer members of these minority groups will be selected into schools, jobs, and training programs than if decisions are made at random or if quotas are imposed. In very selective contexts (e.g., prestigious schools), the use of these tests as the sole means for making decisions will effectively screen out most minority applicants.

There is also clear agreement that differences in test scores are not due solely to irrelevant test bias (Gottfredson, 1986, 1988; Jensen, 1980). Rather, group differences in scores on cognitive ability tests appear to reflect real and meaningful differences in average levels of cognitive ability. Gottfredson (1986, 1988) and Rogers (1988) summarized literature on ability testing and race and noted differences are large, stable, and meaningful. Rogers suggested that massive societal changes will be necessary to significantly affect the discriminatory effects of cognitive ability tests.

Finally, racial differences in cognitive ability test scores are known to be considerably larger than racial differences in measures of job performance (Hattrup, Rock, & Scalia, 1997; Waldman & Avolio, 1991). One implication is that personnel decisions made on the basis of cognitive ability tests will have an unduly large adverse effect on employment opportunities for members of several racial and ethnic minority groups. A workforce selected on the basis of actual performance would be less racially segregated than a workforce selected on the basis of cognitive ability tests. Unfortunately, at the point of making selection decisions, actual performance is unknown, and the best we can normally do is to rely on predictors with well-established records of validity and utility; cognitive ability tests are an exemplar of this class of measures.

Several strategies have been suggested for reducing the adverse impact of cognitive ability tests, none of which has been completely successful. For example, one suggestion for reducing the effects of test bias is to employ multiple methods of assessment. Test bias is most likely to be a societal problem when a single test score determines each person's fate. The use of a broad array of assessment devices that measures many important attributes may provide the ultimate safeguard against the possibility that irrelevant biases in test scores will unfairly handicap individuals taking the test. Although the use of multiple tests or assessment devices can help to reduce the impact of ability tests on workforce diversity (DeCorte,

1999), it is clear that this strategy will rarely eliminate group differences (Hattrup et al., 1997; Ryan, Ployhart, & Friedel, 1998; Schmitt, Rogers, Chan, Sheppard, & Jennings, 1997). If group differences are large on one test (e.g., a cognitive ability test), they must be at least as large and in the opposite direction on a second test to completely eliminate the effects of test bias. This rarely occurs.

Another suggestion for reducing test bias has been to change the testing method (e.g., change from written tests to individually administered oral tests). However, as Schmitt, Clause, and Pulakos (1996) noted, most studies of this hypothesis tend to confound testing methods with test content. That is, comparison of two different methods of assessment (e.g., paper-and-pencil tests vs. work samples) might yield different results because of differences in the way the test is administered and scored, differences in the content of the assessment devices in question, or some combination of the two. In one of the first studies that directly compares differences in methods of test administration, holding test content constant, Chan and Schmitt (1998) obtained some interesting and encouraging results. They developed video-based versus paper-and-pencil versions of a situational judgment test, in which the content of the test was held constant. They showed that group differences were substantially smaller on the video-based version and explained this difference in terms of a number of factors, including differences in reading comprehension and examinees' reactions to the different modes of testing.

Cascio, Outtz, Zedeck, and Goldstein (1991) suggested that, rather than ranking individuals strictly in terms of their test scores, people with similar scores might be grouped together in a test score band. When criteria other than ability test scores are used to rank applicants within bands, it is possible to reduce adverse impact. Sackett and Wilk (1994) reviewed a range of test-score adjustment methods that might be used with cognitive and noncognitive tests. Although it is clear that scores can be transformed in ways that reduce the adverse impact of cognitive ability tests, there are both logical and legal arguments against many methods of test score adjustment (Schmidt, 1991).

To date, there has been little progress in identifying methods that would allow one to take advantage of the validity and predictive power of cognitive ability tests in personnel selection without producing substantial adverse impact. Therein lies the quandary. If you emphasize efficiency criteria, and are willing to live with adverse impact, your choice is easy—that is, rely heavily on cognitive ability tests. If you emphasize equity criteria and are willing to live with lower levels of performance, longer training time, more errors, and so forth, your choice is also easy—that is, remove cognitive tests and other selection devices that have strong cognitive components (e.g., scores on cognitive ability test are correlated with scores on structured interviews and on assessment centers). Many decision makers care about both efficiency and equity, and the choice faced by these decision makers is necessarily more complex.

BALANCING EFFICIENCY AND EQUITY

The decision to use or avoid cognitively loaded measures in personnel selection is usually framed as a conflict between efficiency and equity, and, in many cases, this conflict cannot be resolved without addressing the deeper issue of the relative value of these two criteria. However, it is possible to sketch out circumstances in which there would not be a conflict and to identify the sorts of selection systems that might allow one to satisfy both efficiency and equity goals, and also to identify the circumstances in which these two criteria must come in conflict.

Suppose your task is to choose between two systems for selecting among applicants. Each system might feature some mix of assessment devices (e.g., tests, interviews, biodata, etc.). I will start with the assumption that both efficiency and equity are positively valued by decision makers. That is, all other things being equal, a selection system that did a better job identifying the applicants who were most likely to perform well in a job would be preferred to one that did a worse job in predicting applicant performance. If two selection systems differed in terms of cost (e.g., an assessment center might be much more costly to administer than a paper-and-pencil test), these costs might be factored into the evaluation of the two systems, leading to an emphasis on utility rather than validity, but the same principle would hold. Similarly, all other things being equal, the system that led to less adverse impact would be preferred over the system that led to more adverse impact. That is, if two selection systems showed comparable levels of utility (defined in terms of efficiency criteria), the selection system that had the greater likelihood of screening out applicants from racial and ethnic minority groups would always be less attractive than a system that produced less adverse impact.

Multiattribute utility theory (Edwards & Newman, 1983) suggests that the choice between objects, each of which can be evaluated on multiple dimensions, is often a complex one. Suppose we can describe each of two personnel selection systems in terms of its standing on an efficiency dimension (e.g., this might be indexed in terms of estimated utility, to reflect possible differences in cost, or in terms of estimates of validity for systems that have comparable costs) and an equity dimension (e.g., this might be indexed in terms of the amount of adverse impact against specific groups of applicants). In any case where selection system A is higher on one criterion (e.g., equity) and selection system B is higher on the other (e.g., equity), the choice between A and B cannot logically be made without accomplishing two very challenging goals: (a) scaling efficiency and equity on a common metric, so that trade-offs between the two can be evaluated (e.g., Is a 10% gain in equity comparable to a 10% decrease in equity?; Murphy & Davidshofer, 2000) and (b) deciding the relative value of efficiency and equity. Psychologists can help decision makers understand the potential trade-offs involved and can help them structure their choices among systems, but if the goals of efficiency and equity come into conflict, there is no scientific or empirical resolution to this conflict.

When the two criteria conflict, the choice of one selection system over another is necessarily a matter of values and preferences.

Although conflicts between equity and efficiency are probably common, they are not inevitable. There are a number of scenarios under which the two criteria do not lead you to prefer different selection systems. For example, selection system A must always be preferred over system B when (a) A is higher on both equity and efficiency, (b) A and B are equal in terms of efficiency and A is higher than B in terms of equity, or (c) A and B are equal in terms of equity and A is higher than B in terms of efficiency. In all three cases, A dominates B and should always be chosen. To put this framework into concrete terms, consider a recent article by Gottfredson (1996). She was critical of efforts to reduce the adverse impact of selection tests by lowering their dependence on cognitive abilities (while supposedly mounting somewhat comparable levels of validity) and labeled these efforts "racial gerrymandering."

Viewed from the perspective outlined earlier, efforts to develop noncognitive alternatives that will reduce adverse impact, even at the expense of reducing our reliance on an attribute known to be relevant to job performance (i.e., cognitive ability), are not necessarily a bad idea. Rather, if it works, a "racially gerrymandered" test is arguably preferable to one that is not "gerrymandered." That is, if it is possible to develop a noncognitive test battery that has equal validity and less adverse impact than a cognitively loaded battery, the noncognitive battery would on the whole be preferable to the cognitive one. That is, it would satisfy efficiency criteria just as well as a cognitively loaded battery while producing more favorable results in terms of equity criteria. The question of whether noncognitive batteries can produce validities (or utilities) equal to those attained by cognitively loaded batteries is an empirical one.

Even if you do succeed in developing a noncognitive selection battery that has similar levels of criterion-related validity as would be expected from a cognitive test (which, as I note later, may be very difficult to accomplish), it is important that these two testing methods will lead to qualitatively different outcomes. That is, the two types of tests will select different employees, who bring different strengths and weaknesses to the job, and who are likely to perform different aspects of their jobs well and poorly. Organizations are likely to differ somewhat in their definitions of what constitutes good job performance (Murphy & Shiarella, 1997, examined the implications of differing definitions of performance for the validity of selection tests), and there may be organizations (e.g., those that emphasize only some aspects of the performance domain) in which it is virtually impossible to select good performers without relying to some extent on measures of cognitive ability. Traditionally, we have used the results of validity studies and utility analyses to make statements about the overall value of particular strategies for making selection decisions, but it is useful to keep in mind that different strategies (e.g., rely heavily on g vs. rely heavily on some other attribute that is orthogonal to g) may achieve that value to the organization in fundamentally different ways.

Validity estimates presented by Schmidt and Hunter (1998) suggest that developing such a noncognitive battery will be a daunting task. The validity of general mental ability tests alone is estimated to be .51. Schmidt and Hunter's review suggested that integrity tests, measures of conscientiousness, and structured interviews are among the most valid noncognitive measures (Schmidt & Hunter suggested that scores on these interviews are correlated with measures of cognitive ability, corrected $r = 30$). If integrity tests were combined with a measure of conscientiousness, the estimated multiple R would be .45 (using .36 as an estimate of the corrected correlation between integrity and conscientiousness measures; Murphy & Lee, 1994). If integrity tests were combined with scores on unstructured interviews, the multiple R value might range from .41 to .65, depending on the correlation between these two measures. (Credible estimates of the correlation between integrity test scores and scores form structured interviews are not available.) Finally, if all three measures are combined into a battery, the multiple R might range from .45 to .68, depending on the correlations between unstructured interviews and both conscientiousness and integrity measures. The point is that it might take a combination of the best available noncognitive measures (at least one of which has some overlap with mental ability tests) to reach the same level of validity as that expected from a mental ability test alone. The multiple R values estimated for several of the potential combinations of cognitive tests are near the maximum value of the multiple Rs obtained from batteries of these three noncognitive measures (e.g., Schmidt & Hunter estimated the multiple R resulting from a combination of general mental ability tests and job knowledge tests to be .58).

The search for noncognitive test batteries that perform as well as cognitively loaded batteries as predictors of job performance is clearly going to be a difficult one. Even if you are successful in constructing such a battery, the decision to avoid using cognitive tests is likely to entail potential loss in performance or productivity (i.e., adding a cognitive test to a noncognitive battery is likely to lead to an increased level of validity). Given the difficulty in completely avoiding efficiency–equity trade-offs, it is important that personnel psychologists and human resource managers learn how to approach them.

The problem of choosing among objects, courses of action, policies, and so forth, when they differ on multiple attributes (e.g., equity and efficiency), is one of the key concerns of decision theory (Keeney & Raiffa, 1976). A number of theories and methods have been developed for studying and for aiding decision makers in multiattribute evaluation (Anderson & Zalinski, 1990; Hammond, McClelland, & Mumpower, 1980; Keeney & Raiffa, 1976; Orfelio, 1997), and some broad principles can be drawn from this literature.

First, value comparisons cannot be avoided. The decision to employ a cognitive ability test, knowing that such a test will lead to reduced employment opportunities for members of several racial and ethnic groups, *is* a statement of values (i.e., that the gain in efficiency is worth enough to offset the loss in equity). Similarly, the decision to omit cognitive ability tests, knowing that this is likely to lead to reduced validity and utility, is also a statement of values (i.e., that equity is more important than efficiency). The issues involved in making this choice (validity vs. adverse impact) are so well-documented in the literature that Industrial and Organizational psychologists and Human Resource Management professionals can scarcely plead ignorance, but must rather take a stand on where their values lie and act accordingly. There is nothing wrong with expressing or stating values, but it is to everyone's advantage to make such value statements openly and thoughtfully rather than letting someone else infer your values from the choices you have made.

Second, people have a difficult time making decisions involving value tradeoffs. Normative decision theories often suggest that decision makers should be consistent in their decisions, whereas a key assumption of behavioral decision theories is that decisions often appear illogical and inconsistent (Hammond et al., 1980). A practical result is that asking for one-shot holistic decisions about which selection system should be preferred (e.g., one that is high on efficiency and low on equity vs. one that is low on efficiency and high on equity criteria) might not be reliable or useful. Rather, complex decisions should be broken down into manageable units, and decision makers should receive multiple opportunities to provide input and feedback on the implications of their decision policies (Edwards & Newman, 1983; Hammond et al., 1980). Third, value trade-offs are strongly affected by scaling and by the range of each of the relevant alternatives (Mellers & Cooke, 1994). Equity and efficiency criteria are usually evaluated using different metrics (e.g., dollars vs. employment opportunities), making direct comparisons of the two difficult. One way to attack this problem is to ask decision makers to make choices between hypothetical pairs of systems (e.g., which would you prefer, a system that leads to an increase in productivity worth $15,000 and a 2% reduction in the number of minority group members hired or a system that leads to a $1,000 increase in productivity and no reduction in the number of minority group members hired?). By comparing choices over a range of values for efficiency and equity criteria, it is possible to derive estimated utility functions for decision makers (Luce, 1990). One advantage of deriving such utility functions is that it allows you to help decision makers understand the implicit values that are driving their decisions (e.g., people who choose to rely heavily on cognitive ability tests act as if they value efficiency more strongly than equity, which may or may not correspond to the values they want to put into place).

Value trade-offs cannot be dictated by scientific methods (i.e., the best metaanalysis cannot tell decision makers whether they *should* place more emphasis on efficiency or equity), but they can be substantially informed by scientific research. In particular, we know that selection systems that rely heavily on cognitive ability tests are likely to do the following: (a) predict future performance, (b) do so equally well for members of most groups in society, and (c) limit the employment opportunities of members of several racial and ethnic groups. We know that selection systems that minimize their reliance on cognitive ability tests are likely to (a) be less effective in predicting performance than systems that incorporated cognitive tests and (b) present fewer barriers to the employment opportunities of these same disadvantaged applicants. This information can be very useful to decision makers in making choices that are likely to involve value trade-offs.

One final comment about the role of values in evaluating selection systems is in order. Strongly held values can often distort discussions and evaluations of the scientific evidence. Proponents of equity criteria are sometimes tempted to deny the value of g in selection or to minimize the importance of the substantial body of evidence that tests of cognitive abilities are useful predictors of performance. Proponents of efficiency criteria are sometimes tempted to trivialize the consequences of relying heavily on measures of g in making selection decisions or to impugn the motives of those who seek alternatives to the use of cognitive ability tests. Distorting the evidence on either side of the equity–efficiency conflict does a disservice to everyone, but it is equally a disservice to argue that values are irrelevant to the assessment of selection systems. Efficiency and equity criteria are both valued by many members of society, and in situations where they come into conflict, the choice to emphasize one over the other is a statement of value. The evidence is relatively clear: Reliance on cognitive ability measures in selection is likely to lead to more efficiency (i.e., higher average performance) and less equity (e.g., disparities in selection rates across racial and ethnic groups), whereas avoiding the use of cognitive ability measures is likely to lead to less efficiency and more equity. There is no scientific principal that can tell us which criteria *should* receive more evidence, but scientific research can clearly inform us of the consequences of emphasizing one criterion or the other.

WHOSE VALUES MATTER?

As noted earlier, it is likely that different groups of stakeholders have different opinions about the relative importance of efficiency versus equity, about the appropriateness of cognitive ability tests, and so forth. In particular, groups who tend to receive lower scores on cognitive tests are less likely to regard these tests as valuable and useful (Chan, Schmitt, DeShon, & Clause, 1997). Simple self-interest makes it likely that groups that believe that their employment opportunities will be adversely affected will see cognitive tests as less valuable. However, the converse is also true. There is probably an element of self-interest in the support for cognitive ability testing typically reported for the more privileged social, racial, and ethnic groups. The decision to "live with" a certain amount of adverse impact is probably more easily made by decision makers who will not themselves suffer the adverse effects of these tests. It is reasonable to assume that decisions about which tests and assessments will be used in personnel selection will be largely the province of members of groups who tend to do well on cognitive ability tests, based simply on the relative distribution of wealth, power, credentials, and influence among racial and ethnic groups in American society. It is probably valuable to alert decision makers to the fact that there are real differences in perceptions of the value of these tests and that these tend to fall along lines predictable on the basis of self-interest. Conflicts might be minimized by taking a broad survey of the stakeholders involved in these decisions and, more important, by making the values that drive this decision explicit and public.

REFERENCES

Ackerman, P. L., & Humphreys, L. G. (1990). Individual differences theory in industrial and organizational psychology. In M. Dunnette & L. Hough (Eds.), *Handbook of industrial and organizational psychology, 2nd ed.* (Vol. 1, pp. 223–282). Palo Alto, CA: Consulting Psychologists Press.

Allinger, G. M. (1988). Do zero correlations really exist among measures of different cognitive abilities? *Educational and Psychological Measurement, 48*, 275–280.

Anderson, N. H., & Zalinski, J. (1990). Functional measurement approach to self-estimation in multiattribute evaluation. In N. Anderson (Ed.), *Contributions to information integration theory* (Vol. 1, pp. 145–185). Hillsdale, NJ: Lawrence Erlbaum Associates, Inc.

Carroll, J. B. (1993). *Human cognitive abilities: A survey of factor-analytic studies.* Cambridge, England: Cambridge University Press.

Cascio, W. F., Outtz, J., Zedeck, S., & Goldstein, I. L. (1991). Statistical implications of six methods of test score use in personnel selection. *Human Performance, 4*, 233–264.

Chan, D., & Schmitt, N. (1998). Video-based versus paper-and-pencil method of assessment in situational judgment tests: Subgroup differences in test performance and face validity perceptions. *Journal of Applied Psychology, 82*, 143–159.

Chan, D., Schmitt, N., DeShon, R. P., & Clause, C. S. (1997). Reactions to cognitive ability tests: The relationships between race, test performance, face validity perceptions, and test-taking motivation. *Journal of Applied Psychology, 82*, 300–310.

Coward, W. M., & Sackett, P. R. (1990). Linearity of ability–performance relationships: A reconfirmation. *Journal of Applied Psychology, 75*, 297–300.

Cronbach, L. J. (1975). Five decades of public controversy over psychological testing. *American Psychologist, 30*, 1–14.

DeCorte, W. (1999). Weighing job performance predictors to both maximize the quality of the selected workforce and control the level of adverse impact. *Journal of Applied Psychology, 84*, 695–702.

Edwards, W., & Newman, J. R. (1983). Multiattribute evaluation. Beverly Hills, CA: Sage.

Gottfredson, L. S. (1986). Societal consequences of the g factor in employment. *Journal of Vocational Behavior, 29*, 379–410.

Gottfredson, L. S. (1988). Reconsidering fairness: A matter of social and ethical priorities. *Journal of Vocational Behavior, 33*, 293–319.

Gottfredson, L. S. (1996). Racially gerrymandering the content of police tests to satisfy the U.S. Justice Department: A case study. *Psychology, Public Policy, and Law, 2*, 418–446.

Guilford, J. P. (1988). Some changes in the Structure-of-Intellect Model. *Educational and Psychological Measurement, 48*, 1–4.

Gutenberg, R. L., Arvey, R. D., Osburn, H. G., & Jenneret, P. R. (1983). Moderating effects of decision-making/information processing job dimensions on test validities. *Journal of Applied Psychology, 68*, 602–608.

Guttman, L., & Levy, S. (1991). Two structural laws for intelligence tests. *Intelligence, 15,* 79–103.

Hammond, K., McClelland, G. H., & Mumpower, J. (1980). *Human judgment and decision making.* New York: Praeger.

Hattrup, K., Rock, J., & Scalia, C. (1997). The effects of varying conceptualizations of job performance on adverse impact, minority hiring, and predicted performance. *Journal of Applied Psychology, 82,* 656–664.

Hough, L. M., Eaton, N. K., Dunnette, M. D., Kamp, J. D., & McCloy, R. A. (1991). Criterion-related validities of personality constructs and the effects of response distortion on those validities. *Journal of Applied Psychology, 75,* 581–595.

Humphreys, L. G. (1979). The construct of general intelligence. *Intelligence, 3,* 105–120.

Hunter, J. E. (1986). Cognitive ability, cognitive aptitudes, job knowledge, and job performance. *Journal of Vocational Behavior, 29,* 340–362.

Hunter, J. E., & Hirsh, H. R. (1987). Applications of meta-analysis. In. C. L. Cooper & I. T. Robertson (Eds.), *International review of industrial and organizational psychology* (pp. 321–357). Chichester, England: Wiley.

Hunter, J. E., & Hunter, R. F. (1984). Validity and utility of alternate predictors of job performance. *Psychological Bulletin, 96,* 72–98.

Hunter, J. E., & Schmidt, F L. (1976). Critical analysis of the statistical and ethical implications of various definitions of test bias. *Psychological Bulletin, 83,* 1053–1071.

Jensen, A. R. (1980). *Bias in mental testing.* New York: Free Press.

Keeney, R. L., & Raiffa, H. (1976). *Decisions with multiple objectives: Preferences and value tradeoffs.* New York: Cambridge University Press.

Luce, R. D. (1990). *Utility of gains and losses.* Hillsdale, NJ: Lawrence Erlbaum Associates, Inc.

McClelland, D.C. (1993). Intelligence is not the best predictor of job performance. *Current Directions in Psychological Science, 2,* 5–6.

McHenry, J. J., Hough, L. M., Toquam, J. L., Hanson, M. A., & Ashworth, S. (1990). Project A validity results: The relationship between predictor and criterion domains. *Personnel Psychology, 43,* 335–355.

Mellers, B. A., & Cooke, A. D. (1994). Trade-offs depend on attribute range. *Journal of Experimental Psychology: Human Perception & Performance, 20,* 1055–1067.

Murphy, K., & Davidshofer, C. (2000). *Psychological testing: Principles and applications* (5th ed.). Upper Saddle River, NJ: Prentice Hall.

Murphy, K., & Lee, S. (1994). Does conscientiousness explain the relationship between integrity and performance? *International Journal of Selection and Assessment, 2,* 226–233.

Murphy, K., & Shiarella, A. (1997). Implications of the multidimensional nature of job performance for the validity of selection tests: Multivariate frameworks for studying test validity. *Personnel Psychology, 50,* 823–854.

Orfelio, L. (1997). On the death of SMART and the birth of GRAPA. *Organizational Behavior and Human Decision Processes, 71,* 249–262.

Perloff, R., & Bryant, F. B. (2000). Identifying and measuring diversity's payoffs: Light at the end of the affirmative action tunnel. *Psychology, Public Policy and Law, 6,* 101–111.

Ree, M. J., & Earles, J. A. (1991a). Predicting training success: Not much more than g. *Personnel Psychology, 44,* 321–332.

Ree, M. J., & Earles, J. A. (1991b). The stability of g across different methods of estimation. *Intelligence, 15,* 271–278.

Ree, M. J., & Earles, J. A. (1992). Intelligence is the best predictor of job performance. *Current Directions in Psychological Science, 1,* 86–89.

Ree, M. J., Earles, J. A., & Teachout, M. S. (1994). Predicting job performance: Not much more than g. *Journal of Applied Psychology, 79,* 518–524.

Rogers, E. (1988). Tests, abilities, race, and conflict. *Intelligence, 12,* 333–350.

Ryan, A. M., Ployhart, R. E., & Friedel, L. A. (1998). Using personality testing to reduce adverse impact: A cautionary note. *Journal of Applied Psychology, 83*, 298–307.

Sackett, P. R., & Wilk, S. L. (1994). Within-group norming and other forms of score adjustment in preemployment testing. *American Psychologist, 49*, 929–954.

Schmidt, F. L. (1991). Why all banding procedures in personnel selection are logically flawed. *Human Performance, 4*, 265–277.

Schmidt, F. L., & Hunter, J. E. (1998). The validity and utility of selection methods in personnel psychology: Practical and theoretical implications of 85 years of research findings. *Psychological Bulletin, 124*, 262–274.

Schmidt, F. L., Ones, D. O., & Hunter, J. E. (1992). Personnel selection. *Annual Review of Psychology, 43*, 627–670.

Schmitt, N., Clause, R. Z., & Pulakos, E. D. (1996). Subgroup differences associated with different measures of some common job relevant constructs. In C. L. Cooper & I. T. Robertson (Eds.), *International review of industrial and organizational psychology* (pp. 91-116). New York: Wiley.

Schmitt, N., Rogers, W., Chan, D., Sheppard, L., & Jennings, D. (1997). Adverse impact and predictive efficiency of various predictor combinations. *Journal of Applied Psychology, 82*, 719–730.

Sternberg, R. J. (1977). *Intelligence, information processing, and analogical reasoning: The componential analysis of human abilities.* Hillsdale, NJ: Lawrence Erlbaum Associates, Inc.

Sternberg, R. J., & Wagner, R. K. (1993). The g-ocentric view of intelligence and performance is wrong. *Current Directions in Psychological Science, 2*, 1–5.

Waldman, D. A., & Avolio, B. J. (1991). Race effects in performance evaluations: Controlling for ability, education, and experience. *Journal of Applied Psychology, 76*, 897–901.

HUMAN PERFORMANCE, *15*(1/2), 187–210

The Role of General Cognitive Ability and Job Performance: Why There Cannot Be a Debate

Frank L. Schmidt

Tippie College of Business
University of Iowa

Given the overwhelming research evidence showing the strong link between general cognitive ability (GCA) and job performance, it is not logically possible for industrial-organizational (I/O) psychologists to have a serious debate over whether GCA is important for job performance. However, even if none of this evidence existed in I/O psychology, research findings in differential psychology on the nature and correlates of GCA provide a sufficient basis for the conclusion that GCA is strongly related to job performance. In I/O psychology, the theoretical basis for the empirical evidence linking GCA and job performance is rarely presented, but is critical to understanding and acceptance of these findings. The theory explains the why behind the empirical findings. From the viewpoint of the kind of world we would like to live in—and would like to believe we live in—the research findings on GCA are not what most people would hope for and are not welcome. However, if we want to remain a science-based field, we cannot reject what we know to be true in favor of what we would like to be true.

In light of the evidence in the research literature, can there really be a debate about whether general cognitive ability (GCA) predicts job performance? This was the question that made me ambivalent about the proposal for the 2000 Society for Industrial-Organizational Psychology (SIOP) Conference debate. One explicit assumption underlying the debate proposal was that there is no broad agreement in (I/O) psychology about the role of GCA in job performance. This is not my perception; I think there is broad agreement. Of course, there is never a consensus omnium on any question in science. There are still biologists today who do not accept the theory of evolution. However, broad agreement is another question. Given the

Requests for reprints should be sent to Frank Schmidt, Tippie College of Business, University of Iowa, Iowa City, IA 52242. E-mail: frank-schmidt@uiowa.edu research literature as it exists today, it is almost impossible that there would not be broad agreement. As a telling example of this, I see this agreement in court cases in which expert I/O witnesses for plaintiffs challenging the use of ability tests agree that GCA is generally important in job performance—despite the fact that it would be in the interests of their case to maintain the opposite. Twenty years ago, when the research evidence was less extensive, this was not the case.

In any research-based field, given enough time and effort, research questions are eventually answered. An example is the question of whether GCA and aptitude tests underpredict minority job and training performance. By the early 1980s, hundreds of studies had accumulated making it clear that they do not. Ultimately, two reports by the National Academy of Sciences reviewed this research and confirmed the finding of no predictive bias (Hartigan & Wigdor, 1989; Wigdor & Garner, 1982; see also Schmidt & Hunter, 1999). Thus, this question can now be regarded as settled scientifically (Sackett, Schmitt, Ellingson, & Kabin, 2001).

The question of whether GCA predicts job performance is another example of this: The evidence is so overwhelming that it is no longer an issue among those familiar with the research findings (Sackett et al., 2001). Hence, there cannot be a serious debate. Yet, there was a debate at SIOP 2000—and now there is this special issue. One of my purposes in this article is to explain how such a situation could arise.

SUMMARY OF RESEARCH FINDINGS

General cognitive ability is essentially the ability to learn (Hunter, 1986; Hunter & Schmidt, 1996). From a public relations point of view, it is perhaps unfortunate that psychologists, including I/O psychologists, often refer to GCA as intelligence—because to laymen this term implies genetic potential and not the concept of developed ability at the time the test is administered that psychologists are in fact referencing. This semantic confusion engenders reluctance to accept research findings. Likewise, the term g refers not to genetic potential, but to developed GCA. The fact that GCA scores are influenced—even strongly influenced—by genes does not change the fact that GCA scores reflect more than just genetic potential.

There are abilities other than GCA that are relevant to performance and learning on many jobs: psychomotor ability, social ability, and physical ability. However, validity for these abilities is much more variable across jobs and has a much lower average validity across jobs.

Cognitive abilities that are narrower than GCA are called specific aptitudes—or often just aptitudes. Examples include verbal aptitude, spatial aptitude, and numerical aptitude. Until about 10 years ago, it was widely believed that job performance could be better predicted by using a variety of aptitude measures than by using GCA alone. Multiple aptitude theory hypothesized that different jobs required different aptitude profiles and that regression equations containing different aptitudes for different jobs should therefore optimize the prediction of performance on the job and in training. Despite the fact that to most people this theory had a compelling plausibility, it has been disconfirmed. Differentially weighting multiple aptitude tests produces little or no increase in validity over the use of measures of general mental ability. It has been found that aptitude tests measure mostly GCA; in addition, each measures something specific to that aptitude (e.g., specifically numerical aptitude, over and above GCA). The GCA component appears to be responsible for the prediction of job and training performance, whereas factors specific to the aptitudes appear to contribute little or nothing to prediction. The research showing this is reviewed in Hunter (1986); Jensen (1986), Olea and Ree (1994); Ree and Earles (1992); Ree, Earles, and Teachout (1994); and Schmidt, Ones, and Hunter (1992), among other sources.

Some have turned this argument around and have asked whether GCA contributes anything to prediction over and above specific aptitudes. This question is not as simple as it appears. If this question is asked for any single specific aptitude (e.g., verbal ability), the answer from research is that GCA has higher validity than any single aptitude and contributes incremental validity over and above that aptitude. In the context of GCA theory, this is not surprising, because any single aptitude measure is just one indicator of GCA and thus would be expected to have lower validity than a multiple indicator measure of GCA. However, as discussed in the next paragraph, any combination of two or three or more specific aptitudes is actually a measure of GCA. Comparing the validity of such a combination with the validity of a GCA measure amounts to comparing the validity of two GCA measures. So any difference in validity (typically small) would merely indicate that one measure was a better measure of GCA than the other. The same would be true for any findings of "incremental validity" in this situation.

If the specific aptitudes in the combination of specific aptitudes are differentially weighted (i.e., using regression weights), the composite aptitude measure is still a measure of GCA. The question examined in the research described here pitting specific aptitude theory against GCA is whether such differentially weighted measures of GCA predict job or training performance better than an ordinary measure of GCA. The finding is that they do not—meaning that the differential weighting of the indicators of GCA is not effective in enhancing prediction. There are good theoretical reasons why this should in fact be the case (Schmidt, Hunter, & Pearlman, 1981).

Despite the disconfirmation of specific aptitude theory, a variant of this theory is still used by practitioners, especially in the public sector. Based on my experiences and that of others, those developing tests to select police officers, firefighters, and other public sector employees typically conduct a thorough task analysis of the job. In the next step, they usually attempt to identify the specific cognitive skills required to perform each specific task. Examples of such specific cognitive skills include things such as perceptual skills, memory, and numerical problem solving. The motivation for focusing on such specific skills is often the expectation of reduced adverse impact. Typically, a dozen or more such specific skills are identified and included in the resulting selection test. Such a test—a test that measures performance across a number of such cognitive skills—functions as a measure of GCA. Hence, despite their initial intention to avoid GCA and to focus on the specific cognitive skills actually used, test developers using this approach create and use tests of GCA (Hunter & Schmidt, 1996). They are often unpleasantly surprised when they find that such tests show the usual majority–minority mean differences. A better understanding of GCA research and theory could prevent such surprises.

On the basis of meta-analysis of over 400 studies, Hunter and Hunter (1984) estimated the validity of GCA for supervisor ratings of overall job performance to be .57 for high-complexity jobs (about 17% of U.S. jobs), .51 for medium-complexity jobs (63% of jobs), and .38 for low-complexity jobs (20% of jobs). These findings are consistent with those from other sources (Hunter & Schmidt, 1996; validities are larger against objective job sample measures of job performance, Hunter, 1983a). For performance in job training programs, a number of large databases exist, many based on military training programs. Hunter (1986) reviewed military databases totaling over 82,000 trainees and found an average validity of .63 for GCA. This figure is similar to those for training performance reported in various studies by Ree and his associates (e.g., Ree and Earles, 1991), by Thorndike (1986), by Jensen (1986), and by Hunter and Hunter (1984).

Validity generalization research has advanced the understanding and prediction of job performance by demonstrating that, for most jobs, GCA is the most important trait determinant of job and training performance (Schmidt & Hunter, 1998). Tables 1–4 summarize many validity generalization findings on the validity of GCA and specific aptitudes for predicting both job and training performance. The data in Tables 1-3 illustrate an important research finding: Task differences between jobs do not appear to affect the generalizability of validity. The results presented in Table 1 are for individual jobs (e.g., specific types of clerical jobs), those presented in Table 2 are for broader job groupings (e.g., all clerical jobs combined), and the results presented in Table 3 are from validity generalization studies in which completely different jobs were included in the meta-analysis (e.g., cooks, welders, clerks). Yet, it can be seen that validity generalizes about as well across completely different jobs as it does within a single job. Standard deviations of validities increase very little as jobs become more task-heterogenous. Unlike differences in complexity levels, differences between jobs in task make-up do not affect GCA and aptitude test validity (Schmidt, Hunter, & Pearlman, 1981).

Supervisory ratings of overall job performance were used as the measure of job performance in most of the data summarized in Table 4. In some settings, supervisors have limited ability to observe job performance, making the ratings potentially less accurate. An example of this is the data for law enforcement occupations shown in

TABLE 1
Validity Generalization Findings for Aptitude and Ability Tests— Results With Narrow Job Groupings: All Job Titles the Same

Job	Test Type	$\hat{\rho}$	SD_ρ	Best Case[a]	Worst Case[b]	Criterion
Schmidt, Hunter, Pearlman, and Shane (1979)						
Mechanical Repairman	mechanical comprehension	.78	.12	.93	.63	T
General Clerks	general mental ability	.67	.35	1.00	.22	P
Machine Tenders	spatial ability	.05	.45	.63	-.52	P
First Line Supervisor	general mental ability	.64	.23	.93	.35	P
First Line Supervisor	mechanical comprehension	.48	.27	.83	.14	P
First Line Supervisor	spatial ability	.43	.18	.66	.20	P
Lilienthal and Pearlman (1980)						
Health Aid/Tech	verbal	.59	.20	.85	.33	T
Health Aid/Tech	quantitative	.65	.16	.85	.44	T
Health Aid/Tech	perceptual speed	.39	.03	.43	.36	T
Health Aid/Tech	memory/follow directions	.66	.00	.66	.66	T
Health Aid/Tech	reasoning	.42	.21	.69	.16	T
Health Aid/Tech	spatial	.36	.16	.56	.15	T
Health Aid/Tech	verbal	.48	.12	.63	.33	P
Health Aid/Tech	quantitative	.48	.17	.70	.26	P
Health Aid/Tech	perceptual speed	.36	.06	.44	.28	P
Health Aid/Tech	reasoning	.21	.21	.48	-.06	P
Health Aid/Tech	spatial	.38	.16	.58	.17	P
Science/Engineering Aid/Tech	verbal	.38	.07	.47	.29	T
Science/Engineering Aid/Tech	quantitative	.38	.07	.47	.29	T
Science/Engineering Aid/Tech	perceptual speed	.40	.00	.40	.40	T
Science/Engineering Aid/Tech	reasoning	.52	.29	.89	.14	T
Science/Engineering Aid/Tech	spatial	.61	.15	.80	.43	P
Science/Engineering Aid/Tech	verbal	.58	.14	.80	.40	P
Science/Engineering Aid/Tech	quantitative	.69	.17	.91	.48	P

(continued)

TABLE 1 (Continued)

Job	Test Type	$\hat{\rho}$	SD_ρ	Best Case[a]	Worst Case[b]	Criterion
Science/Engineering Aid/Tech	perceptual speed	.31	.22	.59	.04	P
Science/Engineering Aid/Tech	spatial	.48	.25	.80	.16	P
Pearlman, Schmidt, and Hunter (1980)						
A	general mental ability	.50	.24	.81	.19	P
B	general mental ability	.49	.24	.80	.18	P
E	general mental ability	.43	.00	.43	.43	P
A	verbal ability	.39	.23	.68	.10	P
B	verbal ability	.41	.25	.69	.10	P
C	verbal ability	.37	.00	.37	.37	P
A	quantitative	.49	.13	.66	.32	P
B	quantitative	.52	.16	.72	.32	P
C	quantitative	.60	.09	.72	.49	P
E	quantitative	.45	.00	.45	.45	P
A	reasoning	.38	.00	.38	.38	P
B	reasoning	.63	.12	.78	.47	P
C	reasoning	.31	.18	.54	.08	P
A	perceptual speed	.45	.24	.76	.14	P
B	perceptual speed	.50	.14	.68	.33	P
C	perceptual speed	.45	.00	.45	.45	P
D	perceptual speed	.40	.22	.68	.12	P
E	perceptual speed	.39	.12	.54	.24	P
A	memory	.38	.20	.64	.13	P
B	memory	.42	.00	.42	.42	P
C	memory	.44	.14	.62	.25	P
A	spatial/mechanical	.20	.12	.36	.04	P
B	spatial/mechanical	.42	.19	.66	.17	P
C	sspatial/mechanical	.48	.06	.56	.41	P
A	general mental ability	.80	.00	.80	.80	T
B	general mental ability	.66	.06	.74	.57	T

192

Job	Predictor					Criterion
C	general mental ability	.70	.00	.70	.70	T
D	general mental ability	.54	.11	.68	.41	T
A	verbal ability	.75	.00	.75	.75	T
B	verbal ability	.62	.12	.77	.47	T
C	verbal ability	.60	.00	.60	.60	T
D	verbal ability	.46	.13	.63	.29	T
A	quantitative	.79	.00	.79	.79	T
B	quantitative	.66	.07	.75	.57	T
C	quantitative	.62	.05	.68	.55	T
D	quantitative	.46	.08	.56	.36	T
A	reasoning	.29	.00	.29	.29	T
A	reasoning	.29	.00	.29	.29	T
B	reasoning	.26	.00	.26	.26	T
A	perceptual speed	.46	.27	.81	.11	T
B	perceptual speed	.38	.25	.70	.06	T
C	perceptual speed	.41	.14	.59	.23	T
D	perceptual speed	.36	.17	.58	.53	T
E	perceptual speed	.02	.17	.24	-.20	T
A	spatial/mechanical	.47	.10	.60	.35	T
B	spatial/mechanical	.36	.25	.68	.05	T
C	spatial/mechanical	.26	.15	.45	.07	T
Schmidt, Gast-Rosenberg, and Hunter (1979)						
	Computer programmer	number series (1)	.48	.38	.92	-.05	P
	Computer programmer	figure analogies (2)	.46	.32	.87	.06	P
	Computer programmer	arithmetic reasoning (3)	.57	.34	.72	.13	P
	Computer programmer	sum of (1), (2), & (3)	.73	.27	1.00	.39	P
	Computer programmer	sum of (1), (2), & (3)	.91	.17	1.00	.70	T
Linn, Harnish, and Dumbar (1981)						
	Law School Students	LSAT (Low School Aptitude Test)	.49	.12	.64	.33	T

Note. T = training performance; P = proficiency on the job; Jobs: A = stenography, typing, and filing clerks; B = computing and account receiving clerks; C = production and stock clerks; D = information and message distribution clerks; E = public contact and service clerks.

TABLE 2
Results With Broader Job Groupings

Job	Test Type	$\hat{\rho}$	SD_ρ	Best Case[a]	Worst Case[b]	Criterion
Pearlman (1980)						
All clerical combined	general mental ability	.52	.24	.83	.21	P
All clerical combined	verbal ability	.39	.23	.68	.09	P
All clerical combined	quantitative ability	.47	.14	.65	.30	P
All clerical combined	reasoning	.39	.15	.58	.19	P
All clerical combined	perceptual speed	.47	.22	.75	.19	P
All clerical combined	memory	.38	.17	.60	.17	P
All clerical combined	spatial mechanical	.30	.19	.54	.05	P
All clerical combined	motor ability	.30	.21	.57	.03	P
All clerical combined	performance tests	.44	.43	.99	-.11	P
All clerical combined	general mental ability	.71	.12	.86	.56	T
All clerical combined	verbal ability	.64	.13	.81	.47	T
All clerical combined	quantitative ability	.70	.12	.86	.56	T
All clerical combined	reasoning	.39	.18	.62	.16	T
All clerical combined	perceptual speed	.39	.20	.63	.11	T
All clerical combined	spatial/mechanical	.37	.20	.63	.11	T
Results for law enforcement occupations (Hirsh, Nothup, & Schmidt, 1986)						
All occupations combined	Memory (M)	.40	.00	.40	.40	T
	Quantitative (Q)	.53	.19	.77	.29	T
	Reasoning (R)	.57	.14	.77	.39	T
	Spatial/mechanical	.49	.00	.49	.49	T
	Verbal (V)	.62	.21	.89	.35	T
	*Verbal + reasoning	.75	.00	.75	.75	T
	*V + Q + spatial/mechanical	.76	.00	.76	.76	T
	Memory (M)	.11	.14	.50	-.07	P
	Perceptual speed	.31	.27	.66	-.04	P
	Psychomotor	.26	.15	.45	.07	P

Predictor	Sample					
Quantitative (Q)		.33	.20	.59	.07	P
Reasoning (R)		.20	.10	.33	.07	P
Spatial/mechanical		.21	.10	.34	.08	P
Verbal (V)		.21	.21	.48	-.06	P
V + R		.34	.26	.67	.01	P
V + R + M + spatial/mechanical		.27	.27	.62	.01	P
V + Q +spatial/mechanical		.35	.27	.70	.00	P
Schmidt, Hunter, and Caplan (1981)						
mechanical competence	All petroleum plant operators (1)	.32	.05	.38	.26	P
mechanical competence	All maintenance trades (2)	.36	.20	.62	.11	P
mechanical competence	(1) and (2)	.33	.10	.46	.20	P
mechanical competence	(1), (2) and Lab technicians (3)	.32	.08	.42	.22	P
mechanical competence	(1)	.47	.15	.66	.28	T
mechanical competence	(1) and (2)	.48	.10	.61	.35	T
mechanical competence	(1), (2) and (3)	.46	.12	.61	.30	T
Chemical competence	(1)	.30	.05	.36	.24	P
Chemical competence	(2)	.30	.05	.36	.24	P
Chemical competence	(1) and (2)	.28	.03	.32	.24	P
Chemical competence	(1), (2) and (3)	.29	.00	.29	.29	P
Chemical competence	(2)	.47	.00	.47	.47	T
Chemical competence	(1) and (2)	.28	.03	.32	.24	T
Chemical competence	(1), (2) and (3)	.48	.00	.48	.48	T
General mental ability	(1)	.22	.16	.42	.02	P
General mental ability	(2)	.31	.18	.49	.04	P
General mental ability	(1) and (2)	.26	.18	.49	.04	P
General mental ability	(1), (2) and (3)	.26	.16	.46	.06	P
General mental ability	(1)	.68	.00	.68	.68	T
General mental ability	(2)	.56	.00	.56	.56	T
General mental ability	(1) and (2)	.65	.00	.65	.65	T
General mental ability	(1), (2) and (3)	.63	.00	.63	.63	T

(continued)

TABLE 2 (Continued)

Job	Test Type	ρ̂	SD_ρ	Best Case[a]	Worst Case[b]	Criterion
(1)	Arithmetic reasoning	.26	.20	.52	.01	P
(2)	Arithmetic reasoning	.15	.16	.36	−.05	P
(1) and (2)	Arithmetic reasoning	.31	.18	.54	.09	P
(1), (2) and (3)	Arithmetic reasoning	.31	.17	.53	.09	P
(1)	Arithmetic reasoning	.49	.30	.87	.11	T
(2)	Arithmetic reasoning	.70	.00	.70	.70	T
(1) and (2)	Arithmetic reasoning	.52	.22	.80	.13	T
(1), (2) and (3)	Arithmetic reasoning	.48	.27	.83	.13	T
(1)	Numerical ability	.33	.20	.59	.07	P
(1) and (2)	Numerical ability	.30	.14	.48	.12	P
(1), (2) and (3)	Numerical ability	.30	.11	.44	.15	P
Callender and Osburn (1981)*						
(1), (2) and (3)	General mental ability	.31	.12	.46	.16	P
(1), (2) and (3)	Mechanical competence	.31	.16	.52	.11	P
(1), (2) and (3)	Chemical competence	.28	.00	.28	.28	P
(1), (2) and (3)	Arithmetic reasoning	.20	.19	.44	−.04	P
(1), (2) and (3)	General mental ability	.50	.00	.50	.50	T
(1), (2) and (3)	Mechanical competence	.52	.07	.61	.43	T
(1), (2) and (3)	Chemical competence	.47	.00	.47	.47	T
(1), (2) and (3)	Quantitative ability	.52	.15	.71	.33	T

Note. T = training performance; P = proficency on the job; astericks denotes approximate measures of general cognitive ability.
[a]90th percentile. [b]10th percentile.
*Same Job Groups as in Schmidt, Hunter, & Caplan (1981).

TABLE 3
Results With Extremely Heterogeneous Job Groupings

Job	Test Type	$\hat{\rho}$	SD_ρ	Best Case[a]	Worst Case[b]	Criterion
Schmidt, Hunter and Pearlman (1981)[c]						
35 widely varying	Vocabulary	.51	.12	.66	.36	T
army jobs	Arithmetic reasoning	.56	.13	.73	.39	T
	Spatial ability	.48	.10	.61	.35	T
	Mech. comp.	.50	.11	.64	.36	T
	Perceptual speed	.41	.11	.55	.27	T
Hunter and Hunter (1984)[d]						
Over 500 widely	Gen. mental ability	.45	.12	.61	.29	P
varying jobs	Spatial/perceptual	.37	.10	.50	.24	P
	Psychomotor	.37	.16	.57	.17	P
	Gen. mental ability	.54	.17	.76	.32	T
	Spatial/perceptual	.41	.10	.54	.28	T
	Psychomotor	.26	.13	.43	.09	T

Note. T = training performance; P = proficiency on the job.
[a]90th percentile. [b]10th percentile. [c]35 Widely varying Army jobs. [d]Over 500 widely varying jobs.

TABLE 4
GATB Research Findings: Average Validity of Three Kinds of Ability

Complexity Level of Job	% of Work Force	Performance on the Job			Performance in Training Programs		
		GMA	GPA	PMA	GMA	GPA	PMA
1 (high)	14.7	.58	.35	.21	.59	.26	.13
2	2.5	.56	.52	.30	.65	.53	.09
3	2.5	.56	.52	.30	.65	.53	.09
4	17.7	.40	.35	.43	.54	.53	.40
5 (low)	2.4	.23	.24	.48	—	—	—

Note. Source: J.E. Hunter (1984), *Validity Generalization for 12,000 Jobs: An Application of Synthetic Validity and Validity Generalization to the General Aptitude Test Battery.* Washington, DC: U.S. Employment Service, U.S. Department of Labor.

GATB = General Aptitude Test Battery; GMA = General mental ability, which can be measured by any of a number of commercially available tests (e.g., The Wonderlic Test and The Purdue Adaptability Test); GPA = General perceptual ability, which is a combination of spatial ability and perceptual speed (GPA is measured by the sum of standardized scores on three-dimensional spatial visualization tests - an example is the Revised Minnesota Paper form Board Test) and perceptual speed tests (e.g., The Minnesota Clerical Test); PMA = Psychomotor ability, tests measuring this ability focus on manual dexterity (these are usually not paper and pencil test) they typically require such things as the rapid assembling and disassembling of bolts, nuts, and washers or the rapid placement of differently shaped pegs or blocks in holes of corresponding shape (e.g., The Purdue Pegboard Test). Psychomotor ability is particularly useful in selecting workers for jobs low in cognitive (information processing) complexity.

Table 2 (mostly police jobs; Hirsh, Northrup, & Schmidt, 1986); supervisors typically spend their day in the precinct office and do not observe their officers at work. In law enforcement, the average validity of GCA measures for job performance ratings (last three validities for this occupation in Table 2) is only .32, lower than the average for other occupations (although still substantial). Yet, validities of GCA measures for predicting performance in the police academy are very large, averaging .75 (last two training performance validities), calling into question the mean GCA validity of .32 for performance on the job. Hence, it seems clear that job performance ratings in law enforcement are probably not as accurate as in the case of jobs in which supervisors have greater opportunity to observe their subordinates.

A major concern in the case of GCA measures is lower rates of minority hiring due to the mean differences between groups on GCA measures. These differences in hiring rates can and should be reduced by including valid noncognitive measures in the selection process (Hunter & Schmidt, 1996). However, within the context of GCA measurement per se, there has been interest in the possibility of using video-based tests and other nontraditional vehicles to measure GCA with the objective of reducing adverse impact while holding validity constant. These attempts have generally failed; either group differences have not been reduced or they have but validity has fallen (Sackett et al., 2001). From a theoretical point of view, it is easy to understand these findings. The underlying assumption or hypothesis is that the typical paper-and-pencil approach to measuring GCA creates a bias against minority groups—an hypothesis that is contradicted both by the research findings on predictive fairness and by the broader research findings in differential psychology that I discuss later. If the underlying group differences in GCA are as revealed by previous research, and if a predictor is a measure of GCA, it is not possible to reduce group differences without reducing validity. For a measure of GCA, there are only two ways to reduce group differences. First, one can reduce the reliability of the measure; adding measurement error reduces group differences. This lowers validity. Second, one can modify the measure so that it no longer is a measure only of GCA. This can be achieved by introducing variance from other constructs; for example, one can add personality items and make the measure partly a measure of conscientiousness. This can reduce group differences—and can do so without reducing validity (in fact validity could increase)—but this would no longer be a measure of GCA (Sackett et al., 2001). Hence, for a measure of GCA per se, it is not possible to reduce group differnces in any important way while avoiding loss of validity.

Furthermore, even if one could develop a reliable GCA measure with reduced group differences and with no reduction in validity, such a test would be predictively biased—against the majority group. This is because the mean difference in job performance would remain the same; the reduction in the predictor mean difference would not change the criterion mean difference. For example, if such a hypothetical test showed no mean Black–White differences, it would predict a zero mean difference on job performance, whereas the actual difference would remain the usual *.50 SD*. Hence, such a hypothetical test would be predictively biased; it would underpredict for Whites and overpredict for Blacks.

The relative validity of different predictors of job performance was recently reviewed by Schmidt and Hunter (1998). Among predictors that can be used for entry-level hiring, none are close to GCA in validity. The next most valid predictor was found to be integrity tests (shown by Ones, 1993, to measure mostly the personality trait of conscientiousness). Integrity tests can be used along with a test of GCA to yield a combined validity of .65 (Ones, Viswesvaran & Shmidt, 1993). Among predictors suitable for hiring workers already trained or experienced, only job sample tests and job knowledge tests are comparable in validity to GCA. However, job knowledge and job sample performance are consequences of GCA (Hunter & Schmidt, 1996; Schmidt & Hunter, 1992). That is, GCA is the major cause of both job knowledge and job sample performance. Hence, in using these predictors, one is using an indirect measure of GCA. For the reasons discussed in Schmidt and Hunter (1998), predictors other than ability are best used as supplements to increment the validity of GCA alone. On the basis of available meta-analyses, Schmidt and Hunter (1998) presented estimates of incremental validity for 15 such predictors for job performance and 8 for training performance. Some of these predictors are positively correlated with GCA (e.g., employment interviews) and so are in part measures of GCA.

TAKING A BROADER VIEW: COULD THE FINDINGS ON GCA HAVE BEEN DIFFERENT?

Could the findings summarized earlier have been different? Could it have turned out that GCA was not very important to job performance? Actually, it could not have. In fact, even if no validation studies had ever been conducted relating GCA to job performance, we would still know that GCA predicted job performance. To see why this is so, we must take a broader view; we must broaden the narrow view common in I/O psychology. I/O psychology is not a social science island—it is part of a larger social science continent. Part of the continent is differential psychology: the general study of individual differences. Research in differential psychology has shown that GCA is related to performances and outcomes in so many areas of life—more than any other variable measured in the social sciences—that it would not be possible for job performance to be an exception to the rule that GCA impacts the entire life-space of individuals. The following list is a sampling of some of the life outcomes, other than job performance, that GCA predicts (Brody, 1992; Herrnstein & Murray, 1994; Jensen, 1980; Jensen, 1998):

1. School performance and achievement through elementary school, high school, and college.

2. Ultimate education level attained.
3. Adult occupational level.
4. Adult income.
5. A wide variety of indexes of "adjustment" at all ages.
6. Disciplinary problems in kindergarten through 12th grade (negative relation).
7. Delinquency and criminal behavior (negative relation).
8. Accident rates on the job (negative relation).
9. Poverty (negative relation).
10. Divorce (negative relation).
11. Having an illegitimate child (for women; negative relation).
12. Being on welfare (negative relation).
13. Having a low birth weight baby (negative relation).

GCA is also correlated with a variety of important health-related behaviors (Lubinski & Humphreys, 1997) and a wide variety of tasks involved in everyday life, such as understanding instructions on forms and reading bus schedules, that are not part of one's occupational or job role (Gottfredson, 1997). In fact, the number of life outcomes the GCA predicts are too large to list in an article of this sort. Research in differential psychology has shown there are few things of any importance in the lives of individuals that GCA does not impact. How likely would it be that the one important exception to this rule would be something as important (and cognitively complex) as performance on the job? Not very likely. This means that the research showing a strong link between GCA and job performance could not have turned out differently.

As I/O psychologists, we have a responsibility to take a broader, more inclusive view. We have a responsibility to be aware of relevant research outside the immediate narrow confines of I/O psychology, research that has important implications for conclusions in our field. One such research finding is the finding in differential psychology that GCA is more important than any other trait or characteristic discovered by psychologists in determining life outcomes. It would be irresponsible to ignore this finding in considering the role of GCA in job performance. Yet, this does sometimes happen, even when the individual differences research is conducted by I/O psychologists (e.g., Wilk, Desmarais, & Sackett, 1995; Wilk & Sackett, 1996). Why does this happen? One reason is that most I/O graduate programs no longer include a course in differential psychology. In our program at the University of Iowa, I teach such a seminar, and I find that students are astounded by the recent research findings in such areas as behavior genetics; GCA; personality; interests and values; and trait differences by age, sex, social class, ethnicity, and region of the United States. They are astounded because they have never before been exposed to this body of research. We need to ensure that no one becomes an I/O psychologist without a graduate course in differential psychology.

WHY IS GCA SO IMPORTANT?

It is especially difficult for people to accept facts and findings they do not like if they see no reason why the findings should or could be true. When Alfred Weggner advanced the theory of plate tectonics early in the 20th century, geologists could think of no means by which continents or continental plates could move around. Not knowing of any plausible mechanism or explanation for the movement of continents, they found Weggner's theory implausible and rejected it. Many people have had the same reaction to the empirical findings showing that GCA is highly predictive of job performance. The finding does not seem plausible to them because they cannot think of a reason why such a strong relation should exist (in fact, their intuition often tells them that noncognitive traits are more important than GCA; Hunter & Schmidt, 1996). However, just as in the case of plate tectonics theory, there is an explanation. Causal analyses of the determinants of job performance show that the major effect of GCA is on the acquisition of job knowledge: People higher in GCA acquire more job knowledge and acquire it faster. The amount of job-related knowledge required even on less complex jobs is much greater than is generally realized. Higher levels of job knowledge lead to higher levels of job performance. Viewed negatively, not knowing what one should be doing—or even not knowing all that one should about what one should be doing—is detrimental to job performance. And knowing what one should be doing and how to do it depends strongly on GCA.

However, the effect of GCA on performance is not mediated solely through job knowledge; there is also a direct effect. That is, over and above the effects of job knowledge, job performance requires direct problem solving on the job. Hence, GCA has a direct effect on job performance independent of job knowledge. Space limitations preclude a full description of the causal research that provides this explanation; reviews of this research can be found in Hunter and Schmidt (1996) and Schmidt and Hunter (1992). The key point here is that, even within the confines of I/O research, there is more than just the brute empirical fact of the predictive validity of GCA. There is also an elaborated and empirically supported theoretical rationale that explains why GCA has such high validity. (And, of course, there are also the broader converging and confirming findings in differential psychology, discussed earlier.)

IS THIS THE BEST OF ALL WORLDS?

Would it be better if GCA were less important than it is in determining job performance? In my opinion, it would. From many points of view, it would be better if GCA were less important. For example, it would be better if specific aptitude theory had been confirmed rather than disconfirmed. If specific aptitude theory fit reality, then a larger percentage of people could be high on both predicted and actual job performance. The majority of people could be in, say, the top 10% in predicted job performance for at least one job and probably many. This outcome seems much fairer and more democratic to me. It would also have been much better if noncognitive traits, such as personality traits, had turned out to have the highest validity—rather than GCA. Personality trait measures show minimal group differences, and so adverse impact would have virtually disappeared as a problem. In addition, if all of the Big Five personality traits had high validity, whereas GCA did not, and different, relatively uncorrelated personality traits predicted performance for different jobs, then most people could again be in the top 10% in predicted (and actual) performance for at least one job and probably many. Again, this outcome seems much fairer and more desirable to me. So the world revealed by our research (and research in differential psychology in general) is not the best of all worlds. The world revealed by research is not one that is easy to accept, much less to embrace. However, can we reject what we know to be true in favor of what we would like to be true, and still claim that we are a science-based field?

This is in fact what current social policy does. Current social policy, in effect, pretends that the research findings summarized earlier do not exist. Current social policy strongly discourages hiring and placing people in jobs on the basis of GCA, even when the consequences of not doing so are severe. For example, in Washington, DC, in the late 1980s, GCA requirements were virtually eliminated in the hiring of police officers, resulting in severe and socially dangerous decrements in the performance of the police force (Carlson, 1993a, 1993b). More recently, under pressure from the U.S. Department of Justice, changes in the selection process for police hiring in Nassau County, NY, were made that virtually eliminated GCA requirements (Gottfredson, 1996). In a large U.S. steel company, reduction in mental ability requirements in the selection of applicants for skilled trades apprenticeships resulted in documented dramatic declines in quality and quantity of work performed (Schmidt & Hunter, 1981). As an industrial psychologist, I am familiar with numerous cases such as these resulting from current social policy, most of which have not been quantified and documented. This social policy also has a negative effect on U.S. international competitiveness in the global economy (Schmidt, 1993).

The source of many of these policies has been the interpretation that the government agencies, such as the Equal Employment Opportunity Commission and the Department of Justice, and some courts have placed on Title VII of the 1964 Civil Rights Act (and its subsequent amendments). Some minorities, in particular Blacks and Hispanics, typically have lower average scores on employment tests of aptitude and abilities, resulting in lower hiring rates. The theory of adverse impact holds that such employment tests cause these differences rather than merely measuring them. That is, this theory falsely attributes the score differences and the hiring rate differences to biases in the tests—biases which research has shown do not exist.

A large body of research shows that employment (and educational) tests of ability and aptitude are not predictively biased (Hartigan & Wigdor, 1989; Hunter, 1981b; Hunter & Schmidt, 1982a; Schmidt & Hunter, 1981; Schmidt et al., 1992; Wigdor & Garner, 1982). That is, the finding is that any given GCA test score has essentially the same implications for future job performance for applicants regardless of group membership. For example, Whites and Blacks with low test scores are equally likely to fail on the job. Hence, research findings directly contradict the theory of adverse impact and the requirements that social policy has imposed on employers on the basis of that theory (Schmidt & Hunter, 1999).

The major requirement stemming from the theory of adverse impact has been costly and complicated validation requirements for any hiring and promotion procedures that show group disparities. In particular, employers desiring to select on the basis of GCA must meet these expensive and time-consuming requirements. These requirements encourage the abandonment of ability requirements for job selection, resulting in reduced levels of job performance and output among all employees, not merely for minority employees. In fact, the productivity losses are much greater among nonminority employees than among minority employees (Schmidt & Hunter, 1981).

What should social policy be in connection with GCA in the area of employee selection? Social policy should encourage employers to hire on the basis of valid predictors of performance, including GCA. The research findings discussed earlier indicate that such a policy is likely to maximize economic efficiency and growth (including job growth), resulting in increases in the general standard of living (Hunter & Schmidt, 1982), benefiting all members of society. However, social policy should also encourage use in hiring of those noncognitive methods known to both decrease minority–majority hiring rate differences and to increase validity (and, hence, job performance). That is, social policy should take into account research findings on the role of personality and other noncognitive traits in job performance to simultaneously reduce hiring rate differences and increase the productivity gains from personnel selection (Ones, Viswevaran, & Schmidt, 1993; Sackett et al., 2001; Schmidt et al., 1992).

The goal of current social policy is equal representation of all groups in all jobs and at all levels of job complexity. Even with fully nondiscriminatory and predictively fair selection methods, this goal is unrealistic, at least at this time, because groups today differ in mean levels of job-relevant skills and abilities (Sackett et al., 2001). They also differ greatly in mean age and education level, further reducing the feasibility of this policy goal. The current pursuit of this unrealistic policy goal results not only in frustration, but also in social disasters of the sort that befell the Washington, DC, police force.

This unrealistic policy goal should give way to a policy of eradication of all remaining real discrimination against individuals in the workplace. The chief industrial psychologist in a large manufacturing firm told me that his firm had achieved nondiscrimination in employment, promotion, and other personnel areas. He stated that the firm still had some discrimination against Blacks and women in some locations, but that was balanced out by the discrimination (preference) in favor of Blacks and women in the firm's affirmative action programs. So, in balance, the firm was nondiscriminatory! Actually, the firm simply had two types of discrimination, both of which should not have existed. Both types of discrimination cause employee dissatisfaction and low morale. Discrimination causes resentment and bitterness, because it violates the deeply held American value that each person should be treated as an individual and judged on his or her own merits.

Defenders of the present policy often argue that the task of eliminating all individual-level discrimination is formidable, excessively time consuming, and costly. They argue that the use of minority preferences, hiring goals, time tables, and quotas is much more resource-efficient. However, it is also ineffective, socially divisive, and productive of social disasters of the type described earlier.

RESPONSES TO ISSUES IN THE DEBATE

In this section I discuss some of the contentions advanced by other participants in the SIOP debate. One participant stated that there would be no reluctance to accept the finding of high validity for GCA if it were not for the fact of group differences and adverse impact. I do not think this is the case. Although group differences and adverse impact (in employment and education) do contribute substantially to this reluctance, this is not the whole story. Even if there were no mean differences between groups, a world in which success at work and in life was determined by a large number of relatively independent traits would be fairer and more desirable than the world as revealed by research—a world in which GCA is the dominant determinant of success and half of all people are by definition below average in GCA. Hence, people prefer to believe in the former world and tend to want to reject the research findings on GCA. I find this tendency among students who are not even aware of group differences in GCA. As I indicated earlier, the world as revealed by research is not the best world we can imagine. We can imagine a more desirable world, and we want to believe that that world is the real world. We want to believe a pleasant falsehood. We are in denial.

Another participant stated that the research by Claude Steele on stereotype threat (Steele, 1997; Steele & Aronson, 1995) could explain the lower average GCA scores of some minority groups. However, if this were the case, then GCA scores would of necessity display predictive bias in the prediction of educational and occupational performance. Stereotype threat is hypothesized to artificially lower minority scores, resulting in underestimate of actual GCA. Any artificial depression of scores of a group must logically result in predictive bias against that group. Yet, as noted earlier, the literature is clear in showing no predictive bias against minority groups. There are also other problems. In the typical stereotype threat study, minority and majority students are prematched on some index of GCA (such as Scholastic Assessment Test scores). (For reasons that are not clear, the researchers assume these scores have not been affected by stereotype threat.) Hence, group differences existing in the wider population are artificially eliminated in the study. Participants are then given other GCA tests under both conditions designed to evoke stereotype threat and conditions without stereotype threat (control condition). It is then often found that stereotype threat lowers minority scores somewhat in comparison to the control condition. Therefore, the group difference created in this manner is in addition to the regularly observed group difference. Perhaps the best way to summarize this research is as follows: Minorities typically average lower than nonminorities (and no predictive bias is found for these scores); however, by creating stereotype threat we can make this difference even larger (Sackett et al., 2001). (Note that this means that for scores obtained under stereotype threat, predictive bias against minorities should be found. However, no predictive bias studies have been conducted on GCA scores obtained under conditions of stereotype threat.)

Another proposition advanced during the debate is that GCA is "not unique as a predictor" because meta-analyses indicate that job sample (work sample) tests have even higher validity, as shown in Schmidt and Hunter (1998). This review reported a mean validity of .54 for work sample tests versus a validity of .51 for GCA for medium complexity jobs (63% of all jobs in the United States). The problem with this comment is that performance on work sample tests is a consequence of GCA and hence reflects GCA, as noted earlier. Causal modeling studies have supported the following causal sequence: GCA causes the acquisition of job knowledge, which in turn is the major cause of performance on work sample tests. Hence, work sample tests are not independent of GCA, but rather reflect the effects of GCA. There is also another consideration: Most hiring is done at the entry level, and work sample tests cannot be used for entry-level hiring.

Another participant advanced the hypothesis that "the criterion may be the problem." That is, he suggested that the problem lies in the ways in which I/O psychologists measure job performance, with the implication being that more construct valid performance measures might show that GSA tests are predictively biased against minorities. Job performance is typically measured using supervisory ratings, and the focus of this comment was that such ratings may have construct validity problems as performance measures. Could the research findings of predictive fairness just be a function of construct deficiencies in job performance ratings? This is an example of a case in which triangulation is essential in scientific research. What are the research findings on predictive fairness when other criterion measures are used? Although supervisory ratings are used in most studies, this is not true for all studies. Exceptions fall into two major categories: studies of performance in training using objective measures of amount learned and studies using objective job or work sample measures as the criterion. The military has produced large numbers of training performance studies based on objective measures of amount learned—sometimes objective written tests and sometimes hands-on work sample tests (and sometimes combinations of these). These studies show the same lack of predictive bias as is found in studies based on supervisory ratings. Non-training validation studies using work sample measures obtain the same result. This is true even when those scoring the work sample are blind to the subgroup membership of the participants (Campbell, Crooks, Mahoney, & Rock, 1973; Gael & Grant, 1972; Gael, Grant, & Ritchie, 1975a, 1975b; Grant & Bray, 1970). The findings are similar in the educational domain; different criterion measures used in educational research show the same pattern of lack of predictive bias. Hence, it is not the case that conclusions of predictive fairness rest on the foundation of ratings. All criterion types support the same conclusion. Thus, there is enough research information available to reject the hypothesis that "the criterion is the problem."

One participant emphasized the fact that the structured employment interview appears to have validity comparable to GCA but with smaller subgroup differences, with the implication being that something may be amiss with GCA tests. Although no definitive studies have been conducted showing exactly what constructs are measured by structured interviews, it seems likely that both cognitive and noncognitive constructs are assessed. The finding of positive correlations between structured interview scores and GCA scores (Huffcutt, Roth, & McDaniel, 1996) indicates that GCA is assessed to some degree. Personality traits and other noncognitive traits are probably also assessed. Any predictor score or composite made of both noncognitive constructs and GCA can be expected to show smaller group differences than GCA alone (Sackett et al., 2001). And if the noncognitive dimensions are valid, such a measure may have validity equal to that of GCA measures (Schmidt & Hunter, 1998). This leads to the question raised by the participant: Why not use the structured interview in place of a GCA test and get the same validity with less adverse impact? There is no question that this can be done. However, as noted and demonstrated by Schmidt and Hunter (1998), combinations of predictors lead to higher validity and practical utility than single predictors. Use of a structured interview and a GCA test together (in a compensatory model) yields a validity of .63, versus a validity of .51 for the interview alone. Hence, dropping GCA from the combination results in reduction in both validity and practical utility of nearly 20%. We can also look at this from the opposite view: What would be the consequences of using a GCA test alone, without the structured interview? The answer is lower validity (.51 vs. .63) and greater adverse impact. This example, again, points up the value of using valid noncognitive measures as supplements to GCA measures to increase validity and utility and reduce adverse impact.

Finally, one speaker was concerned that differences between group means are smaller on job performance measures than on GCA. This comment must be considered against the backdrop of the established finding that GCA tests do not show predictive bias against minorities—that is, the finding, discussed in detail, that Blacks, Whites, and Hispanics with the same GCA test scores have essentially the same later average job performance. Because GCA is only one of the determinants of job performance, it is expected statistically that the difference on job performance will be smaller than the difference on GCA scores—given the fact of predictive fairness (Hunter & Schmidt, 1977). For example, given that the difference between Blacks and Whites on GCA is 1 SD and that the validity of GCA measures is typically about .50, the expected difference on job performance must be approximately .50 SD, and this has generally been found to be the case. If the job performance difference were larger or smaller than .50 SD, then research would not find a lack of predictive bias for GCA measures.

Another consideration is reliability. Measures of job performance, especially job performance ratings, are less reliable than measures of GCA. Unreliability artificially reduces apparent group differences—that is, adding the noise of measurement error increases standard deviations, which in turn reduces mean differences in standard deviation units. (This applies on the predictor end as well: GCA tests with low reliability show much smaller group differences than highly reliable GCA measures.) Hence, discussions of group differences that do not take reliability into account are misleading (Sackett et al., 2001). Job sample performance measures are usually more reliable (and more objective) than ratings. Job sample measures typically show Black–White mean differences of about .50 SD or slightly larger (e.g., see Campbell et al., 1973; Gael & Grant, 1972; Gael et al., 1975a, 1975b; Grant & Bray, 1970). At the true score level, these differences are about .55 to .60—about the same as the true score differences on job performance ratings (Hunter & Hirsh, 1987). This complex of research findings is consistent with the theory that GCA is a major determinant of job performance, but there are other determinants that do not show group differences, such as conscientiousness. This is why combining a measure of GCA and a measure of conscientiousness reduces group differences while increasing validity and maintaining predictive fairness.

SUMMARY

The purely empirical research evidence in I/O psychology showing a strong link between GCA and job performance is so massive that there is no basis for questioning the validity of GCA as a predictor of job performance—a predictor that is valid and predictively unbiased for majority and minority groups. In addition to all the purely empirical evidence for the validity and predictive fairness of GCA, there is also a well developed and empirically supported theory that explains why GCA predicts job performance. And even if I/O psychologists had never researched the link between GCA and job performance, research findings on GCA in the broader areas of differential psychology would still compel us to conclude that GCA is predictive of job performance, because it is simply too implausible that GCA could predict all major life performance outcomes except job performance. These findings from differential psychology make the overall theoretical picture for GCA even clearer. Especially when combined with the fact of group differences in mean GCA scores, these findings do not reflect the kind of world most of us were hoping for and hence are not welcome to many people. As a result, we see many attempts—desperate attempts—to somehow circumvent these research findings and reach more palatable conclusions. Such attempts are clearly evident in some of the articles published in this special issue, and I have addressed many of them in this article. Others are addressed in the literature cited. These attempts are in many ways understandable; years ago I was guilty of this myself. However, in light of the evidence that we now have, these attempts are unlikely to succeed. There comes a time when you just have to come out of denial and objectively accept the evidence.

REFERENCES

Barrick, M. R., & Mount, M. K. (1991). The Big Five personality dimensions and job performance: A meta analysis. *Personnel Psychology, 41,* 1–26.

Brody, N. (1992). *Intelligence.* (2nd Ed.). San Diego, CA: Academic Press.

Callender, J. C., & Osburn, H. G. (1981). Testing the constancy of validity with computer generated sampling distributions of the multiplicative model variance estimate: Results for the petroleum industry validation research. *Journal of Applied Psychology, 66,* 274–281.

Campbell, J.T., Crooks, L.A., Mahoney, M.H., & Rock, D. A. (1973). *An investigation of sources of bias in the prediction of job performance: A six year study.* (Final Project Report No. PR-73-37). Princeton, NJ: Educational Testing Service.

Carlson, T. (1993a). D.C. blues: The rap sheet on the Washington police. *Policy Review, 21,* 27–33.

Carlson, T. (1993b, November 3). Washington's inept police force. *The Wall Street Journal,* p. 27.

Gael, S., & Grant, D. L. (1972). Employment test validation for minority and nonminority telephone company service representatives. *Journal of Applied Psychology, 56,* 135-139.

Gael, S., Grant, D.L., & Ritchie, R.J. (1975). Employment test validation for minority and nonminority clerks with work sample criteria. *Journal of Applied Psychology, 60,* 420-426.

Grant, D. L., & Bray, D.W. (1970). Validation of employment tests for telephone company installation and repair occupations. *Journal of Applied Psychology, 54,* 7-14.

Gottfredson, L. S. (1996). Racially gerrymandering the content of police tests to satisfy the U.S. Justice Department: A case study. *Psychology, Public Policy, and Law, 2,* 418–446.

Gottfredson, L. S. (1997). Why g matters: The complexity of everyday life. *Intelligence, 24,* 79–132.

Hartigan, J. A., & Wigdor, A. K. (Eds.). (1989). *Fairness in employment testing.* Washington, DC: National Academy of Sciences Press.

Herrnstein, R., & Murray, C. (1994). *The Bell Curve: Intelligence and Class Structure in American Life.* New York: The Free Press.

Hirsh, H. R., Northrup, L., & Schmidt, F. L. (1986). Validity generalization results for law enforcement occupations. *Personnel Psychology, 39,* 399–420.

Huffcutt, A. I., Roth, P. L., & McDaniel, M. A. (1996). A meta-analytic investigation of cognitive ability in employment interview evaluations: Moderating characteristics and implications for incremental validity. *Journal of Applied Psychology, 81*, 459–473.

Hunter, J. E. (1980). *Test validation for 12,000 jobs: An application of synthetic validity and validity generalization to the General Aptitude Test Battery (GATB)*. Washington, DC: U.S. Employment Service.

Hunter, J. E. (1981). *Fairness of the General Aptitude Test Battery (GATB): Ability differences and their impact on minority hiring rates*. Washington, DC: U.S. Employment Service.

Hunter, J. E. (1983a). A causal analysis of cognitive ability, job knowledge, job performance, and supervisor ratings. In F. Landy, S. Zedeck, & J. Cleveland (Eds.), *Performance measurement theory* (pp. 257–266). Hillsdale, NJ: Lawrence Erlbaum Associates, Inc.

Hunter, J. E. (1983b). *Validity generalization of the ASVAB: Higher validity for factor analytic composites*. Rockville, MD: Research Applications.

Hunter, J. E. (1986). Cognitive ability, cognitive aptitudes, job knowledge, and job performance. *Journal of Vocational Behavior, 29*, 340–362.

Hunter, J. E., & Hirsh, H. R. (1987). Application of meta-analysis. In C. L. Cooper & I. T. Robertson (Eds.), *Review of industrial psychology* (Vol. 2, pp. 321–357). New York: Wiley.

Hunter, J. E., & Hunter, R. F. (1984). Validity and utility of alternative predictors of job performance. *Psychological Bulletin, 96*, 72–98.

Hunter, J. E., & Schmidt, F. L. (1977). A critical analysis of the statistical and ethical definitions of test fairness. *Psychological Bulletin, 83*, 1053–1071.

Hunter, J. E., & Schmidt, F. L. (1982). Ability tests: Economic benefits versus the issue of fairness. *Industrial Relations, 21*, 293–308.

Hunter, J. E., & Schmidt, F. L. (1996). Intelligence and job performance: Economic and social implications. *Psychology, Public Policy, and Law, 2*, 447–472.

Jensen, A. R. (1980). *Bias in mental testing*. New York: Free Press.

Jensen, A. R. (1986). g: Artifact or reality? *Journal of Vocational Behavior, 29*, 301–331.

Jensen, A. R. (1998). *The g factor: The science of mental ability*. Westport, CT: Praeger.

Lilienthal, R. A., & Pearlman, K. (1983). *The validity of federal selection tests for aid/technician in the health, science, and engineering fields*. Washington, DC: U.S. Office of Personnel Management, Office of Personnel Research and Development.

Linn, R. L., & Dunbar, S. B. (1985). Validity generalization and predictive bias. In R. A. Burk (Ed.), *Performance assessment: State of the art* (pp. 205–243). Baltimore: Johns Hopkins University Press.

Lubinski, D., & Humphreys, L. G. (1997). Incorporating general intelligence into epidemiology and the social sciences. *Intelligence, 24*, 159–201.

McDaniel, M. A. (1985). *The evaluation of a causal model of job performance: The interrelationships of general mental ability, job experience, and job performance*. Unpublished doctoral dissertation, George Washington University, Washington, DC.

Mount, M. K., & Barrick, M. R. (1995). The Big Five personality dimensions: Implications for research and practice in human resources management. In G. Ferris (Ed.), *Research in personnel and human resources management* (Vol. 13, pp. 153–200). Greenwich, CT: JAI.

Olea, M. M., & Ree, M. J. (1994). Predicting pilot and navigator criteria: Not much more than g. *Journal of Applied Psychology, 79*, 845–851.

Ones, D. S. (1993). *The construct validity of integrity tests*. Unpublished doctoral dissertation, University of Iowa, Iowa City, IA.

Ones, D. S., Viswesvaran, C., & Schmidt, F. L. (1993). Comprehensive meta-analysis of integrity test validities: Findings and implications for personnel selection and theories of job performance. *Journal of Applied Psychology, 78*, 679–703.

Pearlman, K., Schmidt, F. L., & Hunter, J. E. (1980). Validity generalization results for tests used to predict job proficiency and training criteria in clerical occupations. *Journal of Applied Psychology, 65*, 373–407.

Ree, M. J., & Earles, J. A. (1991). Predicting training success: Not much more than g. *Personnel Psychology, 44,* 321–332.

Ree, M. J., & Earles, J. A. (1992). Intelligence is the best predictor of job performance. *Current Directions in Psychological Science, 1,* 86–89.

Ree, M. J., Earles, J. A., & Teachout, M. (1994). Predicting job performance: Not much for than g. *Journal of Applied Psychology, 79,* 518–524.

Sackett, P. R., Schmitt, N., Ellingson, J. E., & Kabin, M. B. (2001). High-states testing in employment, credentialing, and higher education: Prospects in a post-affirmative action world. *American Psychologist, 56,* 302-318.

Schmidt, F. L. (1988). The problem of group differences in ability scores in employment selection. *Journal of Vocational Behavior, 33,* 272–292.

Schmidt, F. L. (1993). Personnel psychology at the cutting edge. In N. Schmitt & W. Borman (Eds.), *Personnel selection* (pp. 497–515). San Francisco: Jossey-Bass.

Schmidt, F. L., Gast-Rosenberg, I. F., & Hunter, J. E. (1980). Validity generalization results for computer programmers. *Journal of Applied Psychology, 65,* 643–661.

Schmidt, F. L., & Hunter, J. E. (1981). Employment testing: Old theories and new research findings. *American Psychologist, 36,* 1128–1137.

Schmidt, F. L., & Hunter, J. E. (1992). Causal modeling of processes determining job performance. *Current Directions in Psychological Science, 1,* 89–92.

Schmidt, F. L., & Hunter, J. E. (1998). The valadity and utility of selection methods in personal psychology: Practical and theoretical implications of 85 years of research findings. *Psychological Bulletin, 124,* 262-274.

Schmidt, F. L., & Hunter, J. E. (1999). Bias in standardized educational and employment tests as justification for racial preferences in affirmative action programs. In K. T. Leicht (Ed.), *The future of affirmative action* (Vol. 17, pp. 285-302). Stanford, CT: JAI.

Schmidt, F. L., Hunter, J. E., & Caplan, J. R. (1981). Validity generalization results for two job groups in the petroleum industry. *Journal of Applied Psychology, 66,* 261–273.

Schmidt, F. L., Hunter, J. E., Outerbridge, A. N., & Goff, S. (1988). The joint relation of experience and ability with job performance: A test of three hypotheses. *Journal of Applied Psychology, 73,* 46–57.

Schmidt, F. L., Hunter, J. E., & Pearlman, K. (1981). Task differences and the validity of aptitude tests in selection: A red herring. *Journal of Applied Psychology, 66,* 166–185.

Schmidt, F. L., Hunter, J. E., Pearlman, K., & Shane, G. S. (1979). Further tests of the Schmidt–Hunter Bayesian validity generalization model. *Personnel Psychology, 32,* 257–281.

Schmidt, F. L., Ones, D. S., & Hunter, J. E. (1992). Personnel selection. *Annual Review of Psychology, 43,* 627–670.

Steele, C. M. (1997). A threat in the air: How stereotypes shape intellectual identity and performance. *American Psychologist, 52,* 613–629.

Steele, C. M., & Aronson, J. (1995). Stereotype threat and the intellectual test performance of African Americans. *Journal of Personality and Social Psychology, 69,* 797–811.

Thorndike, R. L. (1986). The role of general ability in prediction. *Journal of Vocational Behavior, 29,* 332–339.

Wigdor, A. K., & Garner, W. R. (Eds.). (1982). *Ability testing: Uses, consequences, and controversies* (Report of the National Research Council Committee on Ability Testing). Washington, DC: National Academy of Sciences Press.

Wilk, S. L., Desmarais, L. B., & Sackett, P. R. (1995). Gravitation to jobs commensurate with ability: Longitudinal and cross-sectional tests. *Journal of Applied Psychology, 80,* 79–85.

Wilk, S. L., & Sackett, P. R. (1996). Longitudinal analysis of ability–job complexity fit and job change. *Personnel Psychology, 49,* 937–967.

HUMAN PERFORMANCE, *15*(1/2), 211–231

Agreements and Disagreements on the Role of General Mental Ability (GMA) in Industrial, Work, and Organizational Psychology

Chockalingam Viswesvaran
Department of Psychology
Florida International University

Deniz S. Ones
Department of Psychology
University of Minnesota

General Mental Ability (GMA) has empirical evidence supporting it as a strong predictor of job performance. However, there are agreements and disagreements about the role of GMA in Industrial, Work, and Organizational (IWO) psychology. Some embrace it enthusiastically; some tolerate it; some spend their entire careers looking for ways to minimize the effects of GMA in personnel selection; and, finally, some revile and loath the very concept. The reasons for the divergence vary, and in this special issue of *Human Performance* we brought together leading IWO psychologists and researchers to discuss the potential role of GMA in personnel selection. In this summary, we synthesize, around eight themes, the main points of agreement and disagreements across the contributing authors. The major themes and questions are: (a) predictive value of GMA for real-life outcomes and work behaviors, (b) predictive value of GMA versus specific abilities, (c) the consequences of the criterion problem for GMA validities, (d) is utility evidence for GMA convincing?, (e) are the negative reactions to GMA tests a result of group differences?, (f) is theoretical knowledge of GMA adequate?, (g) is there promise in new methods of testing for GMA?, and (h) what is the current status of non-GMA predictors as substitutes or supplements to GMA?

Requests for reprints should be sent to Chockalingam Viswesvaran, Department of Psychology, Florida International University, Miami, FL 33199. E-mail vish@fiu.edu or Deniz S. Ones, Department of Psychology, University of Minnesota, 75 East River Rd., Minneapolis, MN 55455–0344. E-mail deniz.s.ones-1@tc.umn.edu

Intelligence has been a much debated construct in all of its history. Some swear by it, others swear at it. This is true not only in the area of personnel selection, but across other fields where it has been employed (Jensen, 1980).

Cognitive ability has been used as a predictor in personnel selection for well over 80 years. Although a voluminous literature exists on the topic of cognitive ability, suggesting that it is at least an extensively (if not thoroughly) researched topic, a reading of this (sometimes) contentious literature leads to the conclusion that it may not be well-understood and that there exists less than desirable agreement among Industrial, Work, and Organizational (IWO) psychologists about the appropriate role of cognitive ability in IWO psychology in general, and personnel selection in particular.

Of interest, some of the issues that are debated in this issue about the use and abuse of General Mental Ability (GMA) tests have been around even before intelligence tests were created. The articles in this special issue mirror the literature at large. In any topic of interest to scientists (and especially IWO psychologists), disagreements exist. Consensus omminum is antithetical to science; if everyone agrees on a postulate, no one is likely to conduct research on that postulate. Thus, although some disagreement is expected in any topic, for a topic such as cognitive ability that has played a central role in the practice of IWO psychology for so many years, we would have expected broader agreement.

In this special issue, we brought together distinguished scientists who have grappled with some of the most fundamental issues surrounding the utilization of g in IWO psychology for many years. Of interest, they also disagree with each other on a number of fundamental points. Agreements also exist, but they are few. Even the labels used for the construct are not constant. In the set of 11 articles included in this issue, we see terms such as g, psychometric-g, general mental ability, cognitive ability tests, general cognitive ability, and of course, intelligence tests. In our summary, we refer to this construct as cognitive ability or GMA.

The agreements and disagreements surrounding the use of cognitive ability in selection have to do with both the conclusions that can be drawn from the empirical research conducted on the construct and its measures as well as judgments about the moral obligations IWO psychologists have to society at large. For example, some (see Goldstein, Zedeck, & Goldstein, this issue) question the reliance on GMA not only because of the group differences that result, but also on grounds that it is not a good (enough) predictor. Others level criticisms against reliance on GMA as a predictor because its use results in adverse impact against minorities (Kehoe, this issue).

In this summary, we organize our discussion around eight themes and questions. We underscore the differing opinions expressed on these eight issues by our contributors: their differences on how we should proceed. We hope this summary will enable readers to have an overview of the issues debated as well as the different stances on each issue. The eight themes and questions occurring across the different articles are as follows: (a) predictive value of GMA for real-life outcomes and work behaviors, (b) predictive value of GMA versus specific abilities, (c) the consequences of the criterion problem for GMA validities, (d) is utility evidence for GMA convincing?, (e) are the negative reactions to GMA tests a result of group differences?, (f) is theoretical knowledge of GMA adequate?, (g) is there promise in new methods of testing for GMA?, and (h) what is the current status of non-GMA predictors as substitutes or supplements to GMA?

PREDICTIVE VALUE OF GMA FOR REAL-LIFE OUTCOMES AND WORK BEHAVIORS

In empirical investigations of cognitive ability, by far the most attention has been devoted to predictive validities of GMA for important work and nonwork outcomes.

Ree and Carretta (this issue) as well as Gottfredson (this issue) summarizes the relations between many life outcomes and GMA scores. Drawing on comprehensive and authoritative summaries (Brand, 1987; Herrnstein & Murray, 1994; Jensen, 1980, 1998; Lubinsky & Humphreys, 1997), Schmidt (this issue) states that GMA is positively related to several life outcomes such as educational level, adult income, and positive health-related behaviors; and negatively related to disciplinary problems, delinquency, and crime rates. Gottfredson (1997) presents substantial correlations (.30–.70, depending on which corrections are made) between GMA scores and everyday activities, such as finding which route in a map.

There is general agreement that there has been more than adequate examination of criterion-related validities of cognitive ability tests for different jobs and in different settings. Schmidt (this issue) summarizes most of the validity generalization studies that have been conducted on GMA in his tables. In the special issue, we even have the first validity generalization evidence for two European countries (Salgado & Anderson, this issue).

Reeve and Hakel (this issue) use an analogy from psychological testing literature to underscore the role of GMA in real-life environments. The probability of getting an item correct on a test is hypothesized to be a monotonically increasing function of an underlying trait. Individuals at a given trait level can answer an item of particular item difficulty with a probability of .50, for that item difficulty (and all items of lesser difficulty with greater probability). It is possible, however, that an individual may fail to answer an easier item. Such discrepancies may occur due to carelessness or may be due to good luck or guessing. Similarly, the cognitive complexity of environments vary. Individuals can tackle environments of complexity at or below their cognitive level. Just as a test-taker may miss an item of low difficulty (compared to his or her trait level), it is possible that an intelligent person may fail to succeed in an environment with lower complexity than his or her individual capacity. Thus, cognitive ability is a necessary but not a sufficient condition for success in the real-life outcomes. This idea of individuals needing some level of cognitive complexity to survive and thrive in an environment (with a given level of complexity) is also seen in Gottfredson's article in this issue. Future research can address how this (probabilistic) relation between GMA and real-life outcomes is moderated, mediated, or suppressed by other situational variables and individual traits.

Disagreements arise from interpreting the significance of these findings. On one hand, Reeve and Hakel (this issue) state that if there is only one thing we can know of an individual, then knowing the GMA score will result in the best prediction. Kehoe (this issue), Tenopyr (this issue), as well as Murphy (this issue), accepts that GMA has predictive validity, although they differ in their enthusiasm in endorsing its use.

In contrast, other articles question the relative importance of GMA for real-life outcomes. Criticisms revolve around three main points. First, a central criticism, seen in the articles by Goldstein et al. (this issue), Outtz (this issue), as well as Sternberg and Hedlund (this issue), is that the validities of GMA for predicting real-life outcomes are low. Goldstein et al. state that the percentage variance explained is only 25%, which suggests that 75% of the variance in outcomes are not accounted for.[1] A similar concern is echoed by Sternberg and Hedlund. Goldstein et al. go so far as to state that, given the small amount of variance in work performance explained by cognitive ability, the finding of a generalizable relation between GMA and job performance has inhibited progress in IWO psychology. Murphy also states that we might have become victims of our own success (with GMA).

How high should a correlation be before we can consider it to be substantial? Would researchers and practitioners have been happier if GMA predicted job performance with a validity of 1.00? We think not. Such a scenario would mean that the only determinant of performance would be GMA, and other factors such as motivation, hard work, honesty, and integrity would not matter. It would mean that no other variable could compensate for low cognitive ability test scores. It would mean the complete collapse of IWO psychology as a field: No human resources intervention (e.g., training, development, compensation, and other management interventions) could affect relative rankings on job performance, as the sole determinant of criterion would be GMA. This is not a world in which many of us would like to live.

A second disagreement revolves around whether corrected or uncorrected validities should be interpreted as reflective of the true value of cognitive ability tests. The point of disagreement arises from which corrections, if any, should be applied to observed correlations. For example, Outtz (this issue) noted that observed GMA validities reported in the literature are around .30. His argument is that we should focus on

---

[1]A point worth noting here is that, in gauging the strength of the relation between GMA and performance, the appropriate index of effect size to use is the correlation coefficient (i.e., criterion-related validity) rather than the coefficient of determination, because "evaluating effect size in terms of variance accounted for may lead to interpretations that grossly underestimate the magnitude of a relation" (Ozer, 1985, p. 307).

observed correlations, as these values reflect the state of affairs in practice. The irony of selection is that the more selective one is on the predictor variable, the smaller a correlation one observes with the criterion of interest. If a selection tool has been truly successful, we should observe no or little variance among those selected on that predictor variable. On the other hand, the validity for job applicants (an unselected group) is the value of interest. Range restriction corrections help to gauge the value of the selection tool for applicants (Kuncel, Campbell, & Ones, 1998). Also, if a criterion is unreliably measured, this should not affect judgments about the value of a predictor. Hence, there is a need to correct for unreliability in the criterion as well (Viswesvaran, Ones, & Schmidt, 1996). In passing, we should note that, after deciding to make criterion unreliability and range restriction corrections, another question that arises is which estimates should be used in making them. For example, we recently had an informative exchange on the appropriate reliability coefficient to use for correcting observed validity coefficients for the criterion of supervisory ratings of job performance (Murphy & DeShon, 2000; Schmidt, Viswesvaran, & Ones, 2000). Whether interrater reliabilities, test–retest, or internal consistency reliabilities are used in the corrections will depend on how the criterion construct is conceptualized and measured, as well as on what types of inferences we wish to make.

A third point of disagreement (cf. Sternberg & Hedlund, this issue) is that many psychologists and researchers believe that intelligent behavior is the result of more than just what intelligence tests measure. This may be an educational or public relations issue. Even proponents of GMA validity do not question this view; they merely state that GMA is a major predictor. It is likely that researchers and laypersons use this criticism as a psychological defense mechanism. Given that positive self-delusion is related to well-being, society may need to maintain the viability of this criticism. Future research should investigate how we can promote the use of valid tests without injuring people's self-esteem. Nonetheless, we cannot base research conclusions on what laypersons and researchers believe. That is not science. Many laypersons (and even psychologists?) and researchers in other sciences wonder whether I–O psychology stands for input–output psychology. This misunderstanding does not preclude us from studying industrial–organizational psychology. Thus, misconceptions of laypersons may need to be addressed in educational initiatives and not accepted as truth.

PREDICTIVE VALUE OF GMA VERSUS SPECIFIC ABILITIES

When Ree and colleagues (e.g., Ree & Earles, 1991) titled a series of articles "Not much more than g," a misconception arose about what was being inferred. Many erroneously interpreted "much more than g" as referring to noncognitive measures. The first thing to note is that specific abilities as referred to here do not include personality and motivational constructs or other popular predictors such as interviews that may be designed to assess these. Thus, we can state that all authors in this special issue agree that there are noncognitive predictors or alternatives that could be used to enhance job performance predictions.

Disagreements arise when we focus on specific abilities such as verbal comprehension, block design, number sequencing, finger dexterity, mechanical knowledge, and so forth. Although any specific definition of specific abilities can be challenged, a referral to Carroll (1993) will make clear what we mean by specific abilities here (the boundaries may be fuzzy, but a perusal of the listed specific abilities in Carroll, 1993, will provide a fairly good idea of what we mean by specific abilities in this context). At issue is whether specific abilities increment the validity of GMA.

The attractiveness of specific abilities lies in the desirability of potential outcomes. If specific abilities are important, then we can have a situation where different individuals will be in the top 10% of different specific abilities. Thus, we can conclude that all individuals are in the top 10%, albeit on different specific abilities. This Lake Wobegone effect is comforting to everyone's ego. Schmidt (this issue) elaborates on this psychological process in his article. Thus, multiple aptitude theory is more palatable to all. Reeve and Hakel (this issue) argued that domain-specific performance requires focused, intensive, and deliberate practice. Therefore, GMA may be a necessary and distal determinant of performance, but specific skills obtained by practice are more proximal determinants.

In contrast to what we may desire or believe about domain-specific performance, empirical evidence suggests that the incremental variance when specific abilities are added to GMA is low. All authors who addressed this issue in their articles here (Schmidt, Kehoe, Tenopyr, and Murphy, as well as Ree and Carretta) agree that there is not much more validity to be gained from specific abilities than g (as indexed by incremental validity in the extant literature). However, the authors differ in their evaluation of this empirical finding.

First, Murphy (this issue) states that, although the incremental validity of specific abilities over GMA may be low, it is possible that different people may be selected depending on the specific abilities emphasized. Schmidt (this issue), on the other hand, argues that the military and several police organizations have tried this suggestion, but differential prediction by specific abilities has not been empirically supported. More research on civilian settings (and including a variety of jobs, perhaps across organizations, across industries, and across occupations) will be informative.

Second, Tenopyr (this issue) argues that the low incremental validity of specific abilities may be due to the fact that supervisors have little opportunity to observe specific abilities. The question then arises whether the low opportunity to observe is an accurate reflection of the relative importance of specific abilities or a reflection of criterion deficiency. If the former, then we can dismiss specific abilities as not being important in the workplace; if the latter, we may need to explore methods to refine our criteria. However, Murphy and Cleveland (1995) reported that raters were more accurate in their global evaluations than in recalling specific behavioral acts. If this finding from performance appraisal literature is any guide, tinkering with the criterion may not easily provide incremental validity for specific abilities.

Third, Kehoe (this issue) argues that the low incremental validity may be due to its computation in a restricted population. He noted that GMA is often validated by using samples from the general applicant population, whereas specific ability tests are administered only in restricted samples. However, this explanation appears to be viable only for some exotic specific abilities; most commonly referred to specific abilities can be administered to everyone in the general population. Furthermore, we can correct for range restriction in a third variable to assess the validity of specific abilities in the general population.

Kehoe (this issue) also raises a point that, although the incremental validity may be low for specific abilities, the use of specific abilities may reduce group differences and result in more positive applicant reactions (presumably because these tests are more face valid). Furthermore, Kehoe notes that it might be easier to legally defend a specific ability test. In light of these two advantages of specific abilities over GMA, Kehoe suggests that specific ability tests should be preferred over tests of GMA. He argues that we should require test publishers to demonstrate the incremental validity of GMA over specific abilities. Ree and Carretta (this issue) countered that one cannot measure specific abilities without measuring GMA. Furthermore, a composite of specific abilities is by definition a measure of GMA.

Unlike specific abilities, g-loaded tests are not domain dependent. Measuring GMA enhances generalizability across jobs and criterion facets also. We suspect the general factor observed in job performance measures (see Viswesvaran, 1993; Viswesvaran & Ones, 2000) is partially caused by the GMA that cuts across job performance dimensions as a determinant.

Nevertheless, perhaps another point to note is that empirical findings that relate to the lack of incremental validity of specific abilities over GMA have been limited to a handful of criteria (e.g., overall job performance, training success). We cannot help but wonder if future research will find the same pattern of results for other criteria, such as counterproductive behaviors. The bandwidth and fidelity of what is being predicted is crucial (Ones & Viswesvaran, 1996).

THE CONSEQUENCES OF THE CRITERION PROBLEM FOR GMA VALIDITIES

The criterion problem has been with us for almost a century (Austin & Villanova, 1992; Landy & Farr, 1980). Most research on GMA has demonstrated the predictive validity for training performance, overall job performance, and technical performance. Disagreements exist on the adequacy of these criteria.

Questions are raised about the fact that some of the validation studies have used training performance as the criterion (cf. Goldstein et al., this issue). Because training performance involves the same or similar cognitive tasks as those used in GMA tests, these validity coefficients are called into question. However, Ree and Carretta (this issue) notes that, before anyone can perform the job tasks, they have to learn what to perform and how to perform (declarative and procedural knowledge), rendering training performance a crucially important criterion. Goldstein et al. (this issue) also stresses the distinction between task and contextual performance (Borman & Motowidlo, 1993, 1997) and that GMA, although valid for task performance, may not be as valid as personality variables for predicting contextual performance. Of course, this is countered by Gottfredson (this issue) that no organization would forego selecting individuals for core task performance.

Outtz (this issue) points out that race differences in GMA are greater than race differences in job performance. This is a result of GMA tests having less than perfect predictive validity. Schmidt (this issue) notes that, given the criterion—related validity of GMA for predicting job performance is around .50; a difference of 1 SD in GMA should only translate to a difference of .50 SD in job performance. If this were not the case, it would actually be an indication of differential prediction and test bias (Rotundo & Sackett, 1999). However, Outtz stresses that even the reduced (0.5 vs. 1.0 SD) differences reported in the literature (Ford, Kraiger, & Schechtman, 1986; Kraiger & Ford, 1985) may be misleading, and that actual race differences in job performance may be much less than .50 SD units (Pulakos, Oppler, White, & Borman, 1989; Sackett & DuBois, 1991). Unreliability in performance ratings needs to be taken into consideration. As Schmidt points out, there is voluminous research that triangulates the findings from supervisory ratings with those obtained from objective records and work sample tests (e.g., Bommer, Johnson, Rich, Podsakoff, & MacKenzie, 1995; Borman, 1978, 1979; Heneman, 1986; Schmidt & Hunter, 1998).

Goldstein et al. (this issue) also argues that IWO psychologists should not restrict themselves to individual job performance, but should consider team and organizational performance. That is, in addition to showing validity of GMA for predicting individual job performance, we may need to explore the validity of GMA for organizational effectiveness. Of course, utility analysis does just that, but Goldstein et al. (along with Tenopyr, this issue) do not have much confidence in those utility estimates.

IS UTILITY EVIDENCE FOR GMA CONVINCING?

Schmidt (this issue) and Hunter and Schmidt (1996) estimate the utility of GMA as substantial to both organizations and to the economy at large. As Schmidt also notes, the social consequences of ignoring the role of GMA in job performance may be large (as in the case of police performance). Salgado and Andersen (this issue) provides empirical data suggesting the utility of GMA in European contexts.

However, other articles in this special issue also raise several caveats about utility estimates. For example, Outtz (this issue) wonders how observed correlations of .30 can translate into the gargantuan estimates of utility being paraded. Tenopyr (this issue) notes how even the conservative utility estimates (Schmidt & Hunter, 1981) strain credulity so much that she avoids using such estimates.

It may be worthwhile to remember that the decision theoretic models used to express the utility for tests of GMA are not applicable only to these tests. There is nothing methodologically wrong with the dollar value estimates. Furthermore, even if dollar value estimates are dismissed, other indicators of value (e.g., reduction in workforce to maintain same productivity; training costs; training time reductions; percent increase in output) can provide compelling utility statements. However, utility analyses, as currently carried out, do reductionistically focus on productivity as the primary goal.

Murphy (this issue) maintaines that the statement that we should develop and recommend to employers' selection systems that maximize productivity is a value statement in itself. For example, one can argue that the goal should be to develop a selection system that maximizes opportunities for all groups in society. Outtz (this issue) cites a study by Silva and Jacobs (1993) that suggests that the utility loss from increased minority hiring is not substantial. Outtz suggests that organizations may find a competitive advantage in diversity, especially in a world of increasing diversity.

Future research should explore the stakeholder model that Murphy (this issue) describes in his article. Specifically, research from economics, judgment, and decision making can be used to understand how individuals make utility estimates. The question of which interests to include in a stakeholder model is still an unanswered one. Other issues to consider will have to include whether stakeholders have accurate insights into their own values. Much of the policy capturing studies in human judgment and decision making are not optimistic regarding this question.

ARE THE NEGATIVE REACTIONS
TO GMA TESTS A RESULT OF GROUP DIFFERENCES?

In the United States, there are inescapable group differences on cognitive ability measures. In making desirability judgments about using various predictors as part of selection systems, IWO psychologists compare group differences across different predictors. We saw it in this special issue, when various authors argued for using predictors with smaller group differences in lieu of GMA tests. Yet, no mention is made of the fact that if GMA tests are more reliable than other predictors, the advantage of lower group differences predictors might be illusory. Outtz (this issue) states that GMA produces racial differences that are 3 to 5 times that produced by interviews, biodata, and work sample tests. We wonder about the magnitude of group differences masked by measurement error in predictors such as interviews. In a similar vein, Kehoe (this issue) states that specific abilities show smaller group differences than GMA. This may be a case of unreliability and range restriction masking the true nature of group differences on measures of specific abilities (specific abilities may typically be measured in more select samples than GMA). It may be important to know both the observed and the true (corrected) magnitudes of group differences on predictor measures. The former gives an indication of the differences that are likely to be observed in using the test, whereas the latter can provide insights into whether the construct being measured or statistical artifacts (e.g., measurement error and range restriction) are at the root of differences observed.

On another front, in the interest of making progress in our science, future research should be careful about the terminology used. Clarity demands it. For example, it is dramatic to use the word *discrimination*. But what does it mean? As another example, note how Murphy (this issue) argues about the trade-off between efficiency and equity. On reflection, it is clear that he is talking about group and not individual equity, especially if it is defined from an unqualified individualism perspective (Hunter & Schmidt, 1977). Terms such as *group differences, discrimination, adverse impact, bias*, and *fairness*, although related, are distinct. Carefully crafted and used definitions are crucial to science.

Yet another issue is to consider the logic of the four-fifths rule. Mean differences on predictors may or may not translate themselves into adverse impact. Selectivity also matters. As organizations become more selective, the adverse impact resulting from observed group differences increases. The four-fifths rule infers adverse impact when the selection rate for the low scoring group is less than four-fifths the selection rate for the high scoring group. However, this is only an administrative convenience to balance several social claims (Sackett & Ellingson, 1997). Gottfredson (this issue) notes how job complexity varies across jobs, and as a result the extent of adverse impact varies across jobs when GMA is used for selection. Reeve and Hakel (this issue) compares the cognitive complexity of environments to test item difficulty. Given this gradation in complexity across jobs, it might be intriguing to explore the possibility of a sliding adverse impact rule (e.g., infer adverse impact when the ratio of selection ratios is .50 for high complexity jobs, .80 when considering low complexity jobs). Alternatively, we can eschew the tendency to think in dichotomies (whether or not there is any adverse impact). If we decide to avoid dichotomies, then the question raises as to what the plaintiff has to show to demonstrate adverse impact.

Would the controversy surrounding GMA be less intense if there were no group differences? Although it is only academic to consider such hypothetical scenarios, such considerations can help us better understand the nature and the sources of debate. Some of the authors (Murphy, Kehoe, Outtz) view group differences as a major drawback of GMA assessment. For example, Murphy (this issue) states that GMA is the best predictor of job performance, but also the predictor with most adverse impact. Kehoe (this issue) asserts that the dilemma stems primarily from three key findings about GMA and work performance: (a) GMA tests are at least as predictive of work performance as other more job-specific tests in the cognitive domain and other assessments outside the cognitive domain, such as personality (Schmidt & Hunter, 1998); (b) specific abilities have little incremental validity; and (c) there are substantial group differences on GMA tests that are not due to bias in the measurement (Wigdor & Garner, 1982). According to Kehoe, the first two conclusions suggest efficient and effective selection strategies in which GMA is a primary component, but the third suggests undesirable social consequences. Similarly, Outtz (this issue) states that GMA predicts job performance, but the controversy comes from the fact that cognitive ability tests produce racial differences that are 3 to 5 times larger than other predictors—such as biodata, personality inventories, and the structured interview—that are valid predictors of job performance. According to Gottfredson (this issue), most of the criticism against GMA is at least partly driven by a motivation to meet the socially desirable outcome of reducing group differences.

In contrast, Schmidt (this issue) argues that the controversy about GMA would have been just as intense even if there were no group differences on GMA measures. Schmidt notes that even students who are not aware of group differences have negative reactions. In relatively homogenous societies, there are also negative reactions to GMA tests (Salgado & Anderson, this issue). Salgado and Anderson (this issue) reports on applicant reactions from European countries, where group differences (especially racial group differences) are not as much a salient issue as they are in the United States. Their review suggests that negative reactions to GMA tests exist in the European countries. Why are there negative feelings toward a high validity predictor?

Reeve and Hakel (this issue) notes how the past abuses of testing for GMA still haunt us. The relation between GMA assessment and social movements such as eugenics has stigmatized the societal view of GMA. Equality for all has been touted as the cornerstone of Western democracy. The curious thing is that GMA can be used to create a society of equal opportunity for all.

Research on applicant reactions in general, and reactions to GMA assessment, can be valuable in discovering the roots of dislike for GMA tests (Rynes, 1993). However, the study of applicant reactions is still in its infancy (Smither, Reilly, Millsap, Pearlman, & Stoffey, 1993). The existing work focuses on general psychological principles such as perceptions of justice (Gilliland, 1993). Most of the existing research in organizational research has taken the organization's perspective, and very little work has focused on the applicant's perspective (Gilliland, 1995; Schuler, Farr, & Smith, 1993). Most of the existing research focuses on applicants reactions to various selection system characteristics and very little addresses the question why such reactions occur or what could be done specifically to address or mitigate such concerns.

Goldstein et al. (this issue) and Sternberg and Hedlund (this issue) provids another potential reason for the limited support GMA assessments enjoy among the general public. These authors points out that the laypeople may be convinced that cognitive ability is not the only determinant, or even the most important determinant of intelligent behavior. This line of reasoning may also partially explain Tenopyr's (this issue) point that, although research suggests validity of GMA increases with increasing job complexity, organizations are less likely to emphasize GMA for high-level jobs than they do for lower level jobs. As discussed earlier, face validity probably also comes into play here.

IS THEORETICAL KNOWLEDGE OF GMA ADEQUATE?

There is more disagreement than agreement on this question across the set of articles in this special issue. Some authors even questioned the existence of anything meaningful in GMA, beyond an abstraction. For example, Goldstein et al. (this issue) noted that there is no agreement on the definition and measurement of GMA and quoted Gould (1994) for how reification of an abstract concept results in absurdities. This lack of agreement is also echoed by Sternberg and Hedlund (this issue). Reeve and Hakel (this issue) observed that all constructs are abstractions, and, thus, the criticism of GMA as only an abstraction is misguided. They also noted that discussions of "Psychometric g" involve a redundant adjective; all factors are psychometric. The use of terms such as "psychometric g" or "the so-called general factor," as though GMA is a statistical phenomenon with no practical importance, makes sense for scoring debate points, but is scientifically meaningless.

In criticizing the theoretical basis of GMA for predicting job performance, Goldstein et al. (this issue) charges that the finding of a simple, linear relation generalizable across jobs between GMA and job performance has (a) stunted the development of the theoretical basis and refinements of other predictors and influences on job performance and (b) restricted us to linear models to the exclusion of an exploration of nonlinear, configural models. Dissenting, Gottfredson (this issue) points out that theoretical obtuseness should not be used to discredit or confuse the literature to satisfy socially motivated goals. She points out the presence of a general factor in many test batteries, in different samples, in different cultures, and so forth. Gottfredson notes the lawful relation between the g-loadedness of tests and their validity in predicting complex task performance. The case of personality assessment is invoked to stress that the presence of a general factor cannot be an artifact of factor analyses.

What process mechanisms explain the effects of cognitive ability on performance and other work outcomes? Ree and Carretta (this issue) as well as

Schmidt (this issue) summarize existing path models developed to test process mechanisms of the effects of GMA on work outcomes. Although the research is not discussed by the contributing authors, we would also note the several laboratory experiments that clarify the role of GMA in work-relevant task performance. There may be more explorations of the theoretical rationale for GMA-outcome relations in IWO psychology than other fields.

Ree and Carretta (this issue) summarize the several psychological and biological correlates of GMA. Reeve and Hakel (this issue) state that knowledge of how GMA is important for a wide variety of life outcomes is sparse. After reviewing the material from behavior genetics, they proposed some potential reasons for racial group differences. Future research should explore other mechanisms to better understand how and why GMA differs across individuals and across groups defined by ethnic origin. Advances in biological sciences, and behavior genetics in particular, may advance our understanding of GMA, notably on these questions.

Several authors advise the incorporation of findings from other fields in the quest to better understand the theoretical basis of GMA. Schmidt (this issue) suggest that a course in differential psychology must be compulsory for all industrial–organizational psychologists. Tenopyr (this issue) stress the need to assimilate the recent advances in cognitive and developmental psychology to understand the development of GMA in individuals. She called for linking the study of individual differences and organizational research. Tenopyr also mentioned the research on person–environment fit and the concept of "typical intellectual engagement" proposed by Ackerman and his colleagues (e.g., Ackerman 1989) as potentially fruitful avenues for future research to explore. In Tenopyr's view, although current theories of GMA enjoy some support, (a) they can all be criticized, and (b) the possibility of a viable new theory cannot be dismissed.

Finally, we should stress that the theoretical knowledge of GMA is much more than what we have for other predictors. Murphy (1996) characterizes this state of affairs noting that research on predictors in personnel selection can be classified as either those exploring cognition or those exploring variables other than cognition. In fact, Goldstein et al. (this issue) use this massive (compared to other predictors) theoretical database on GMA as evidence of how GMA has stunted development and refinement of other predictors. It appears that there are important unresolved questions about GMA, but we know more about GMA than any other construct used as a predictor in personnel selection.

IS THERE PROMISE IN NEW METHODS
OF TESTING FOR GMA?

Goldstein et al. (this issue) suggest that the low cost of paper-and-pencil tests has killed the demand for other types of testing media. Some efforts have been made to assess GMA with different technologies. To reduce group differences on paper-and-pencil GMA tests, a strategy that seems to be gaining in popularity appears to be changes in test medium (Sackett, Schmitt, Ellingson, & Kabin, 2001). Computerized and video-based assessments (cf. Chan & Schmitt, 1997) are some examples. Salgado and Anderson (this issue) discussed a virtual reality technology used in Europe for selection. Sternberg and Hedlund (this issue) listed alternative approaches to assessing practical intelligence. If the use of a different medium reduces adverse impact without reducing validity for a criterion, then the new method of testing is preferable.

In pursuing alternative media and test format changes, care must be taken not to alter the construct being assessed. "Format changes" may rarely be truly format changes alone. Scores on new formats of assessing GMA may reflect individual differences in GMA plus individual differences in responding to the new medium of testing. If the latter source of variance also reduces group differences but is unrelated to the criterion of interest, then changing the medium of assessment may be beneficial. Murphy (this issue) suggests that this might be one approach to try to balance efficiency and (group) equity. However, Schmidt (this issue) as well as Kehoe (this issue) correctly argue that, given the lack of differential prediction for paper-and-pencil GMA tests, any reduction in group differences resulting from changes in testing medium will result in differential prediction. Also, in assessing the relative reduction of group differences resulting from format changes, measurement error must also be taken into account (see the previous section for a discussion). What might be perceived as a medium effect may actually be a reliability effect. Emphasizing this point, Gottfredson (this issue) and Schmidt (this issue) suggest that most of the recent attempts to reduce group differences by changes to GMA test format may have been due to changes in the level of measurement error in GMA assessments.

The next few decades will be interesting, as new tools based on physiological, biological, and even genetic markers are identified for GMA. Whether these potentially more invasive assessments are developed and become available for use depends on how society decides to balance the privacy rights of individuals against the needs of organizations.

WHAT IS THE CURRENT STATUS OF NON-GMA PREDICTORS AS SUBSTITUTES OR SUPPLEMENTS TO GMA?

The search for alternative predictors to GMA has already had a long history (Hunter & Hunter, 1984; Schmidt & Hunter, 1998). The first issue where we note differences across our 11 sets of contributors is whether we should consider the different predictors as substitutes to GMA or as supplements to GMA. Outtz (this issue) argue that because GMA produces 3 to 5 times the adverse impact as other equally valid predictors, it is indefensible to use GMA as a major component in a selection system. Murphy (this issue) states that we cannot defend the use of GMA if alternate predictors of equal validities can be found. On the other hand, Schmidt (this issue) noted that alternatives are not substitutes, but supplements. This is also echoed by Gottfredson (this issue), who classified predictors as can do, will do, and have done predictors. GMA tests capture a can do construct, personality measures reflect will do constructs, and work sample tests are prototypical examples of have done predictors. Gottfredson noted that GMA predicts task performance, whereas personality variables could better predict contextual performance (Borman & Motowidlo, 1997). However, she stresses that no organization would forego selecting for core technical performance. Thus, alternative predictors can at best serve as supplements, but never as substitutes for GMA.

This view is also echoed by Goldstein et al. (this issue), whose emphasis is on increasing the percentage variance explained in job performance by using more complex models and incorporating non-GMA measures into selection systems. Similar views are also expressed by Sternberg and Hedlund (this issue). We should note that, although reductions in group differences are possible by combining GMA and noncognitive measures with negligible group differences such as integrity tests (Ones & Viswesvaran, 1998; Ones, Viswesvaran, & Schmidt, 1993), this strategy cannot completely erase the group differences (Sackett & Ellingson, 1997).

The alternate predictors frequently cited in the literature include personality variables, job knowledge measures, and work sample tests. Tenopyr (this issue) notes that, despite the recent favorable reviews of personality assessment for predicting job performance, the actual validities are just as low as those reported by Guion and Gottier (1965). She also raises issues of faking and the need to develop applicant level norms. Not all personality constructs and measures have equal validity in predicting overall job performance. As we have noted elsewhere, compound personality measures such as integrity tests (Ones et al., 1993) and Criterion-focused Occupational Personality Scales (Ones & Viswesvaran, 2001) produce validities in upper .30s and lower .40s for overall job performance. Such criterion-related validities are certainly superior to those reported for the Big Five personality dimensions (Barrick & Mount, 1991; Hurtz & Donovan, 2000). As for social desirability influences on the validity of personality measures, extensive research has shown that faking among job applicants does not destroy criterion-related validity (Hough, 1998; Ones & Viswesvaran, 1998; Ones, Viswesvaran, & Reiss, 1996). However, applicant norms may be essential to appropriately interpret the meaning of scores in personnel selection settings.

Research on job knowledge and work samples has concentrated on several predictors such as job knowledge tests, tacit knowledge tests, situational judgment tests, and so forth. Gottfredson (this issue) note that these "have done" predictors cannot be used with untrained applicants, for most entry-level positions, or with inexperienced individuals (a point also made by Schmidt, this issue). Furthermore, job knowledge and job sample performance are partly consequences of GMA.

Sternberg and Hedlund (this issue) promote the use of tacit knowledge as an alternate predictor. However, many authors (Gottfredson; Ree, & Carretta; Reeve & Hakel; Tenopyr; all this issue) express concern about the construct definition of tacit knowledge. Sternberg and Hedlund note that tacit knowledge is a specific kind of procedural knowledge. There is also added clarity that Sternberg and colleagues consider practical intelligence a determinant of tacit knowledge. Sternberg and Hedlund argue that the empirical evidence to date suggests that tacit knowledge is independent of GMA. However, correlations between the measures have been examined in very range restricted samples (e.g., Yale undergraduates; see Kuncel et al., 1998, and Kuncel, Hezlett, & Ones, 2001, for detailed discussions of this point). More important, if tacit knowledge is indeed a type of procedural knowledge, it may be misleading to measure it among those who have had no opportunity to gain this knowledge (e.g., college students). Among art majors, it would be relatively easy to show that physics knowledge does not correlate with GMA, but this does not mean that acquiring physics knowledge is unrelated to one's intelligence!

As Goldstein et al. (this issue) note in their article, often the distinction between cognitive abilities and noncognitive predictors is not as clear cut as we would like it to be. The distinction is fuzzy at the boundaries. This raises questions as to whether the predictive validity of alternate predictors is partly due to GMA. Tenopyr (this issue) wonder whether some of the incremental validity of interviews and biodata reported in some studies are due to interviews and biodata measuring cognitive abilities, not measured by the GMA test used in those studies. For alternate predictors such as personality and psychomotor ability tests, the assessment process may invoke GMA. Goldstein et al. note how cognitive demands can exist even in personality assessments, and a similar point is made by Ree and Carretta (this issue) with respect to assessment of psychomotor ability. Finally, Goldstein et al. note that working memory capacity may influence both performance in GMA tests as well as on alternate predictors.

In general, the theoretical foundation of alternate predictors is nowhere near that accumulated for GMA (Murphy, 1996). In evaluating alternate predictors, one should apply the same standards to these as those applied to GMA tests. Unfortunately, most of the extant literature fails to do this. It is also important to note that, if alternatives are used as substitutes rather than as supplements, by forgoing use of GMA tests we may be missing an important predictor of performance (particularly core task performance).

There are two issues that future research should address with respect to the development of alternate predictors. First, there seems to be some confusion between constructs and methods (Hough & Oswald, 2000; Schmitt & Chan, 1998). It is not clear what one refers to when the validity of (or group differences in) interviews, biodata, assessment centers, and so forth, are discussed. Interviews, assessment centers, and biodata can be used to measure all sorts of different constructs from social skills to abstract mathematical problem-solving skills. Furthermore, an interview used as a first selection hurdle is likely to differ in content and form from an interview used as a final step in the selection process.

A second issue is the lack of empirical data on the predictor intercorrelations. Both to build comprehensive theories of work performance as well as to design personnel selection systems to maximize validity and reduce group differences, we need to accurately and precisely estimate predictor intercorrelations. Schmitt, Rogers, Chan, Sheppard, and Jennings (1997) compiled a meta-analytically derived matrix (cf. Viswesvaran & Ones, 1995) to estimate these intercorrelations. Bobko, Roth, and Potosky (1999) cautioned us about the methodological choices involved in putting together such a matrix. More important, it is clear that there is very sparse empirical evidence to guide us here.

A related issue in assessing predictor intercorrelations is the type of selection system under consideration. The implicit assumption in using these predictor intercorrelation matrices to investigate the validity and adverse impact of different combinations (Sackett et al., 2001; Schmitt et al., 1997) is that the selection systems are fully compensatory. When predictors are used in different stages, then there is a need to account for different levels of range restriction. That is, in considering the intercorrelation of one predictor with other predictors, we need to consider the order in which the predictors will be used. Thus, if there are six predictors, then we may need to construct $2^6 - 1 = 63$ intercorrelation matrices for the different combinations. Ultimately, the needs of organizations might dictate how predictor incorrelation matrices are put together and used.

A final crucial point to note in considering other predictors is to be aware that equal validity may not imply equal value. This view underlies even the Uniform Guidelines on Employee Selection Procedures (U.S. Equal Employment Opportunity Commission, 1978) in that the guidelines suggest that when there are equally valid predictors, those with less adverse impact should be employed. This assumption that equal validity implies equal value is also reflected in utility models. However, as Kehoe (this issue) notes

A correlation coefficient of .25 between a personality composite and a measure of overall performance does not necessarily reflect the same value for an organization as a .25 correlation between GMA and overall performance. The people chosen based on the personality measure would not be the same, and they would not have the same attribute profile, as the people chosen based on GMA. The two equal correlations would reflect different construct mappings of predictors onto the criterion, although the variance accounted for is the same. Operationally, the organization might experience the differences in a variety of tangible ways. For example, the "personality" employees might achieve their overall performance by being relatively more dependable, persistent, attentive, helpful, and so on. The "cognitive" employees might achieve their overall performance by being relatively more accurate, faster, effective problem solvers, and the like.

This view of equal validity being different from equal value should be kept in mind when considering the multiattribute utility models discussed by Murphy (this issue). Murphy states that, logically, decision makers should prefer selection system A over system B if (a) A is higher in both equity and efficiency, (b) A equals B in efficiency but A is greater than B in terms of equity, and (c) A equals B in equity but A is greater than B in efficiency. The key point to note here is that efficiency cannot be defined solely in terms of validity, and equity has to be clearly taken into consideration.

CONCLUSION

The set of 11 articles in this special issue are thought-provoking and raise several important points. These articles summarize what psychologists have discovered about GMA thus far. Of interest, contributors also diverge on the future importance of GMA for job performance. Predictions are diametrically opposing: The role of GMA in the sphere of work may (a) increase (Kehoe, this issue) and (b) decrease (Goldstein et al., this issue). We tend to believe that, with increasing complexity in our environments, the former is more likely than the latter. Increasing technological sophistication of the workplace as well as globalization of economic activities (see Salgado and Anderson, this issue) are likely to contribute to the increase in the importance of GMA. Hopefully, this special issue of *Human Performance* will serve as a summary for practitioners and guide future research. We recognize that goals of any society are not determined solely by research findings or the scientific literature. Research and literature can only point out whether the goals set by society are likely to succeed or to fail. It is our hope that a clearer understanding of GMA and its role in IWO psychology will maximize GMA's usefulness for applied purposes and will increase decision quality when setting public policy.

ACKNOWLEDGMENT

Both authors contributed equally to this article; the order of authorship is arbitrary.

REFERENCES

Ackerman, P.L., (1989). Within task intercorrelations of skilled performance: Implications for predicting individual differences. Journal of Applied Psychology, 74, 360–364.

Austin, J. T., & Villanova, P. (1992). The criterion problem: 1917–1992. *Journal of Applied Psychology, 77,* 836–874.

Barrick, M. R., & Mount, M. K. (1991). The Big Five personality dimensions and job performance: A meta-analysis. *Personnel Psychology, 44,* 1–26.

Bobko, P., Roth, P. L., & Potosky, D. (1999). Derivation and implications of a meta-analytic matrix incorporating cognitive ability, alternative predictors, and job performance. *Personnel Psychology, 52,* 561–589.

Bommer, W. H., Johnson, J. L., Rich, G. A., Podsakoff, P. M., & MacKenzie, S. B. (1995). On the interchangeability of objective and subjective measures of employee performance: A meta-analysis. *Personnel Psychology, 48,* 587–605.

Borman, W. C. (1978). Exploring the upper limits of reliability and validity in job performance ratings. *Journal of Applied Psychology, 63,* 135–144.

Borman, W. C. (1979). Format and training effects on rating accuracy and rater errors. *Journal of Applied Psychology, 64,* 410–412.

Borman, W. C., & Motowidlo, S. J. (1993). Expanding the criterion domain to include elements of contextual performance. In N. Schmitt & W. C. Borman (Eds.), *Personnel selection in organizations* (pp. 71–98). San Francisco: Jossey-Bass.

Borman, W. C., & Motowidlo, S. J. (1997). Task performance and contextual performance: The meaning for personnel selection research. *Human Performance, 10,* 99–109.

Brand, C. (1987). The importance of general intelligence. In S. Modgil & C. Modgil (Eds.), *Arthur Jensen: Consensus and controversy* (pp. 251–265). New York: Falmer.

Carroll, J. B. (1993). *Human cognitive abilities: A survey of factor-analytic studies.* New York: Cambridge University Press.

Chan, D., & Schmitt, N. (1997). Video-based versus paper-and-pencil method of assessment in situational judgment tests: Subgroup differences in test performance and face validity perceptions. *Journal of Applied Psychology, 42,* 143–159.

Ford, J. K., Kraiger, K., & Schechtman, S. L. (1986). Study of race effects in objective indices and subjective evaluations of performance: A meta-analysis of performance criteria. *Psychological Bulletin, 99,* 330–337.

Gilliland, S. W. (1993). The perceived fairness of selection systems: An organizational justice perspective. *Academy of Management Review, 18,* 694–734.

Gilliland, S. W. (1995). Fairness from the applicant's perspective: Reactions to employee selection procedures. *International Journal of Selection and Assessment, 3,* 11–19.

Gottfredson, L. S. (1997). Why *g* matters: The complexity of everyday life. *Intelligence, 24,* 79–132.

Gould, S.J., (1994). Curveball. *The New Yorker,* November 28.

Guion, R. M., & Gottier, R. F. (1965). Validity of personality measures in personnel selection. *Personnel Psychology, 18,* 135–164.

Heneman, R. L. (1986). The relationship between supervisory ratings and results-oriented measures of performance: A meta-analysis. *Personnel Psychology, 39,* 811–826.

Herrnstein, R. J., & Murray, C. (1994). *The bell curve: Intelligence and class structure in American life.* New York: Free Press.

Hough, L.M., (1998). Effects of distortion in personality measurement and suggested palliatives. *Human Performance, 4,* 209–244.

Hough, L. M., & Oswald, F. L. (2000). Personnel selection: Looking toward the future—Remembering the past. *Annual Review of Psychology, 51,* 631–664.

Hunter, J. E., & Hunter, R. F. (1984). Validity and utility of alternative predictors of job performance. *Psychological Bulletin, 96,* 72–98.

Hunter, J. E., & Schmidt, F. L. (1977). A critical analysis of the statistical and ethical definitions of test fairness. *Psychological Bulletin, 83,* 1053–1071.

Hunter, J. E., & Schmidt, F. L. (1996). Intelligence and job performance: Economic and social implications. *Psychology, Public Policy, and Law, 2,* 447–472.

Hurtz, G. M., & Donovan, J. J. (2000). Personality and job performance: The Big Five revisited. *Journal of Applied Psychology, 85*, 869–879.

Jensen, A. R. (1980). *Bias in mental testing.* New York: Free Press.

Jensen, A. R. (1998). *The g factor: The science of mental ability.* Westport, CT: Praeger.

Kraiger, K., & Ford, J. K. (1985). A meta-analysis of ratee race effects in performance ratings. *Journal of Applied Psychology, 70*, 56–65.

Kuncel, N. R., Campbell, J. P., & Ones, D. S. (1998). The validity of the Graduate Record Exam: Estimated or tacitly known? *American Psychologist, 53*, 567–568.

Kuncel, N. R., Hezlett, S. A., & Ones, D. S. (2001). A comprehensive meta-analysis of the predictive validity of the graduate record examinations: Implications for graduate student selection and performance. *Psychological Bulletin, 127*, 162–181.

Landy, F. J., & Farr, J. L. (1980). Performance rating. *Psychological Bulletin, 87*, 72–107.

Lubinski, D., & Humphreys, L. G. (1997). Incorporating general intelligence into epidemiology and the social sciences. *Intelligence, 24*, 159–201.

Murphy, K. R. (1996). Individual differences and behavior in organizations: Much more than *g.* In K. R. Murphy (Ed.), *Individual differences and behavior in organizations* (pp. 3–30). San Francisco: Jossey-Bass.

Murphy, K. R., & Cleveland, J.N. (1995). *Understanding performance appraisal: Social organizational, and goal-based perspectives.* Thousand Oaks, CA: Sage Publications.

Murphy, K. R., & DeShon, R. P. (2000). Interrater correlations do not estimate the reliability of job performance ratings. *Personnel Psychology, 53.* 873–900.

Ones, D.S., Viswesvaran, C. (2001). Integrity tests and other criterion-focused occupational personality scales (COPS) used in personnel selection. International Journal of Selection and Assessment, 9, 31–*39.*

Ones, D. S., & Viswesvaran, C. (1996). Bandwidth-fidelity dilemma in personality measurement for personnel selection. *Journal of Organizational Behavior, 17*, 209–226.

Ones, D. S., & Viswesvaran, C. (1998). Gender, age and race differences on overt integrity tests: Analyses across four large-scale applicant data sets. *Journal of Applied Psychology, 83*, 35–42.

Ones, D. S., Viswesvaran, C., & Reiss, A. D. (1996). Role of social desirability in personality testing for personnel selection: The red herring. *Journal of Applied Psychology, 81*, 660–679.

Ones, D. S., Viswesvaran, C., & Schmidt, F. L. (1993). Comprehensive meta-analysis of integrity test validities: Findings and implications for personnel selection and theories of job performance [Monograph]. *Journal of Applied Psychology, 78*, 679–703.

Ozer, D. J. (1985). Correlation and the coefficient of determination. *Psychological Bulletin, 97*, 307–315.

Pulakos, E. D., Oppler, S. H., White, L. A., & Borman, W. C. (1989). Examination of race and sex effects on performance ratings. *Journal of Applied Psychology, 74*, 770–780.

Ree, M.J., & Earles, J.A. (1991). Predicting training success: Not much more than g. *Personnel Psychology, 44*, 321–332.

Rotundo, M., & Sackett, P. R. (1999). Effect of rater race on conclusions regarding differential prediction in cognitive ability tests. *Journal of Applied Psychology, 84*, 815–822.

Rynes, S. L. (1993). Who's selecting whom? Effects of selection practices on applicant attitudes and behavior. In N. Schmitt & W. C. Borman (Eds.), *Personnel selection in organizations* (pp. 240–274). San Francisco: Jossey-Bass.

Sackett, P. R., & DuBois, C. L. Z. (1991). Rater–ratee race effects on performance evaluation: Challenging meta-analytic conclusions. *Journal of Applied Psychology, 76*, 873–877.

Sackett, P. R., & Ellingson, J. E. (1997). The effects of forming multi-predictor composites on group differences and adverse impact. *Personnel Psychology, 50*, 707–721.

Sackett, P. R., & Roth, L. (1996). Multi-stage selection strategies: A Monte Carlo investigation of effects on performance and minority hiring. *Personnel Psychology, 49*, 549–572.

Sackett, P. R., Schmitt, N., Ellingson, J. E., & Kabin, M. B. (in press). High-states testing in employment, credentialing, and higher education: Prospects in a post-affirmative action world. *American Psychologist*.

Schmidt, F. L., & Hunter, J. E. (1981). Employment testing: Old theories and new research findings. *American Psychologist, 36*, 1128–1137.

Schmidt, F. L., & Hunter, J. E. (1998). The validity and utility of selection methods in personnel psychology: Practical and theoretical implications of 85 years of research findings. *Psychological Bulletin, 124*, 262–274.

Schmidt, F. L., Viswesvaran, C., & Ones, D. S. (2000). Reliability is not validity and validity is not reliability. *Personnel Psychology, 53*, 501–912.

Schmitt, N., & Chan, D. (1998). *Personnel selection: A theoretical approach*. Thousand Oaks, CA: Sage.

Schmitt, N., Rogers, W., Chan, D., Sheppard, L., & Jennings, D. (1997). Adverse impact and predictive efficiency of various predictor combinations. *Journal of Applied Psychology, 82*, 719–730.

Schuler, H., Farr, J. L., & Smith, M. (1993). (Eds.). *Personnel selection and assessment: Individual and organizational perspectives*. Hillsdale, NJ: Lawrence Erlbaum Associates, Inc.

Silva, J. M., & Jacobs, R. R. (1993). Performance as a function of increased minority hiring. *Journal of Applied Psychology, 78*, 591–601.

Smither, J. W., Reilly, R. R., Millsap, R. E., Pearlman, K., & Stoffey, R. W. (1993). Applicant reactions to selection procedures. *Personnel Psychology, 46*, 49–76.

U.S. Equal Employment Opportunity Commission, Civil Service Commission, Department of Labor, & Department of Justice. (1978). Uniform guidelines on employee selection procedures. *Federal Register, 43*, 38290–38315.

Viswesvaran, C. (1993). *Modeling job performance: Is there a general factor?* Unpublished doctoral dissertation, University of Iowa, Iowa City.

Viswesvaran, C., & Ones, D. S. (1995). Theory testing: Combining psychometric meta-analysis and structural equations modeling. *Personnel Psychology, 48*, 865–885.

Viswesvaran, C., & Ones, D. S. (2000). Perspectives on models of job performance. *International Journal of Selection and Assessment, 8*, 216–227.

Viswesvaran, C., Ones, D. S., & Schmidt, F. L. (1996). Comparative analysis of the reliability of job performance ratings. *Journal of Applied Psychology, 81*, 557–560.

Wigdor, A. K., & Garner, W. R. (Eds.). (1982). *Ability testing: Uses, consequences, and controversies. Part 1: Report of the committee*. Washington, DC: National Academy Press.

T - #0122 - 270225 - C0 - 229/152/13 - PB - 9780805896848 - Gloss Lamination